PSYCHOLOGY PRACTITIONER GUIDEBOOKS

EDITORS

Arnold P. Goldstein, Syracuse University
Leonard Krasner, Stanford University & SUNY at Stony Brook
Sol L. Garfield, Washington University in St. Louis

BEHAVIORAL FAMILY INTERVENTION

Titles of Related Interest

BEHAVIORAL FAMILY INTERVENTION

MATTHEW R. SANDERS
MARK R. DADDS

University of Queensland
Brisbane, Australia

ALLYN AND BACON

Boston • London • Toronto • Sydney • Tokyo • Singapore

Library of Congress Cataloging in Publication Data

Sanders, Matthew R.
    Behavioral family intervention / by Matthew R. Sanders, Mark R. Dadds.
        p.   cm. -- (Psychology practitioner guidebooks)
    Includes bibliographical references.
    Includes index.
    ISBN 0-205-14599-X (paper) -- ISBN 0-205-14600-7 (cloth)
    1. Family psychotherapy. 2. Behavior therapy. 3. Adolescent psychotherapy. I. Dadds, Mark R. II. Title. III. Series.
    [DNLM: 1. Behavior Therapy Methods. 2. Child Behavior Disorders--therapy. 3. Family Therapy. 4. Parent-Child Relations.
    WM430.5.F2 S215b] 1990
    RC488.5.S195 1990   90-14342
                                                             CIP

British Library Cataloging-in-Publication Data

Sanders, Matthew R.
    Behavioral family intervention.
    1. Medicine. Family therapy
    I. Title II. Dadds, Mark R. III. Series
    616.89156
    ISBN 0-205-14600-7
    ISBN 0-205-14599-X pbk

Printed in the United States of America

10 9 8 7 6 5 4 3 2 1   96 95 94 93 92

Table of Contents

Contents

Acknowledgments

This book is dedicated to the many children and their families who have participated in the Family Intervention Research Program in the Behavior Research and Therapy Center at the University of Queensland, Brisbane, Australia. We thank our graduate students, research assistants, and professional colleagues whose experience and feedback helped to refine the intervention process described in this book. We also thank typists Sheryl Bradley, Carla Reid, Sue Maccaroni, and Kath Begg, who prepared this manuscript on a tight time line. Special thanks to Tricia and our two children, Emma and Ben, whose ideas about enriching family life and support have strongly influenced my views on family intervention (M. S.); many thanks to friends and loved ones who endured and supported me through this challenging time (M. D.).

Preface

Parenthood is a complex and demanding role. It can also be a challenging and rewarding one. Prospective parents typically receive no training or preparation for parenthood, despite its importance. Most parents learn to parent on the job through trial and error, and many parents have to tackle the task under less than ideal circumstances. Some have become parents accidentally; some struggle as single parents with little social support and severe financial burdens. Parents may also experience other problems, such as marital conflict or depression, which complicate an already difficult task.

The effective resolution of a wide variety of behavioral and emotional problems of childhood and the promotion of positive family life rest on being able to develop a close working collaboration between the clinician, parents, and children. This book provides a detailed account of the clinical consultative process involved in using behavioral family intervention with families of behaviorally-disturbed preadolescent children.

The book is divided into three parts. Part 1 provides a broad overview of the clinical and empirical bases of behavioral family intervention as a treatment approach. Chapter 1 discusses the relationship between family interaction processes and the development of psychopathology. Chapter 2 traces the development of behavioral family intervention as an approach to assisting troubled families, and highlights some recent promising trends in the field. Part 2 provides a detailed account of the procedures used in assessing family dysfunction. Chapters 3, 4, and 5 highlight the importance of therapeutic process variables in laying the foundations for the introduction of specific intervention procedures and in maintaining the motivation of parents and children throughout the treatment process. Chapter 3 covers in detail the intake assessment process. Chapter 4 describes observational and self-report procedures used in assessing family problems, and chapter 5 introduces a guided-participation model for discussing the results of assessments with parents to lay the foundation for treatment.

Part 3, which consists of the remaining five chapters, presents a detailed description of the intervention process. Chapter 6 details a treatment model for teaching parents a variety of positive family interaction and child management skills. Chapter 7 describes procedures for training parents to generalize these skills to a variety of interactional contexts and to maintain therapeutic gains. Specifically, chapter 7 deals with the management of anger and depression in parents and cognitive coping skills training for children as an adjunctive treatment. Chapter 8 discusses the importance of liaison with schools in the treatment of many forms of childhood disturbances, gives a case example of a home-and-school contract, and discusses strategies for overcoming disruptive behavior at school and homework problems. Chapter 9 discusses the relationship between marital problems and parenting difficulties and describes a brief adjunctive marital therapy intervention for use with families with concurrent marital and child management problems. Chapter 10, the final chapter, discusses the limitations of clinical models of service delivery, highlighting some new developments in behavioral family intervention and indicating several exciting future directions for clinical research and practice.

About the Authors

Matthew R. Sanders, Ph.D., is an Associate Professor in Clinical Psychology in the Department of Psychiatry at the University of Queensland. Dr. Sanders was a foundation director of the Behavior Research and Therapy Centre, established the Family Intervention Research Program, and coordinates a behavioral pediatrics research group at the University of Queensland. His research interests include the application of behavioral family intervention methods to a variety of childhood disturbances including conduct problems, depression, feeding disorders, recurrent pain syndromes, and chronic illness. His recent research has been published in *Behavior Therapy, Journal of Consulting and Clinical Psychology, Behavior Modification, Journal of Social and Clinical Psychology, Cognitive Research and Therapy,* and *Behavioral Psychotherapy.* He is editor-elect of *Behavior Change,* a former state and national president of the Australian Behavior Modification Association, a member of the Clinical Courses Approval Committee of the Australian Psychological Society, and program coordinator for the Fourth World Congress of Behavior Therapy. Dr. Sanders is also a practicing clinical psychologist, maintains his own private practice, and conducts workshops and training seminars for professionals.

Mark R. Dadds, Ph.D., is Co-Director in Psychology of the Behavior Research and Therapy Centre and a Senior Lecturer in Clinical Psychology at the University of Queensland. He also holds a number of honorary positions, including Director of Research at the Abused Child Trust of Queensland, and has served as both state and national president of the Australian Behaviour Modification Association. His clinical and research interests include the treatment of conduct disorder, depression and anxiety in children, the process of family therapy, interactional and cognitive processes in child abuse, behavior therapy, and behavioral pediatrics in general. His work on the role of the family in the development and treatment of child psychopathology has been published in several leading international journals, and he has twice won research achievement awards from the Australian Behavior Modification Association. He currently serves on the editorial boards of *Behavior Change, Australian Developmental and Educational Psychologist,* and *Journal of Child and Family Studies.* In 1991, he received an Early Career Award for contributions to psychology from the Australian Psychological Society, Division of Scientific Affairs.

BEHAVIORAL FAMILY INTERVENTION

Part I
Introduction to Behavioral Family Intervention

Chapter 1

Nature and Causes of Behavioral Disorders in Children

Research into the nature, causes, and treatment of behavior problems in children and adolescents represents major areas of comparative neglect in the study of psychopathology. However, the last few decades have witnessed a steady growth in effort devoted to understanding children's problems. Various treatment approaches that focus on changing the child's social environment (particularly the family) have provided a new optimism for clinicians, researchers, children, and their families. This book presents a practical, process-oriented model of behavioral family intervention for children with behavior disorders. The model is process oriented in that its central tenet is that successful intervention depends as much on the process of consultation as it does on the selection and application of specific treatment techniques. We present a treatment model that highlights process issues that begin with the first contact with the child and family, and continues through assessment, diagnosis, treatment selection and implementation, to termination and planning for the maintenance of positive change. Our focus is mainly on children who display disruptive behavior or conduct problems in the home; however, there are a number of indications that the same process model can be applied, with minor adjustments, to a range of other childhood disorders.

Conduct problems are found in approximately 70% of children with any psychiatric diagnosis (Rutter, Cox, Tupling, Berger, & Yule, 1975), and many different forms of child psychopathology contain similar discrete behavior problems. For example, aggression is commonly associated with conduct disorders, attention deficit disorder with hyperactivity, some forms of developmental delay, adjustment disorders, and depression (Kaz-

3

din, 1987a). Similarly, social withdrawal can occur in children with anxiety disorders, social skills problems, conduct disorders, developmental delay, and depression. Research comparing nonclinical and clinical populations has highlighted the similarity of the types of behavior found in all children. In some studies, the only difference is the quantity or severity of problems (Kazdin, 1988).

Irrespective of the nature or causes of a child's behavior problems, they are invariably influenced by the social context in which they occur. Problem behaviors typically occur within family, school, or community settings and frequently disrupt these settings. Positive change in the child's behavior often depends on a corresponding change in parents', teachers', or other caregivers' behavior. Regardless of the specific type of intervention (e.g., more effective discipline, positive communication, giving a child medication, physical therapy, a homework program), the social system caring for the child invariably must change and accommodate, if not be fully responsible for, the implementation of the treatment. The process of consulting with parents and other caregivers demands similar considerations regardless of the specific details of the treatment intervention itself.

Our goal in this book has been to be as practical and specific as possible. Details are provided on all phases of the treatment process, and the actual materials we use in working with families are included. In addition, case examples are provided. The book is directed to the practicing clinician or advanced graduate student. We assume that the reader has basic knowledge and skills in interviewing and counseling, child development and psychopathology, behavior modification, and social learning theory.

BEHAVIORAL AND EMOTIONAL DISTURBANCE IN CHILDREN

Behavior problems in children and adolescents must be viewed within a developmental context and the task of developmental psychopathology is to map the origins and course of individual patterns of maladaptive behavior (Rutter, 1989). This necessarily involves developing an understanding of both continuities and discontinuities (stability and change), in behavior patterns throughout the child's development. Recent data have indicated that the different types of childhood disturbances vary in the extent to which they persist into adolescence and adulthood. This section briefly reviews literature on the prevalence and outcome of common childhood disorders and discusses methods of classifying behavioral disorders.

Recently, classification of behavior disturbance in children has received increased attention, and it is clear that current systems are far from satisfactory (Kazdin, 1983, 1988). The three most common methods of classifying and describing children's problems are the diagnostic taxonomy, the dimensions of dysfunction approach, and the behavioral approach. The best-known taxonomical system is based on the *Diagnostic and Statistical Manual of Mental Disorders*, third edition, revised (DSM-III-R; see American Psychiatric Association, 1987), and it assumes that psychopathology can be classified into symptom clusters that are indicative of discrete forms of psychopathology. Table 1.1 summarizes the major types of childhood disturbance identified by the DSM-IIIR. Such a system is unavoidable if clinicians and researchers are to share a common international language of child psychopathology. However, a taxonomy that assumes discrete types of disorders is fraught with problems, especially when used at the clinical level, which focuses on individual patterns of psychopathology (Kazdin, 1988).

The second approach assumes that a child can show a pattern of disturbance across a number of dimensions of dysfunction such as aggression, social withdrawal, depression, and anxiety. These dimensions vary with the age and sex of the child and are usually derived from empirical and statistical studies of a large population of children. This dimensional approach is exemplified by the rating checklists developed by Quay and Peterson (Revised Behavior Problem Checklist; Quay & Peterson, 1983) and Achenbach (Child Behavior Checklist; Achenbach & Edelbrock, 1983). The approach assumes that different disorders vary in the number and intensity of problems children experience. Assessment attempts to determine the degree to which a referred child differs from a normative comparison group on constellations of problems.

The third approach assumes that any attempt to move beyond a detailed description of the actual behaviors a child displays is fraught with methodological and conceptual problems that render it of limited value in treatment planning. Thus, the behavioral approach to assessment emphasizes the clear description of the individual's behavioral repertoire without the inferential process of transforming specific problems to more general diagnostic labels or dimensions of dysfunction. All of the aforementioned systems have their advantages and disadvantages, both in terms of their role in research and in clinical work with families and children. We argue that each has a useful role to play at the clinical level, and a comprehensive approach should incorporate all three methods at various stages in the assessment and treatment process. This is emphasized and elaborated on in the following sections describing the assessment of childhood dysfunction and the discussion of assessment findings with families.

Studies that have examined children in the general population have found that between 5 and 30% of children meet the criteria for at least one DSM-IIIR diagnosis (Kashani, Orvaschel, Rosenberg, & Reid, 1989; Rutter et al., 1975). Estimates tend to be higher when children's self-report data

Table 1.1. Disorders First Evident in Infancy, Childhood, or Adolescence

Disorder	Characteristic
Mental Retardation	General intellectual functioning significantly below average, associated with deficits or impairments in adaptive behavior, with onset before the age of 18.
Autistic Disorder	Severe deficits or disturbance in social interactions, communication, and language, and a restricted repertoire of activities (e.g., stereotyped body movements).
Arithmetic Disorder	Arithmetic skills are significantly below the child's intellectual level, and problems are not due to visual, hearing, or other neurological disorders.
Expressive Writing Disorder	Writing skills are markedly below the child's intellectual capacity. The disturbance is not due to visual, hearing, or other neurological problems and interferes with the composition of written material.
Reading Disorder	Reading achievement markedly below the child's intellectual capacity. The disturbance is not due to visual, hearing, or other neurological problems and interferes with academic achievement and activities requiring reading skills.
Articulation Disorder	Consistent failure to use developmentally expected speech sounds.
Expressive Language Disorder	Use of language that is markedly below what would be expected given the child's nonverbal intellectual capacity. The disturbance significantly interferes with academic and other performance requiring verbal expression.
Receptive Language Disorder	Comprehension of language is markedly below what would be expected given the child's nonverbal intellectual capacity. The disturbance significantly interferes with academic and other performance requiring the comprehension of language.
Coordination Disorder	Performance in daily activities requiring motor coordination is markedly below the expected level, given the child's chronological age and intellectual capacity. The disorder is not due to a known physical disorder.
Attention Deficit Hyperactivity Disorder	Excesses of inattention, impulsivity, and hyperactivity lasting at least 6 months with onset prior to age 7.

Table 1.1. *Continued*

Disorder	Characteristic
Conduct Disorder	Disturbance of conduct, lasting at least 6 months, in which either the basic rights of others or major age-appropriate societal norms or rules are violated.
Oppositional Defiant Disorder	A pattern of noncompliant, negativistic, and oppositional behavior to authority figures lasting at least 6 months.
Separation Anxiety Disorder	Persistent and excessive anxiety on separation from major attachment figures, home, or other familiar surroundings, lasting at least 2 weeks with onset prior to age 18.
Avoidant Disorder	Fearful avoidance of contact with unfamiliar people lasting at least 6 months in a child of 2½ years or older.
Overanxious Disorder	Excessive worrying and fear about future or past events that is not confined to a specific situation or object, is not due to a recent psychological stressor, and persists for 6 months or more.
Anorexia Nervosa	Intense fear of gaining weight, disturbance of body image, body weight at least 15% below expected, and amenorrhea (in females).
Bulimia Nervosa	Recurrent episodes of binge eating, accompanied by lack of control over eating, use of diet, vigorous exercise, vomiting, or medication to prevent weight gain, and persistent concern about body. At least two binge eating episodes per week for at least 3 months.
Pica	Repeated eating of a nonnutritive substance for at least 1 month. No aversion to food exists.
Rumination Disorder of Infancy	Repeated regurgitation without nausea or associated gastrointestinal illness with weight loss or a failure to make expected weight gain. Duration of at least 1 month following a period of normal functioning.
Gender Identity Disorder of Childhood	Persistent and intense distress of being a girl (for females) or a boy (for males) with marked aversion to normative sex-typed clothing and insistence on wearing clothing of the opposite sex. Child repudiates his or her own sexual anatomy. Child has not yet reached puberty.

Continued

Table 1.1. *Continued*

Disorder	Characteristic
Transsexualism	Persistent discomfort and sense of inappropriateness about one's assigned gender and preoccupation with acquiring sex characteristics of the other sex, lasting at least 2 years in a child who has reached puberty.
Cross-Gender Disorder (Nontranssexual)	Persistent discomfort about one's assigned gender with recurrent cross-dressing in the role of the other sex and no preoccupation of changing one's sex characteristics, in a child who has reached puberty.
Tourette's Disorder	Involuntary, repetitive motor movements and vocal productions lasting at least 1 year with onset prior to age 21.
Chronic Motor or Vocal Tic Disorder	Involuntary, repetitive, rapid movements or vocal productions. Duration for more than 1 year with onset prior to age 21.
Transient Tic Disorder	Involuntary, repetitive motor or vocal tics with duration at least 2 weeks but no longer than 12 consecutive months.
Functional Encopresis	Repeated passage of feces into places not appropriate for that purpose, not due to any physical disorder. At least one such event a month for 6 months in a child of at least 4 years of age.
Functional Enuresis	Repeated voiding of urine during the day or at night into places not appropriate for that purpose, not due to any physical disorder. Child is at least 5 years old.
Cluttering	A disorder of speech fluency involving both the rate and rhythm of speech resulting in impaired speech intelligibility. Speech is erratic and dysrhythmic, consisting of rapid and jerky spurts that may also involve faulty phrasing.
Stuttering	Frequent repetitions or prolongations of sounds or syllables that markedly impair the rhythmic flow of speech.
Elective Mutism	Persistent refusal to speak in one or more major social situations, including at school, despite ability to comprehend spoken language and to speak.
Identity Disorder	Severe subjective distress regarding uncertainty about identity issues (career, friends, moral values) with resultant impairment in functioning lasting at least 3 months.

Table 1.1. *Continued*

Disorder	Characteristic
Reactive Attachment Disorder of Infancy and Early Childhood	Lack of age-appropriate signs of social responsiveness, apathetic mood, and problems with physical development (failure to thrive), with onset before the age of 5, because of lack of adequate caretaking, including psychological and physical abuse or neglect.
Stereotypy and Habit Disorder	Intentional, repetitive, and nonfunctional behaviors such as handshaking or waving, body rocking, headbanging, and mouthing of objects that markedly interfere with normal activities.

Note. Other adult diagnoses may be used, unless specified for each diagnosis, for diagnosing a child. These include depression, adjustment disorder, organic mental syndromes, and substance use disorders.

are compared with parents' or teachers', but considerably lower when rigorous criteria of impaired functioning are used.

Some studies assessing the frequency of psychiatric problems in community samples of 7- to 17-year-olds have found that anxiety disorders are the most common diagnosis overall, being more frequent in females but tending to diminish in frequency with age (Garralda & Bailey, 1986; Kashani et al., 1989; Vikan, 1985). However, studies employing large population samples have typically found that attention deficit, oppositional, and conduct problems are the next most common overall (Anderson, Williams, McGee, & Silva, 1987; Rutter et al., 1975). These disorders tend to increase with age from middle childhood through adolescence and are the most common referral problems for boys (Kashani et al., 1989; Kazdin, 1987a). Further, conduct disorders persist into adulthood for a substantial proportion of children and are predictive of a broader range of adult disorders (Rutter, 1989). The most common complaints among preschool children are disruptive noncompliant behaviors, which are frequent in boys and tend to decrease overall with age. Other common complaints are problems with the child's toileting, eating behavior, and social withdrawal (Beautrais, Fergusson, & Shannon, 1982; McGuire & Richman, 1986). Table 1.2 shows the most common problems reported by parents and teachers as a function of the age of the child in a comprehensive large-scale longitudinal study of New Zealand children who were followed from birth until age 12.

Our focus in this book is on the child within the family, and this approach assumes that the family is implicated in the origins, maintenance, and management of childhood behavior problems. In the last several decades there has been a dramatic increase in emphasis on the family in

Table 1.2. Reports of Child Behavior Problems, Age 6 to 12 Years

Problem	6 Years (N = 1,115)		8 Years (N = 1,092)		10 Years (N = 1,067)		12 Years (N = 1,020)	
Maternal Reports								
Bullies other children	13.0	(2.2)	13.6	(2.8)	14.7	(2.9)	13.6	(1.9)
Has temper outbursts	26.2	(5.7)	30.0	(7.6)	29.1	(6.8)	31.0	(7.1)
Destroys own or others' belongings	10.6	(2.3)	7.4	(1.9)	4.3	(0.7)	5.0	(1.1)
Irritable, quick to fly off the handle	34.2	(8.1)	27.8	(6.9)	27.0	(5.2)	34.7	(5.5)
Disobedient	27.7	(6.8)	16.0	(4.3)	21.5	(3.7)	29.8	(2.2)
Tells lies	21.2	(2.9)	15.8	(3.1)	17.3	(2.2)	25.8	(3.6)
Steals	9.6	(1.3)	5.4	(1.3)	5.9	(1.0)	7.5	(2.2)
Frequently fights with other children	13.1	(2.2)	6.6	(1.6)	10.9	(1.2)	8.5	(1.0)
Restless, overactive	37.8	(15.2)	27.5	(10.7)	24.4	(7.7)	24.7	(8.1)
Excitable, impulsive	—		32.6	(11.9)	29.3	(10.9)	31.6	(7.9)
Inattentive, easily distracted	—		30.1	(11.5)	33.6	(13.3)	35.9	(12.2)
Constantly fidgeting	—		24.4	(10.3)	21.4	(8.1)	21.6	(7.3)
Can't settle to anything	10.0	(3.2)	11.5	(3.7)	10.2	(2.6)	8.7	(2.5)
Always climbing	—		18.8	(9.9)	13.0	(6.7)	7.5	(3.3)
Afraid of new things or situations	27.3	(5.9)	26.0	(5.2)	25.7	(5.7)	33.1	(7.5)
Shy with other children	—		16.1	(2.1)	12.7	(1.4)	14.9	(2.2)
Often worried about things	36.7	(9.3)	23.5	(6.0)	25.3	(5.5)	31.1	(4.8)
Often appears miserable, unhappy	12.8	(1.6)	10.1	(2.0)	12.3	(2.4)	14.0	(2.3)
Not much liked by other children	3.4	(0.6)	3.2	(0.4)	6.4	(0.9)	9.2	(1.6)
Rather solitary	44.5	(15.2)	53.1	(20.1)	42.7	(15.7)	49.1	(14.5)
Teacher Reports								
Bullies other children	14.5	(2.6)	11.2	(1.1)	13.1	(1.8)	11.3	(2.3)
Has temper outbursts	—		7.0	(0.8)	9.3	(2.2)	11.3	(3.0)
Destroys own or others' belongings	7.1	(1.1)	3.5	(0.5)	5.4	(0.9)	6.7	(1.0)
Irritable, quick to fly off the handle	11.1	(1.9)	9.6	(1.3)	11.6	(3.0)	11.7	(3.1)
Disobedient	17.1	(3.2)	12.9	(1.4)	17.7	(2.2)	14.4	(2.4)
Tells lies	13.1	(2.2)	7.5	(1.2)	9.2	(1.3)	8.8	(1.5)
Steals	5.4	(0.6)	2.5	(0.4)	2.8	(0.4)	1.8	(1.8)
Frequently fights with other children	18.1	(2.8)	16.4	(1.9)	15.2	(2.5)	13.4	(2.9)
Restless, overactive	27.5	(5.0)	24.9	(5.3)	26.1	(5.0)	24.6	(5.1)
Excitable, impulsive	—		31.5	(6.4)	33.5	(7.3)	30.3	(7.1)
Inattentive, easily distracted	—		43.7	(12.5)	46.4	(12.5)	43.7	(12.4)
Constantly fidgeting	26.7	(6.3)	37.0	(7.7)	37.2	(7.8)	33.3	(6.3)
Short attention span	33.4	(8.7)	28.0	(7.2)	34.4	(9.2)	31.3	(11.1)
Afraid of new things or situations	31.6	(4.8)	27.0	(2.2)	33.7	(4.9)	28.9	(3.1)
Shy with adults	—		39.7	(5.9)	46.6	(8.0)	43.2	(8.0)

Table 1.2. *Continued*

Problem	6 Years (N = 1,115)		8 Years (N = 1,092)		10 Years (N = 1,067)		12 Years (N = 1,020)	
Often worried about things	39.9	(5.7)	32.4	(4.2)	35.3	(4.7)	28.6	(4.1)
Often appears miserable, unhappy	17.4	(2.0)	14.1	(1.2)	13.6	(2.1)	11.8	(2.2)
Overly sensitive	—		29.0	(4.0)	32.9	(4.1)	28.7	(4.3)
Isolates self from other children	—		13.6	(2.1)	18.6	(2.1)	19.4	(3.8)
Not much liked by other children	15.0	(1.7)	12.6	(2.4)	20.5	(4.7)	19.0	(4.1)

Note. The data for this table were kindly provided by Dr. David Fergusson of the Christchurch Child Development Study, Christchurch School of Medicine, University of Otago (Fergusson, personal communication, September 1990). A dash (—) indicates an item not measured. The figures not in parentheses show the percentages of mothers or teachers reporting that the item applies somewhat. The figures in parentheses give the percentages reporting that the item certainly applies. Items adapted from the Rutter Behavior Questionnaire (Rutter, Tizard, & Whitmore, 1970) and the Connors Rating Scale (Connors, 1969).

the genesis and management of all forms of psychopathology. Currently, family therapy models tend to dominate the landscape of many disorders such as childhood aggression and depression. Given this enthusiasm for family models, it is crucial that empirical research clarifies the role of the family in the development of child psychopathology. Historically, the family has been argued to be causally implicated in severe disorders such as schizophrenia (Bateson, Jackson, Haley, & Weakland, 1956). However, later research indicated that these views were overly simplistic if not incorrect. Recently, a number of authors have argued that the role of the family in the genesis of psychopathology has been overestimated (e.g., Sines, 1987). Sines reviewed studies indicating that we must exercise caution when ascribing causal relationships between individual psychopathology and family variables.

However, one does not have to assume or demonstrate a causal relationship between the family interaction variables and the child's problems as a prerequisite to adopting a family-based intervention approach. There are many clinical problems of children which are influenced by extrafamilial variables, but for which the family still represents the child's best hopes for change. For example, psychosocial family variables cannot be held responsible for mental retardation, yet one of our best methods of helping such a child develop to his or her full potential is to help the parents cope with the child's problems and train them to foster and develop new behavioral skills in the child. In many clinical situations, we need not assume that the family has caused a child's problem to work with the family. Emphasizing the family's role in the maintenance and remediation of the problem can lead to important clinical outcomes.

CAUSES OF BEHAVIOR
PROBLEMS IN CHILDREN

From the moment of conception, children's development is influenced by their inherited genetic makeup, the family environment in which they are raised, and the broader culture in which they live. Heredity and environment play an interactive role in shaping the child's behavioral repertoire and influencing whether behavioral and emotional problems develop. However, the relative importance of genetic and environmental influences varies depending on the type of problem being discussed. In severe developmental disorders such as autism, genetic influences are probably dominant causal factors. In other problems, such as severe conduct problems, depression, and anxiety, research has indicated that genetic characteristics may predispose the child to developing the problem (Rutter et al., 1990). However, a wealth of evidence also indicates that the child's environment, in particular family interactions, plays an important role in the development and maintenance of behavioral and emotional problems (Dadds, 1987; Patterson, 1982; Rutter, 1989). Even if children are biologically predisposed to developing problems, they are not born knowing how to steal, lie, or be violent.

Characteristics of Children

Recent research has shown that children may inherit varying degrees of vulnerability to behavioral and emotional problems. The review by Rutter et al. (1990) indicates that the evidence of genetic vulnerability differs across different disorders, with autism, major affective disorder, severe delinquency, and multiple tic disorders having a clear genetic component. The evidence with regard to anxiety, oppositional conduct, substance abuse, and hyperactivity disorders in children, however, is too weak to make any definitive conclusions. Where genetic inheritance predisposes a child to psychological problems, a number of hypotheses regarding the mechanisms of influence exist. Genetic influences may operate through temperamental features, vulnerability to react poorly to stress, predisposition for a particular disorder, or through a range of other pathways. In clinical practice, one of the first signs of potential problems can be seen in the infant's temperament.

The temperament of newborn children has an important influence on their future development and can be considered as a combination of three factors.

1. *Emotionality* refers to an infant's arousal level in response to environmental stimuli. Highly emotional infants cry and fuss or show angry or fearful reactions to sudden changes in stimulation levels.

2. *Activity level* refers to the amount of gross motor movement and activity that the infant displays. Children with high activity levels tend to explore their environment, engage in vigorous play, and may have problems settling or concentrating on activities for prolonged periods.

3. *Sociability* refers to an infant's preference for interaction with people. Sociable infants show interest in human faces and are responsive to attention from others. Unsociable infants may become distressed when forced to interact with people, preferring to withdraw from social contact.

About 10% of infants have temperaments that make them difficult to rear and place them at risk for later problems (Rutter, 1989). Such infants place extra stress on the family. For example, if an infant cries frequently but cannot be comforted, the parents' attending and comforting behaviors may be extinguished or punished, leading the parents to become less responsive and the child to escalate demanding to receive attention (Donovan, Leavitt, & Balling, 1978). The parents may begin to feel negatively toward the child, arguments between parents over how best to manage the child may develop, and the whole family may suffer. While infants with difficult temperaments cannot be labeled as having a behavioral or emotional disorder, intervention with difficult infants should become an important part of mental health services for children and families.

While a difficult temperament places a child at risk for later problems, many children are referred to clinics who may have been "perfect" babies. Further, there is evidence that a child's temperament is influenced by the family environment during pregnancy and birth. For example, the mother's personal and marital adjustment during pregnancy and expectations of the child and childbirth experience all appear to predict the child's later temperament (Scholom, Zucker, & Stollack, 1979; Zeanah, Keener, Stewart, & Anders, 1985). Thus, it appears that infant temperament and family environment are reciprocally determined from pregnancy onward.

As children enter the school years, a number of other risk factors for psychopathology appear. Learning and language difficulties place the child at risk by establishing a pattern of educational, and later occupational, failure (Loeber, 1990; Piacentini, 1987; Rutter, 1989). Cognitive factors may also be associated with the development and maintenance of specific disorders. Depressed children show the same negative attributional set about self and others that has repeatedly been observed in depressed adults (Kazdin, 1990a). Recent research has also indicated that adolescents with conduct problems may be less skilled at interpreting social messages, tending to overdetect, and thus elicit hostility and rejection in other people (Dodge, 1985; Rutter, 1989). Many of the foregoing factors may increase the risk for psychopathology by disrupting the developing child's social competence and peer relationships (Parker & Asher, 1987).

Factors Affecting the Child's Behavior

Environmental variables related to the development of childhood disorders fall into two broad categories. First, there are those concerning the interactions of children with their primary caregivers and peers. Second, much research has demonstrated that emotional and behavioral disturbances often follow disruptive environmental events such as divorce, arrival of a sibling, and so on. These two categories of stressors may have many commonalities, and it appears that the second category affects the child's behavior by producing change in the first category; that is, by affecting parent-child interactions. Demonstration of the relationship between child and caregivers' behaviors requires at least two empirical components. First, it must be shown that behavior problems in children can be reliably observed to covary with selected caregiver behaviors in the natural environment. Second, experimental manipulations of the selected caregiver behaviors under controlled conditions must be reliably followed by concomitant changes in the child's behaviors. Research to date has met both of these conditions to varying degrees for a range of common forms of child psychopathology.

Parents of disturbed children engage in significantly more aversive behaviors toward their child than parents of nonproblem children (Patterson, 1982; Sanders, Dadds, & Bor, 1989). Aversive behaviors are usually defined to include the use of aversive voice content and tone, and physical aggression. The most frequently observed behaviors are aversive instructions that are yelled at the child, often accompanied by threats (Wahler, 1969). The siblings of disturbed children are more likely to start conflicts with one another during home observations than are those in nonclinic families, and the observed occurrence of these conflicts reliably discriminates clinic from nonclinic families at a group level (Patterson, 1982). Thus, it appears that the families of children with conduct problems provide the children with an environment conducive to learning a repertoire of aggressive behavior. Similarly, recent research has indicated that parents of depressed children may model depressive behaviors to their children and selectively reinforce cognitions and behaviors associated with depression (Billings & Moos, 1983; Cole & Rehm, 1986).

Studies demonstrating that experimental manipulations of parent behavior result in concomitant changes in aggressive, noncompliant child behaviors have been common in the child behavior therapy literature (Lochman, 1990). These clinical trials have provided strong evidence of the dependent relationship between oppositional behavior in children and interactional patterns with parents. Similar evidence exists for recurrent abdominal pain problems (Sanders, Rebgetz et al., 1989) and some anxiety disorders (Strauss, 1987); however, evidence that family changes are reliably associated with improvements in childhood depression is lacking.

Disturbed children tend to come from families who engage in relatively high rates of disturbed behavior in their day-to-day interactions. The aggressive child is regularly exposed to conflict among family members and is likely to receive high rates of aversive instructions; many of his or her behaviors will be followed by aversive consequences regardless of their appropriateness. Depressed children are likely to have depressed parents who similarly reinforce the problem in the child. Behavioral conceptualizations of these interactional patterns focus on the functional relationships between individual behaviors and their social consequences. That is, prosocial responses may be punished or ignored while problematic behavior may be maintained by the consequences it produces. Bandura (1973) provided convincing data on the tendency of children to imitate specific behaviors and more general response classes (for example, aggression) after witnessing others perform the behavior. Further evidence exists that children, in particular boys, may show a generalized stress reaction associated with displays of aggressive behavior in response to open parental disagreements (Cummings, Ianotti, & Zahn-Waxler, 1985).

Rather than review the large range of possible environmental events that can have adverse effects on children (Goodyer, 1990), the effects of one common stressor are used as an example. The impact of parental divorce and/or separation on the child has been relatively well researched, and marital breakdown affects a substantial proportion of families in most developed countries (Emery, 1982). One of the first attempts to develop a model of the relationship between divorce and child behavior came from Hetherington, Cox, and Cox (1982). Two hypotheses arising from this work bear special relevance to this discussion.

The first is that children from separated households are at greater risk to develop behavioral and emotional problems. The relevant data have left little doubt that this is indeed the case (Emery, 1982). These children are more likely to develop problems of undercontrol (that is, oppositional and conduct disorders) than problems of overcontrol, and this effect is more readily observable in boys than in girls. No consistent relationship between the age of the child and the effects of separation has been clearly noted, and there is considerable evidence to suggest that a positive relationship with one of the parents can minimize, but not overcome, the adverse effects of the separation on the child.

The second hypothesis is that the effects of divorce on children may be mediated by the amount and type of conflict between the parents. This is in stark contrast to psychodynamic explanations of the effects of divorce, which emphasize the direct effects of emotional separation from a parent as the key factor in the impact on children (Bowlby, 1973). As Emery (1982) pointed out, this belief is common and has resulted in a number of axioms about the need for parents to stay together for the child's sake, despite extremes of marital discord. However, research emanating from a number of countries and using different methodologies has indicated that it is the discord and not the separation that has the most visible effect on the child. Children from broken or intact homes characterized by open marital discord are at greater risk to develop a behavioral disorder than children from broken or intact homes that are relatively nondiscordant.

Hetherington et al. (1982) found that the likelihood that the child's behavior would deteriorate following divorce was related to observed changes in the mother's discipline practices. Mothers, the most common custodians following divorce, tended to show decreases in their use of limit setting, maturity demands, affection, and clear communication. These were accompanied by increases in disturbed behavior in children, which tended to peak approximately 1 year after the divorce. Further, boys were exposed to more of this inconsistency than were their sisters. There is evidence that the effects of severe economic hardship on developing children are mediated by changes in the interactional patterns of parents and their children (Elder, Nguyen, & Caspi, 1985). Further, the established relationship between parental psychopathology and behavior disorders in children may also be mediated by the impact of the psychopathology on the marital relationship and related parenting styles (Billings & Moos, 1983; Emery, 1982).

Environmental conditions, both in the form of day-to-day interactions with family members and disruptive events such as divorce, are important determinants of the development and course of behavior disorders in children. Further, it appears that some of the effects of disruptive events on children may be mediated through changes in the parent-child interactions. The presence of parental discord and open conflict between parents is predictive of the development of conduct problems in children.

Characteristics of Parents

The personal adjustment of family members, particularly parents, has a central impact on the developing child. One of the most widely researched areas of parental adjustment with respect to child psychopathology is maternal depression. Children of depressed mothers have significantly more emotional, somatic, and behavioral problems than children of nondepressed mothers (Billings & Moos, 1983). As with many of the factors reviewed so far, it appears that the effects of maternal depression on the child may be influenced by the marital relationship and the parenting styles and skills of the parents. There is substantial evidence that one of the major causes of maternal depression is marital discord (Schafer, 1985; Waring & Patton, 1984). People with identifiable psychopathology have relatively more discordant marriages (Molholm & Dinitz, 1972). Emery, Weintraub, and Neale (1982) found that the effects of a parent's psychopathology on the child were largely ameliorated if the parents had a nondiscordant marriage.

Fathers of boys with severe conduct problems show a disproportionately high incidence of antisocial personality disorder (Rutter et al., 1990) and may use severe forms of discipline with their children. These fathers are also more likely to be in highly discordant marriages or to have separated from the family (Lahey et al., 1988). Other factors acting primarily at the level of individual adjustment in families include the presence of a handicapped member. Siblings of handicapped children have been shown to be at increased risk for behavioral disturbances, and male siblings are at particular risk for developing conduct disorders (O'Connor & Stachowiak, 1971). Again, there is evidence that the degree of disturbance shown by siblings is largely mediated by the quality of the parents' marital relationship and parenting skills (Warren, 1974).

Factors Affecting Families

Major steps toward understanding the development of childhood problems, in particular conduct disorders, have recently been made by attempts to clarify the observed relationship between these disorders and low socioeconomic status. The level of social support available to parents appears to be an important variable that may mediate the relationship. Wahler (1980) demonstrated that in a group of socially isolated mothers with an oppositional child, the number of friendly extrafamiliar encounters and the occurrence of behavior problems in the child covaried on a daily basis. Wahler and Afton (1980) showed that the total number of extrafamilial interactions for mothers was inversely correlated with the total number of parent-child problems. Wahler, Hughey, and Gordon (1981) found that mothers with low rates of extrafamilial contact were more likely to engage in longer, coercive parent-child interactions than were mothers of oppositional children with higher rates of social contact. Wahler's conceptualization of these findings draws on the idea of a perceptual or cognitive bias. As a result of minimal or aversive social contacts, mothers are less able to monitor and accurately label their child's behavior, predisposing them to react aversively to their child in an indiscriminate way.

It is unclear from Wahler's work whether the social contacts characterizing these insular mothers function because of their quality, quantity, or both. Aversive social contacts may propagate coercive parent-child interactions because they both belong to the functional response class of aggression and are elicited by the same existing stimuli in the environment on any given day. Patterson's coercion trap hypothesis and life stress theories (Rutter, Tizzard, & Whitmore, 1970) emphasize this relationship. Alternatively, the relative poverty of positive social contacts may be the functional variable. This could be tested empirically by comparing groups of mothers who experience varying combinations of aversive–nonaversive and high-frequency versus low-frequency social contacts. However, much research is available on the effects of low-frequency social contacts, usually termed lack of a social support system.

In a review of the research on social support and psychological well-being, Winefield (1984) concluded as follows:

1.   The presence of an adequate social network is predictive of fewer psychological and medical problems in the general population. Individuals' subjective rating of the adequacy of their social support network is a better predictor than objective quantifications of their network.

2.   There is much support for a buffer hypothesis. That is, adequate social support protects the individual against the adverse effects of life stressors.

3.   There is some support for the existence of a relationship between the adequacy of an individual's support network and ability to deal effectively with personal problems.

These general conclusions become more interesting in light of Wahler's work and the following findings related to child behavior. Lamb and Elster (1985) found that the amount of a father's engagement with the mother and children was predictive of parental perceptions of social support and of negative life stressors. Parents who reported inadequate social support networks experienced a greater impact of negative life stressors and showed deficits in father-mother and father-child engagement. This finding is based on direct observations of parent-child interactions and relates the area of social support to the earlier discussion of marital discord and maternal depression.

Webster-Stratton (1985) monitored a group of parents for 1 year subsequent to participating in a behavioral treatment program that focused on their child's oppositional behavior. The two factors that best predicted objective ratings of poor treatment outcome at 12-month follow-up were low socio-economic status (SES), including single-parent status, and a report of low negative life stress. The best predictors of the mother having a negative attitude toward the child at follow-up were low SES and a report of high negative life stress.

Mothers who had a negative perception of the child at follow-up tended to be low-SES, single parents who reported high levels of stress during the preceding year. This finding is consistent with the conceptual approaches reviewed earlier in that external stressors appear to predispose the mother to perceive the child in a negative way. Comparisons of the components of the low-SES measure revealed, however, that these mothers were no different from the positive-attitude group on measures of income, occupation, and education. The only difference between the groups appeared to be the adequacy of the social support they had received during the preceding year.

In conclusion, it appears that factors discussed earlier, such as parent-child interactions, maternal depression, marital discord, and a parent's personal adjustment, may need to be seen in the context of the family's interactions with the local community. The observation that day-to-day social contacts and subjective evaluations of social support are predictive of a range of parent-parent and parent-child interaction patterns is an excellent example of clinical and research approaches to the analysis of interacting hierarchical systems (Wahler & Dumas, 1984) and emphasizes the relationship between "molar" (e.g., SES, delinquency) and "molecular" (e.g., parent-child interaction) variables (Patterson & Reid, 1984).

Community Factors

A number of factors have been identified that may increase the stress on parents involved in raising a child under 18 years of age. Risley, Clark, and Cataldo (1976) pointed out that the decline in extended families in most Western countries may be producing parents who have had few role models for successful child-rearing techniques and who receive minimal support in raising children. Single parenting is an increasing social phenomenon, and 90% of single parents are women who may have relatively low income and lack support networks and social status. These conditions may intensify the problems associated with child rearing (Blechman, 1982). Mothers in the paid work force may have less time available to spend with children and may find their parenting at variance with the techniques used by childcare personnel. Loss of extended family supports, worsening of economic conditions, increases in single-parent households, modeling of violence in the media, and the growth of suburban overcrowding and isolation may all contribute to the growing salience of parenting problems.

Conclusions

The conclusions about the determinants of behavioral problems in children derived from this review are best regarded as hypotheses.

1.   While further research is needed, it appears that genetic vulnerability to childhood psychopathology exists for many disorders, particularly autism, major affective disorders, multiple tic disorders, and severe delinquency.

2.   The earliest identified precursor of childhood disorders is the bio-

logical state of the newborn infant (i.e., temperament, irritability) in interaction with the personal, marital, and social adjustment of the parents
during and after pregnancy.

3.   Oppositional behavior appears to stem from the infant's repertoire
of distress signals and nurturance-soliciting behavior and is maintained
and shaped within the interactions of the child with his or her caregivers.

4.   The establishment of a repertoire of oppositional, depressed, anxious, or withdrawn behaviors may preclude the child from learning more
prosocial behaviors that protect against psychopathology. The parents of
disturbed children appear to model and reinforce problem behaviors in
their children, especially in their child's development from infancy to
middle childhood.

5.   A range of variables are associated with the parents' perceptions of
the aversiveness or deviance of their children's behavior and the likelihood
that they will engage in conflict with their children. These variables are
marital discord, maternal depression, lack of social support, minimal father
engagement in family life, and other stressors such as economic disruption,
divorce, and the presence of an ill member in the family.

6.   The quality of the parental marriage and social support network
appears to mediate between the effects of stress (within and upon the
family) and child development. The most likely explanation is that social
and marital support can buffer the parent against stressors, thereby mini-
mizing the likelihood of negative changes in his or her perceptions of and
behavior toward the children.

Figure 1.1 emphasizes the reciprocal relationship between the hypothesized causal variables. The causes of childhood disorders are best seen as
a set of systems, subsystems, and components of systems interacting at the
biological, interpersonal, and social levels. This does not mean that all
children will be influenced by all of the hypothesized causal variables.

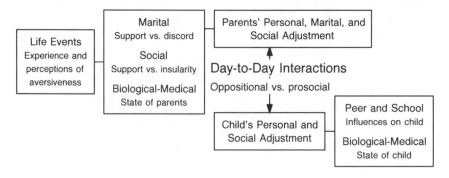

FIGURE 1.1. A model of the reciprocal influences implicated in the development of
childhood behavior disorders.

Rather, it is likely that different causal paths may lead to the same end point of a behavioral disorder. For example, two similar boys presenting with aggression, noncompliance, and school failure may have strikingly different histories involving divorce and familial aggression, on the one hand, and maternal depression and deficits in social support, on the other. For a rational or empirically based science, it is assumed that there must be common elements in both boys' histories that were and are maintaining the disorders, even though their superficial histories are dissimilar. At this stage, the most likely contenders are the child's predetermined characteristics and the interactional style of his or her family.

PATTERNS OF FAMILY INTERACTION AMONG PROBLEM CHILDREN

All children have behavioral and emotional upsets in their lives. Problems of disobedience, anxiety, fears, lying, aggression, crying, and social withdrawal happen in many children at some point in their development, but for most children these will be temporary or infrequent occurrences. Behaviors become problematic and warrant professional intervention when they persist at such intensity or frequency that they interfere with the child's or family's functioning. In this section we discuss various characteristics of parent-child interactions that help maintain or escalate childhood problems. We draw heavily on the theoretical and clinical models of Patterson, Forehand, Wahler, and others that emphasize social learning processes in the development of psychopathology.

Reinforcement Traps

Reinforcement traps can occur in two ways. First, it is common to find that parents inadvertently reinforce problematic behaviors in children. Consider the following example: Sam, age 7, is complaining to his mother that he does not want to go to bed. Rather, he wants to continue watching TV.

Sam: It's not fair, I want to watch this.
Mother: [irritated] Now come on, young man, you know the rule, now get off to bed.
Sam: [starting to cry] No, it's not fair.
Mother: Come on, I'll read you a story. Get up and brush your teeth. [Mother starts to pick up the child.]

Sam: [starts to scream and cry] Just let me watch this show, then I promise to go to bed, I promise.

Mother: All right, just to the end of this show and then you're off to bed with no fuss. Do you hear me? [yelling]

Sam: Yes, mom.

In this example, Sam's protests are positively reinforced by receiving permission to keep watching, and negatively reinforced by the termination of his mother's verbal and physical demands. Simultaneously, the mother's demanding is reinforced by the immediate termination of her son's screaming (negative reinforcement) and the promise of compliance with the new rule about bedtime (positive reinforcement). Given this interaction, we would expect that Sam's protests will increase when this scenario next occurs.

There are a number of ways that parents inadvertently reinforce problematic behaviors. *Attentional rewards* occur when a child's problem behaviors produce an increase in parental attention (looking, touching, speaking, frowning, smacking, and so on). This is probably the most common and yet inconspicuous reward for problem behavior. Patterson (1982) clearly demonstrated that a child's whining and crying results in an immediate increase in the parent talking to the child. *Material and food rewards* refer to sweets, toys, and other things that parents might give to a child contingent on certain behaviors. This is a problem when the reward is for aggressive, demanding, or other problem behaviors. *Activity rewards* occur when parents schedule a pleasant activity as a consequence of a child's problematic behaviors. Many parents use distraction to a pleasant activity to avoid escalating aggression, demanding, or complaining in their children.

The second way in which a reinforcement trap works is by diminishing the contrast between problematic and desirable behavior. The more a child engages in (is reinforced for) problem behaviors, the less likely the child will be reinforced for positive behaviors. If parents feel they are spending hours engaged in unpleasant interactions with a child (sorting out fights, arguing over chores, having attention demanded), the less likely it is that the parents will notice and attend to positive behaviors by the child. Thus, a vicious circle entraps the parent and the child in which the parent has a break whenever the child is not misbehaving, and the child must escalate problem behaviors to obtain the parent's attention.

The foregoing examples refer to problem interactions between two persons; however, reinforcement traps can occur in more complex forms. Parent-child interactions are sometimes influenced by interactions between and with parents, siblings, the extended family, and various people in the community. A number of family therapists have argued that such complex interactions are best understood using concepts that apply to overall structures or systems characterizing families — for example, enmeshment, alliances, and power (Minuchin, 1974). We argue that the use of these global theoretical descriptions is not scientifically justified and at a clinical level sacrifices the efficacy of focusing on specific, clearly definable targets for change. Further, reinforcement theory can be used to describe complex interactions between multiple people. Consider the following examples.

A father and mother are referred because of management problems with their 10-year-old son, who is frequently aggressive, noncompliant, destructive, and moody. Assessment reveals that the mother frequently becomes trapped in escalating conflicts with the son over such issues as chores, homework, and choice of friends. The father, however, spends long hours at work and other outside activities and feels that the mother exaggerates the problems with the son. On a bad day, the following scenario occurs: During the afternoon, mother and son engage in repeated conflicts over chores. By the time the father comes home that night, the mother is exhausted and feels frustrated with the son and unsupported by the father. She expresses her concerns about the son, but the father is unsympathetic because he feels he should not have to come home to a house full of conflict and that the mother should be able to manage the problem. However, sometimes the father acquiesces to her wishes and has a long talk with the son about his behavior.

All three family members are now caught in a number of reinforcement traps. The mother's complaints are aversive to the father and cause him to increase the amount of time he spends away from the family (negative reinforcement). The more the father is away, the more the mother feels unsupported and initiates aversive behavior to the son. Thus, the son is more likely to misbehave with the mother, she is more likely to complain to the father, he withdraws, and so on. The son is also intermittently reinforced for misbehavior by receiving a long talk from his otherwise absent father, and by the temporary increase in marital engagement his behavior produces.

Shirley, 32, is a single parent of daughters aged 5 and 11. She has sought help with the older daughter, who is often angry, sullen, and aggressive to her younger sister. The older daughter frequently hits, bites, and verbally abuses her sister, and often complains that her mother loves her sister more than her. Assessment reveals a common interaction pattern. While Shirley is busy with household chores, a fight usually will occur between the sisters and escalate quickly to aggression. The mother's inquiries consistently reveal that the older sister has been aggressive, and thus the older sister is chastised. The situation repeats itself throughout the day with the younger sister increasing her complaints to the mother that she is being picked on, is not loved, and so on. Finally, the older sister's aggression becomes intolerable to the mother, and the child is sent to bed early. A normal part of Shirley's routine is to read the girls a bedtime story. At first, only the younger sister is read a story, but the older sister's crying is more than Shirley can tolerate, and she ends the night having a talk with the older sister, reassuring her that she is loved and expressing hope that her behavior will improve.

In this example, both girls are reinforced for fighting because of the attentional rewards their fighting receives from an otherwise occupied mother. Because the older sister is bigger and more rapidly provoked into aggression than the younger sister, the older sister is blamed and punished for the fighting. This is a discriminative stimuli to her signaling that she is unlikely to receive any positive attention from her mother for the next few hours, and so the cycle begins again. The younger sister, ostensibly innocent of fighting in the mother's eyes, is reinforced for provoking the older sister to aggression by attentional rewards and increased favoritism she receives from the mother. The mother is reinforced for intervening by the temporary reduction in fighting it produces. Thus, the whole pattern escalates through the day until all players are reinforced. The older sister receives her mother's reassurances of equal love, the younger receives her mother's sole attention during the bedtime story, and Shirley has temporarily stopped the conflict and relieved the feelings of guilt that her oldest daughter's complaints evoke in her.

Table 1.3 summarizes the risk factors for parent-child problems and shows various problems parents can experience in interacting with their children. These difficulties frequently serve as the focus of behavioral family intervention.

SUMMARY

About 10% of children display behavioral and emotional problems that cause concern for the child or their caretakers. The type of problems commonly reported by children and parents vary as a function of age and sex of the child, and many of the problems that indicate child psychopathology are also prevalent in nonclinic children. A child's family is an important factor in the development, maintenance, and treatment of behavioral and emotional problems. However, a comprehensive model of disturbance in children emphasizes the interacting roles of characteristics of the child; factors acting on the child that are internal and external to the family; the personal, marital, and social adjustment of the parents; family interaction patterns; and the influence of the community in which the family lives.

Many childhood disturbances are learned or maintained through the interactions children have with their caretakers. Further, the impact on the child of negative life events such as divorce, maternal depression, and poverty appears to be mediated by the quality of day-to-day parent-child

Table 1.3. Risk Factors for Parent-Child Problems

Risk Factor	Description
Characteristics of the Child	Inherited predisposition to psychopathology, irritable temperament, learning, language, and attention deficit problems, social skills problems, health problems, poor problem-solving skills.
Characteristics of Parents	Poor child-rearing skills, low self-confidence, low satisfaction and efficacy in parenting role, poor problem-solving skills, low tolerance levels, anger and impulse control problems, physical and mental health problems, marital problems, social isolation, inaccuracies in observing and labeling child behavior.
Interactional Problems	Ineffective use of instructions (too many, vague, not pitched at child's developmental level, aversive voice tone), failure to reinforce appropriate child behavior, punishment used impulsively, unpredictably, too rarely, or form of punishment too severe, frequent use of criticism and sarcasm, lack of expression of affection.
Family Environment Problems	Problems with household rules (too few, too many, vague or inappropriate), disorganized and chaotic schedules, few stimulating activities available for children, lack of space, privacy, or quiet, inequitable workload sharing, few opportunities for discussions and problem solving.
Community Factors	Lack of social support from friends and family, interfering extended family, inadequacy of childcare help, mobility problems, unemployment and poverty, lack of medical and psychological services, crowding or isolation.

interactions. Thus, the aim of behavioral family intervention is to identify and remediate parent-child interaction patterns that create and maintain child problems, and identify and remediate contextual factors both within and outside the family that support these problematic parent-child interactions.

Parent-child interactions that are associated with the development and maintenance of problems in children include coercion traps in which both parent and child are reinforced for aggressive behavior; deficits in positive attending, communication, and problem solving; and poor use of instructions and punishment. Broader risk factors that predict these specific parent-child problems are parental distress and psychopathology, marital discord, lack of social support, social isolation, and financial stress.

Chapter 2

Clinical and Empirical Foundations of Behavioral Family Intervention

Parenthood is almost universally acknowledged as being a complex and demanding social role (Dangel & Polster, 1984). Numerous commentators have lamented the lack of adequate preparation of parents to undertake arguably the most important job in the community, namely, raising the future generation of children. Many parents presenting to mental health services concerned about their child's behavior and development want information and concrete practical advice on how to deal more effectively with the problems they confront on a day-to-day basis. Behavioral family intervention is one such approach to assisting families with concerns about their children's behavior and development. This chapter examines the current status of behavioral approaches to working with families of children with behavioral or emotional problems.

BEHAVIORAL FAMILY INTERVENTION: AN INTRODUCTION

Behavioral family intervention is a generic term describing a therapeutic process which aims to effect change in a child's behavior and adjustment through corresponding changes in those aspects of the family environment which are implicated in the maintenance of the child's problem behavior. This may include attempting to change parents' behavior, including the marital relationship, and other aspects of family functioning such as the

26

behavior of siblings, grandparents, babysitters, household organization, the division of labor among caregivers, elimination of safety hazards from a child's play environment, and the provision of age-appropriate toys and activities in the home. It involves the systematic application of social learning principles and behavioral techniques with an emphasis on the reciprocity of change among family members.

Therapeutic Options in Behavioral Family Intervention

Several types of interventions are encompassed within behavioral family intervention and may be incorporated into an intervention protocol, depending on the nature and complexity of the presenting problem and its maintaining conditions. Successful behavioral family intervention must be a flexible approach allowing tailoring of intervention components to a family's requirements. Table 2.1 outlines the therapeutic options in developing an intervention plan for a family. These interventions vary in complexity and the level of clinical sophistication required to effect change. They range from brief, focal interventions using written materials which parents implement with minimal or no training (Azrin & Foxx, 1974) to more complex intervention programs which involve concurrently dealing with a variety of other family issues (e.g., marital problems, maternal depression, financial difficulties, social isolation of parents) in addition to child management problems (Dadds, Schwartz, & Sanders, 1987). Between these two extremes is the behavioral parent-training technology which constitutes the therapeutic centerpiece of the approach. The therapeutic options are not mutually exclusive, and individual families may require interventions at several different levels at different stages of the therapeutic process.

Written Information and Advice. This type of intervention attempts to effect behavior change by providing parents with clear, specific written guidelines they can employ in dealing with a particular behavior problem. Generally, the parent is observed to have sufficient skill and motivation to implement a proposed solution with little professional help. While there are many self-help and parenting books on the market that parents can buy, few of these materials have been properly evaluated. Notable exceptions in the literature include books on specific topics such as toilet training by Azrin and Foxx (1974), taking children shopping (Clarke et al., 1977), handling bedtime disruptiveness (Seymour, Brock, During, & Poole, 1989), and children's use of car restraints (Christophersen & Gyulay, 1981).

Another type of minimal intervention uses the medium of television to convey specific information and advice to parents about child management

Table 2.1. Therapeutic Options in Behavioral Family Intervention with Children

Description of Option	Intervention Methods	Possible Target Behaviors	Examples in Literature
1. Written advice alone	Brief written instructions on how to solve specific child problems. No therapist contact.	Sleep disturbances, toilet training, supermarket behavior problems.	Seymour, Brock, During, & Poole (1989) McManmon, Peterson, Metelenis, McWhinter, & Clark (1982)
2. Written advice plus minimal therapist contact	Written instructions combined with brief therapist contact.	Mealtime behavior problems, bedtime disruption, thumb-sucking.	Christensen & Sanders (1987) Sanders, Bor, & Dadds (1984)
3. Written advice plus active training	Combination of instructions, modeling, rehearsal, and feedback focused on teaching parents how to manage specific problems.	Temper tantrums, noncompliance.	Dadds, Sanders, & Bor (1984)
4. Intensive behavioral parent training	Training methods similar to item 3 above, but focus is on parent-child interaction and the application of diverse parenting skills to a variety of child problems. Includes training in antecedent stimulus control and contingency management techniques.	Oppositional behavior or aggression as a response-class.	Forehand & McMahon (1981) Sanders & Plant (1989) Wells & Egan (1988)
5. Behavioral family intervention	May involve all of the above but, in addition, other family problems are addressed such as marital problems, depression, and anger management.	Concurrent child and parent problems, severe conduct disorder, child depression. Mixed depression and anxiety disorders.	Dadds, Schwartz, & Sanders (1987) Wahler (1980)

techniques. For example, Webster-Stratton (1981, 1982, 1987), in a series of studies, developed a videotaped modeling program which depicts approximately 250 two-minute vignettes involving parent-child interaction, designed to teach parents play skills, use of praise and tangible rewards, and nonpunitive discipline techniques. Parents of children with conduct problems who received a self-administered version of the videotaped modeling program achieved improvements comparable to participants in a therapist-led group which employed the same videotaped program. The self-administered program was more cost-effective.

Written Advice Plus Minimal Therapist Contact. The major difference between this type of intervention and the two previous ones is the availability of back-up professional consultation. This type of intervention occurs when a professional (after preliminary assessment) decides that the problem is relatively mild and can be dealt with by providing the parent with specific practical guidelines (usually written) on how to manage the problem. Such an intervention might be useful as part of well-child care in pediatrics to discuss common developmental issues in raising normal children (Christophersen, 1982). It might be the only type of intervention that is accessible to parents in isolated rural areas, which tend to be more poorly serviced by mental health facilities. Examples of intervention at this level include a study by Sanders, Bor, and Dadds (1984) which trained parents to implement a stimulus control and contingency management program to manage bedtime disruptiveness in preschool children. The program involved brief nightly telephone calls to discuss any problems parents were having in carrying out an extinction program. This type of intervention is not recommended for severe or chronic behavioral problems.

Written Advice Plus Active Training. This intervention involves providing parents with specific instructions; however, it involves more extensive therapeutic involvement whereby the parent is trained through performance-based methods combining instructions, modeling, rehearsal, and feedback. The parent is trained to reach some criterion level of acceptable performance of the behavior change skills being taught. Treatment targets focus on the management of discrete individual behaviors, rather than on developing a broad range of interactional skills. An example of an intervention at this level includes a study by Dadds, Sanders, and Bor (1984) which involved training parents to implement a contingency management program to handle mealtime behavior problems.

Intensive Behavioral Parent Training. Behavioral parent training involves training parents in the application of techniques of behavior change (e.g., use of praise, clear specific instructions, time out) which are implemented in the home under close therapist supervision (Graziano, 1977). Of the approaches that behavioral family intervention encompasses, parent training has the most accumulated evidence regarding its therapeutic value (Kazdin, 1987b; Wells & Forehand, 1981). This is mainly due to the large number of studies which demonstrate its efficacy in the treatment of oppositional behavior disorders (Forehand & Long, 1988). We use the generic term *behavioral family intervention* in preference to *behavioral parent training* because of the greater flexibility it permits in tailoring the focus of intervention to the requirements of individual families. Intensive behavioral parent training programs typically teach parents a variety of interactional and child management skills. Examples of some of the skills taught in our program are outlined in Table 2.2.

Behavioral Family Intervention. Behavioral family intervention may involve interventions at all of the preceding levels; however, additional family problems such as marital difficulties, parents' psychological state (e.g., problems of depression, anger, and irritability), financial difficulties, household organization, and division of labor are also dealt with. Usually, the family is observed to be multidistressed, and problems external to the parent-child relationship are observed to affect parents' interaction with the child and their capacity to acquire and maintain new child management skills. Examples of interventions at this level include work by Wahler and Dumas (1984) and Blechman (1984) with multiproblem parents, Lutzker (1984) with abusive parents, and work by the authors with maritally distressed couples of oppositional children (Dadds, Schwartz, & Sanders, 1987).

Within this broad spectrum of interventions the solution to a child's problem can be matched to the characteristics of the problem and the complexity of its maintaining conditions (Blechman, 1981; Embry, 1984). For example, a parent who presents to her family doctor with a relatively

Table 2.2. Skills Commonly Taught in Behavioral Family Intervention Programs

Skills to Promote Desirable Behavior	Skills to Decrease Problem Behavior
Observing desired behavior	Observing problem behavior
Using descriptive praise	Establishing ground rules in new situations
Attending to desirable behavior	Using good-behavior charts
Using contingent physical contact	Giving clear, calm instructions
Conversing with children	Using response cost and other contingencies
Using incidental teaching	Using quiet time
Modeling desirable behaviors	Using time out
Using prompting, fading, and reinforcement to promote independence	Planned ignoring
Providing engaging activities	Planning activities in high-risk situations

uncomplicated problem of sleep disturbance in an otherwise healthy 2-year-old may not require extensive skills training to implement a new nighttime routine that incorporates planned ignoring of crying once the child is placed in bed. A simple written protocol delivered by the family doctor may suffice. On the other hand, if the child's mother and father frequently argue over the handling of the child's nighttime crying, an intervention to address the associated marital conflict may be essential to ensure that the treatment plan is accurately implemented and the child's difficulty is resolved. In our experience, a skills-oriented intervention dealing with parenting is often an essential element in successful intervention with children, even in cases where the family experiences other additional problems.

In summary, behavioral family intervention is a flexible, action-oriented, educationally focused intervention that attempts to equip family members with the skills and knowledge necessary for resolving pressing family problems with children. The interventions can be relatively brief or alternatively involve a relatively time-consuming, multilevel intervention process, depending on the nature of the family's problem.

ORIGINS OF BEHAVIORAL FAMILY INTERVENTION

The history of behavioral family intervention is closely linked to the history of behavior modification itself. Traditionally, it has emphasized the importance of involving parents, teachers, and other significant people (e.g., institution staff) as mediators or behavior change agents to bring about lasting therapeutic change (Patterson, 1969; Tharp & Wetzel, 1969). Behavior analysts argue that effective intervention with children must access those aspects of the child's social environment that contribute to problem behavior (Patterson, 1982; Wahler, 1969). As we saw in chapter 1, there is substantial evidence implicating parents and other family members in both the development and maintenance of a variety of disturbed behaviors in children (e.g., Dadds, 1987; Hetherington & Martin, 1979; Patterson & Reid, 1984). Training parents to provide different social contingencies for specific problem behaviors as a therapeutic approach provides fairly direct and immediate access to social interaction factors within the family (particularly coercive parent-child relationships) which help to maintain problem behaviors. Many of the management techniques used were directly derived from contemporary learning theory, particularly models of operant behavior (Baer, Wolf, & Risley, 1968; Skinner, 1953) and to a lesser extent from social learning theory (Bandura, 1977) and developmental theory (Bijou & Baer, 1961; Harris & Ferrari, 1983).

Behavioral parent training (by far the most influential approach to working with families from a behavioral perspective) began as an attempt to apply laboratory-derived principles of learning to children's problems. Most of the early studies were devoted to demonstrating that parents could be reliably trained (using fairly simple training methods such as giving the parent instructions) to change their existing management practices, in particular the contingencies of reinforcement and punishment associated with problem behavior. For example, Williams (1959), who is credited with the first published therapeutic application of parent-training techniques, demonstrated that a 21-month-old boy's bedtime tantrum behavior could be eliminated through the use of an extinction procedure. The parents were instructed to put the child to bed at his usual bedtime, to close the bedroom door, and to ignore subsequent screaming and protests. This procedure was effective in eliminating the tantrums completely and was maintained over a 2-year follow-up period.

Other early applications of parent training (Hawkins, Peterson, Schweid, & Bijou, 1966; Patterson & Brodsky, 1966) similarly focused on the oppositional behavior problems of young children. In the process of treating a 4-year-old's tantrums, aggression, and noncompliant behavior, Bijou and his colleagues showed that specific parent and child behaviors could be measured reliably. The effects of the parenting intervention were assessed through the use of a single-subject design (a reversal design), which allowed conclusions regarding cause-and-effect relationships to be made. During the 1960s, several other investigators demonstrated that parents could be trained to modify problem behaviors by "reprogramming" the child's social environment (Patterson, McNeal, Hawkins, & Phelps, 1967; Wahler, Winkel, Peterson, & Morrison, 1965). While early applications of parent training focused on relatively circumscribed problem behaviors, in the latter half of the 1960s more complex and severe behavioral disturbances were investigated.

In the 1970s, parent-training research mushroomed with demonstrations of the usefulness of this type of intervention with an increasing range of clinical problems. Numerous individual studies and several reviews showed that parents can be trained to overcome their own children's problems using behavioral techniques (Berkowitz & Graziano, 1972; Graziano, 1977; O'Dell, 1974). Problem behaviors treated through this approach included oppositional and negativistic behaviors such as noncompliance, temper outbursts, and aggression (Forehand & McMahon, 1981; Patterson, Chamberlain, & Reid, 1982; Patterson, Reid, Jones, & Conger, 1975; Sanders & Glynn, 1981); somatic problems such as recurrent abdominal pain and headaches (Sanders, Rebgetz et al., 1989); enuresis, encopresis; nervous habits such as nail biting and thumbsucking (Christensen & Sanders, 1985); common behavior problems in the home of otherwise normal children such as bedtime and mealtime problems (Dadds et al., 1984; Hall et al., 1972; McMahon & Forehand, 1978; Sanders et al., 1984); problems on shopping trips or in restaurants (Clark et al., 1977); language problems (Laski, Charlop, & Schreibman, 1988); academic learning problems (McNaughton, Glynn, & Robinson, 1987); attention deficit disorders (Pisterman et al., 1989); and children's fears and phobias (Graziano, 1977). Much of this research supported the basic conclusion that when parents accurately implement specific behavior change strategies, there is often a corresponding improvement in their child's behavior and adjustment.

During the 1970s, as research and clinical experience increased and the parent training technology became more widely disseminated, some of the limitations of behavioral family interventions became apparent. Questions were raised regarding the generalization and maintenance effects of treatment (Forehand & Atkeson, 1977); the social acceptability of specific treatment technologies (Kazdin, 1980; Wolf, 1978); the difficulties involved in working with multiproblem families, particularly socially isolated mothers (Wahler, Leske, & Rogers, 1979); maritally distressed couples (Cole & Morrow, 1976); parents from lower socioeconomic groups (Webster-Stratton, 1985); and depressed mothers (Dumas & Wahler, 1983).

During this time, a variety of instructional formats, training methods, and service delivery models were developed to determine optimal methods of teaching parents to implement behavior change strategies (Graziano, 1977). Treatment has been provided in the clinic on either an individual or a group basis, in various community settings, including schools, and during training sessions conducted in the child's own home. Research comparing the effects of different training methods has been less prominent in recent years, and there is a reasonable consensus in the literature that parent training, particularly for more severe behavioral problems, works best when parents are involved in an active, multicomponent learning process. This training process often consists of a combination of providing specific instructions or information, modeling of specific child management techniques (either live or via videotaped demonstrations), rehearsal of skills via role-plays, and provision of in vivo feedback and support as parents attempt to implement techniques in the home or in the clinic (Forehand & McMahon, 1981; Sanders & Glynn, 1981).

There is little direct evidence that specific teaching of behavioral principles is an essential component in producing generalized and lasting behavior change in parents (Hudson, 1982; Sanders & James, 1983). Hudson (1982) compared the effects of three training methods: verbal instruction, verbal instruction plus teaching of behavior principles, and verbal instructions plus modeling and role-play with parents of multihandicapped children. These three groups were compared with a waiting list control group.

The results of this study showed that the teaching of behavioral principles did not enhance the effectiveness of training. The group receiving the modeling and role-playing performed as well as the group taught behavioral principles on a knowledge test of principles, suggesting that parents can acquire some knowledge of principles incidentally.

The selection of educational methods for working with parents depends somewhat on the training objective. For example, if the training goal is to teach a parent how to implement a limited number of specific behavior change techniques to modify a troublesome behavior, relatively straightforward training methods such as giving clear instructions, modeling the procedure, and giving support and feedback may be sufficient. On the other hand, if the training goal is to teach the parent how to apply specific interactional and behavior change skills to a variety of problems, in a variety of situations, with all (relevant) siblings in the family, and to adapt procedures to novel situations the parent might encounter in the future, then the training methods employed may need to be different. The training goal in the latter situation has to do with the generalization and maintenance of parent behavior change. It is not clear how this latter therapeutic goal can best be achieved, although several studies have begun to address this question. We return to this issue in more detail in chapter 7.

During the 1980s, the clinical and empirical basis of behavioral family intervention continued to expand with new applications and new challenges stemming from research which showed that parental characteristics, particularly marital and social adjustment and level of depression, are influential determinants of response to treatment. Contemporary approaches to behavioral family intervention continue to be shaped by theoretical considerations which stress the importance of the child's social environment in determining behavior (Patterson, 1982), evidence from controlled research which shows that parent training is an effective way of managing difficult children, and contingencies provided by families who reinforce and punish therapeutic efforts.

The field has been reasonably responsive to the data that have emerged on the strengths and limitations of interventions. For example, research suggesting that some parents have difficulties in generalizing their parenting skills across settings or over time led to several studies designed to promote better generalization and maintenance effects (Forehand & Atkeson, 1977; Koegel, Glahn, & Nieminen, 1978; Sanders & Glynn, 1981). This contrasts markedly to other family-based approaches, particularly systemic family therapy (Hoffman, 1981), which have relied more on theoretical assumptions and clinical experience than evidence from controlled research.

In many ways, behavioral parent training was a response to the paucity of empirically validated advice available to parents on a range of child-rearing issues. The development of behavioral parent training filled an important gap in the delivery of clinical services to children. For the first time, specific methods of child management were carefully scrutinized using intrasubject replication, group comparison research designs, and reliable measures of outcome.

Effectiveness and Limitations

Behavioral family intervention shares a commitment with behavioral approaches in general to the close empirical scrutiny of the effects of intervention procedures. This process of ongoing empirical evaluation and attention to methodological and measurement issues in general constitutes a core defining feature of the behavioral approach and has been one of the field's single most important contributions to mental health research and clinical practice (Graziano, 1977). During the past 3 decades, behavioral family intervention has evolved as a viable, empirically supported approach to working with behaviorally and emotionally disturbed children (Forehand & Long, 1988; Twardosz & Nordquist, 1988; Webster-Stratton, Kalpacoff, & Hollinsworth, 1988; Wells & Egan, 1988). The strongest empirical support for the efficacy of parent training is for children with oppositional behavior problems. Many studies have been conducted which have clearly established the usefulness of behavioral parent training as a treatment approach (Forehand & McMahon, 1981; Graziano, 1977; Kazdin, 1987b).

Short-term Treatment Effects. There is a considerable body of evidence that parent training produces significant short-term behavioral change in both parents and children immediately following treatment. Desirable outcomes have been demonstrated repeatedly using a variety of outcome criteria including observations in the home by trained independent observers, parent-completed questionnaires measuring parental perceptions of child behavior, parental attitudes toward the child, and parental satisfaction with treatment (Forehand, Griest, & Wells, 1979; Kazdin, 1987b).

Consumer Satisfaction. Parents undergoing behavioral parent training are generally satisfied consumers and view the specific behavioral techniques (e.g., praise, time out) taught in these training programs as both effective and acceptable (McMahon & Forehand, 1983; Webster-Stratton, 1989). Much less is known about how children view the treatment process, although Dadds, Adlington, and Christensen (1987) found that both nonclinic and oppositional children rated time out as an acceptable strategy for parents to use. Furey and Basili (1988) found that the child's level of deviant behavior was unrelated to parental consumer satisfaction, but having a noncompliant daughter, low SES, depression, and poor parenting skills were all predictors of dissatisfaction.

Durability of Treatment Gains. Several studies have examined the durability of treatment effects (Forehand & Long, 1988; Sanders & James, 1983). In general, these studies have shown good maintenance of treatment gain, particularly when the child's problem is not complicated by parent-related difficulties or social adversity. The treatment program employed by Forehand and his colleagues represents the most thoroughly evaluated parent-training program. Many studies with acting-out children whose primary presenting problem is noncompliance have shown that immediately post-treatment, target children display reduced levels of oppositional behavior, and their parents increase positive attending, decrease aversive attention, perceive their children as better behaved, evaluate the intervention (e.g., time out) as effective and acceptable, and are satisfied with the treatment they received. In a recent long-term follow-up study of adolescents who had been treated with this program 4 to 10 years previously, results showed that on most measures of adolescent functioning, treated children were indistinguishable from a comparison group of nonclinic adolescents (Forehand & Long, 1988). However, one third of the treated group had received other treatment since leaving the program and were performing significantly more poorly academically. These findings highlight the importance of school-based intervention with disturbed children. The parents of the treated children were functioning just as well as parents of nonclinic adolescents on measures of depression, marital adjustment, and parenting competence.

Generalization Effects. Several studies have also investigated the generalization effects of treatment (Feldman, Case, Rincover, Town, & Betel, 1989; Koegel et al., 1978; Laski et al., 1988; Miller & Sloane, 1976; Sanders & Dadds, 1982; Sanders & Glynn, 1981; Sanders & Plant, 1989). In general, this research shows that parents can be trained successfully to generalize their skills (e.g., use of praise and time out) across settings, siblings, and time. (See Sanders & James, 1983, for a review.) We return to this issue later in this chapter and again in chapter 7.

Predictors of Response to Treatment.

As the field of behavioral parent training has matured, both empirical evidence and clinical experience suggest that not all parents or families benefit to the same extent from treatment (Bernal, Klinnert, & Schultz, 1980; Eyberg & Johnson, 1974; Johnson & Christensen, 1975; Wahler & Graves, 1983). Several commentators have highlighted difficulties which can be encountered when there are concurrent yet unresolved marital problems, maternal depression, and other family difficulties such as economic hardship (Furey & Basili, 1988; Griest & Wells, 1983). These concerns have prompted two lines of inquiry. First, several studies sought to identify parental characteristics which predict successful treatment outcome (e.g., Furey & Basili, 1988; McMahon, Forehand, Griest & Wells, 1981). A second group of studies tried to clarify more clearly the obstacles to change by defining the ecological context within which parents are expected to implement treatment strategies (e.g., Sanders, Dadds, & Bor, 1989; Wahler & Graves, 1983). This involves a different approach to the problem of nonresponding in that explanations were not sought in terms of the personal characteristics of parents but by examining the ecological context within which parents were expected to implement change strategies.

The research has shown that behavioral parent training has limited effects when there is a concurrent unresolved marital problem (Dadds, Schwartz, & Sanders, 1987), when the mother suffers from depression (McMahon, Forehand, Greist, & Wells, 1981), when the family lives in adverse socioeconomic circumstances (Dumas, 1986; Kazdin, 1990b; Webster-Stratton, 1985), and when the mother has a low level of social support available to her (Wahler, 1980).

Several authors have lamented the apparent difficulty in working with multidistressed families and have made various proposals to improve the outcome of treatment by expanding the focus of treatment (Wahler, 1980). These suggestions have included providing additional skills training to overcome problems which are hypothesized to be related to child management difficulties. Such adjunctive interventions include teaching parents self-management skills (Griest et al., 1982), providing concurrent marital therapy (Dadds, Sanders, Behrens, & James, 1987; Dadds, Schwartz, & Sanders, 1987), providing training in the selection and arrangement of activities for children in high-risk situations (Sanders & Christensen, 1985; Sanders & Dadds, 1982), anger management (Goldstein, Keller, & Erne, 1985), social support training (Dadds & McHugh, in press), and the development of better liaison between home and school for the management of school-based behavioral problems (Blechman, 1984). While each of these suggestions has merits with selected cases, our clinical experience with multidistressed families indicates that it is better to use the least cluttered intervention as possible in achieving the desired goal. This means including in an intervention only those components required to achieve the therapeutic objectives negotiated with a family. Adjunctive treatment should only be used when there is clear evidence (from either case data or the research literature) to link the additional problem (e.g., depression) to the parents' capacity to alter dysfunctional parenting practices. The mere coexistence of the two problems does not constitute such proof. In chapter 7 we return in more detail to the issue of how to design effective adjunctive interventions.

RECENT INNOVATIONS IN BEHAVIORAL FAMILY INTERVENTION

As the field of behavioral family intervention has matured, there have been several calls for changes in the parent-training technology to enhance its effectiveness with specific populations (Griest & Wells, 1983). These changes have included the need to develop strategies that promote the generalization and maintenance of changes in parental behavior; the need to change the emphasis of intervention away from controlling children's problem behavior to a focus on prosocial behavior; the identification of clinical and consultation skills used by effective therapists; and the emergence of an ecological perspective in parent training.

Generalization of Parent Behavior

It is generally recognized in behavior therapy research that effective treatment frequently requires helping clients generalize their skills to conditions outside the initial training setting where the skills were first learned (Stokes & Osnes, 1989). In the case of parents and children learning to deal with family conflict more effectively, it might involve the parent applying the same behavior change strategy used with one child in the family to a sibling who displays similar problem behavior (sibling generalization). It might also involve the parent learning to deal with situations outside the home in which a child is disruptive (e.g., in a supermarket) in the same or similar ways (setting generalization). Alternatively, the child who is taught to speak pleasantly when making requests of one adult (e.g., the father) should be able to display similar polite behavior when speaking to other adults, such as the mother (person generalization). The foregoing examples illustrate the importance of identifying the extent to which treatment facilitates the appropriate generalization of parent and child behavior. At the same time, parents and children must learn to discriminate conditions in which generalization is not desirable (Sanders, 1984). For example, using the same unmodified token reinforcement program with a 14-year-old teenager as was used with a 7-year-old is likely to be ineffective.

While only a small number of studies have examined the generalization effects of behavioral parent-training procedures (Koegel et al., 1978, Miller & Sloane, 1976; Sanders & Dadds, 1982; Sanders & Glynn, 1981; Sanders & Plant, 1989), the results of this research suggest that generalized implementation of new parenting strategies is indeed a realistic and feasible clinical goal. These findings show that some parents generalize their implementation of behavioral skills across different childcare settings with relatively minimal or no prompting, while other parents do not (Sanders & Glynn, 1981). Furthermore, there is some evidence that reductions in negative parental behavior seem to generalize and maintain better than increases in positive or nonaversive behavior (Sanders & Dadds, 1982).

Several specific adjunctive interventions have been employed with parents who fail initially to generalize across settings, including training parents in self-management skills (Sanders & Glynn, 1981) and planned activities training, which involves training parents to arrange suitable activities for children in high-risk situations in the community (Sanders & Dadds, 1982). These and a variety of other possibilities for promoting or restricting the generalization of parental behavior change are discussed in detail in chapter 7.

Importance of Social Competency

It is unfortunate that so much of the research in the field of behavioral family intervention has involved working with oppositional and conduct-disordered children. This has resulted in much of the research focusing on the reduction of behavioral excesses such as noncompliance with parental instructions, aggression, demanding, and tantrum behaviors. Relatively little work has focused on using family interventions to promote socially competent or prosocial behavior in children. These concerns have been reflected by a move within clinical child psychology research toward examining the determinants of social competence in children and their caregivers (Blechman, Tinsley, Carella, & McEnroe, 1985; Gardiner, 1987) and its relationship to behavioral disturbance. Children who have low levels of social competence are rated by teachers as having higher levels of behavioral disturbance (Blechman et al., 1985).

Some research shows that behaviorally disturbed children differ from nonclinical samples not only on measures of aversive behavior but on a variety of indices of positive parent-child interaction as well. Gardiner (1987), using home observations, found that preschoolers with conduct problems spent significantly less time than nonproblem children in cooperative activities, joint activities, and conversations with their mother. They also watched more television or spent more time doing nothing and less time in constructive play.

Training techniques that have been used successfully in teaching parents specific behavior change techniques to reduce problem behavior or to increase desirable behaviors in children can be adapted to teach parents how to model, prompt, and reinforce prosocial or socially competent behaviors. For example, parents can be taught how to arrange activities in situations where children might otherwise have little or nothing to do (e.g., traveling in the car) or when a parent is necessarily busy (e.g., in the bank). Important relationship-enhancing skills include behaviors such as giving positive affection, soliciting children's opinions and ideas about family activities or the child's own experiences, prompting and reinforcing independence and decision making, and learning social skills such as receiving and making telephone calls appropriately or issuing and receiving invitations from other children. For example, Sanders and Dadds (1982) successfully taught mothers of oppositional children to arrange engaging activities for children in community situations in an effort to prevent problem behavior.

Much more detailed attention must be given to the selection of behavioral targets which attempt to improve children's proficiency at dealing constructively with relationship conflict and their interactions with peers. Parents may be crucial in determining the extent to which children acquire and maintain prosocial behaviors.

Importance of Process Variables

The importance of the therapist-client relationship in behavior therapy has received increased attention recently (Chamberlain & Baldwin, 1987; Chamberlain, Patterson, Reid, Kavanagh, & Forgatch, 1984; Dadds, 1989; Sweet, 1987; Twardosz & Nordquist, 1988). Several authors have noted that there is an emerging convergence of opinion in the literature that successful clinicians working with families should be warm, empathic, supportive, encouraging, and humorous. However, there is little direct empirical evidence which examines the relationship between therapist variables and outcome in behavioral parent training. Within the behavioral family intervention literature, the descriptions of parent-training technology have been incomplete and therefore less than completely accurate.

The technological descriptions of parent training as reflected in scientific journals and books on the subject have largely ignored important process variables that affect the acceptability (to parents) of the behavior change techniques advocated by therapists. These techniques include a diverse range of clinical and interpersonal skills which provide the relationship context within which family intervention takes place. There is little doubt that therapists differ markedly in their effectiveness as parent trainers. For example, some therapists develop techniques of providing negative feedback to parents which prompt parents to question how they currently manage family problems. However, when other therapists attempt to convey the same message, the parent feels criticized, devalued, and fails to return for the next appointment. Therapist variables in delivering effective behavioral family services involve more than simply having a liberal dose of empathy, humor, warmth, and genuineness. These characteristics do not lead to replicable descriptions of specific clinical skills that exemplify competent clinical offerings to families.

Behavioral family intervention from a therapist's perspective involves a series of interrelated consultation tasks that occur within an interpersonal context of a therapeutic relationship. Kanfer and Schefft (1988) described a seven-phase therapeutic process model which outlines the specific tasks to be accomplished in therapy. These phases are (a) role structuring and creating the therapeutic alliance, (b) developing a commitment to change, (c) conducting the behavior analysis, (d) negotiating treatment objectives and methods, (e) implementing treatment and maintaining motivation, (f) monitoring and evaluating progress, and (g) maintenance, generalization, and termination of treatment. As this model applies generally to working with adults, some modification is needed to depict the consultation process involved in working with children and their families.

It is useful to differentiate between consultation tasks and consultation skills. The former includes the process steps or tasks clinicians must accomplish, and the latter includes the interpersonal, communication, and therapeutic skills the clinician must have to carry out the required tasks. While the precise form of the intervention required must depend substantially on the results of a comprehensive clinical assessment and behavioral analysis, the basic consultation tasks involved remain fairly constant. Table 2.3 summarizes the key consultation tasks and associated clinical skills required of therapists to carry out an intervention plan.

Emergence of an EcoBehavioral Perspective

The plea for ecologically oriented inquiry has been a strong trend within psychology over the past 2 decades. Bronfenbrenner (1977) proposed an experimental ecological approach to developmental psychology. He conceived of the ecological environment as a topographically nested arrangement of structures. Each structure has elements which are contained within the next structure. To understand the acquisition and maintenance of problem behaviors within the family from an ecological perspective, research is required at all system levels (micro, meso, exo, and macro). The so-called ecobehavioral perspective in the family intervention field fundamentally argues for the importance of considering variables external to the moment-to-moment encounters between parent and child as important determinants of parenting, and hence the child's learning environment. Parental behavior toward children is clearly a function of more than the pattern of antecedent and consequent events children provide contingent on parental conduct, although these contingencies are important. Variables

Table 2.3. Consultation Tasks and Clinical Skills

Consultation Tasks	Important Clinical Skills
1. Creating a therapeutic alliance	1. Effective listening, empathic, and other interviewing and rapport-building skills
2. Negotiating an assessment protocol	2. Translating vague or nonspecific concerns of clients into concrete, specific goals for change
3. Discussing assessment results	3. Providing a rationale for data collection tasks
4. Negotiating goals of intervention	4. Negotiating with parents and school personnel regarding data collection requirements
5. Designing an intervention	5. Conveying assessment results clearly and succinctly; dealing with client defensiveness and resistance
6. Implementing treatment	6. Formulating with the parent a shared explanation for the problem behavior
7. Monitoring and evaluating progress	7. Conducting a behavioral rehearsal with the parent as a skill-training strategy
8. Programming for generalization and maintenance of therapeutic gains	8. Providing constructive negative feedback without being critical
	9. Dealing with dependency problems

such as a couple's marital interaction, occupational demands and stresses, interactions with relatives and neighbors, psychological state, and the family's financial resources influence either directly or indirectly parents' behavior toward their children. For example, a father who works 80 hours per week has little time to devote to child rearing. A mother who experiences frequent criticism from a mother-in-law who looks after a child 3 days per week is exposed to a hostile environment which may be difficult to avoid if alternative care is not readily available.

Wahler argued that the conceptual basis for understanding family problems must be broadened to encompass the wider social context within which the family lives. For example, Wahler (1980) found that families characterized by poor parental education, single parenthood, residence in high crime areas, crowded living conditions, and low incomes were at high risk for failure in behavioral parent training. High-risk mothers reported lower rates of social contacts; lower rates of self-initiation of contacts; higher rates of interaction with relatives judged as aversive; lower rates of help for their children from friends, relatives, and informal networks; and more frequent use of social agencies. Wahler argued that high-risk mothers become socially insulated from the community support systems used by nonproblem families for advice, guidance, and feedback on child-rearing matters.

Other examples of research examining parent-child relationships from an ecobehavioral perspective include an observational study by Sanders,

Dadds and Bor, (1989). These authors observed oppositional and nonproblem children in each of five childcare settings in the home (breakfast, getting ready for school or preschool, a structured play interaction, bathtime, and bedtime). The study attempted to identify contextual variables which predict levels of oppositional behavior in children and aversive behavior in parents. The observation system allowed for recording the child's and the mother's aversive and nonaversive behavior and their location, ongoing activity, and who was in their immediate vicinity. The results of a stepwise multiple regression analysis showed that while deviant behavior in children was best predicted by corresponding levels of maternal aversive behavior, in some 63% of individual cases the addition of contextual variables significantly increased the amount of unique variance explained. In other words, in some families the variables of maternal activity, people present, and the child's location affect how disruptive a child is.

These findings point to the need to determine more precisely the elements that define a parenting environment. Difficult children may be much more difficult for a parent to manage in some situations than in others. Situations in which a parent has competing demands on time or attention, in which there are time constraints (e.g., getting ready to go out), or in which parents disagree about how to deal with the child may represent high-risk occasions for returning to maladaptive or coercive styles of interaction with children. However, it is unclear what combinations of contextual, cognitive, and affective variables best define a high-risk parenting environment. Sanders and Plant (1989) defined a high-risk setting as "a combination of contextual variables that serve to increase the probability that parents experience difficulties in managing their child and fail to implement trained skills" (p. 285).

Several studies have investigated the extent to which child management training procedures produce changes in parent behavior which generalize across different childcare settings. For example, Sanders and Glynn (1981), Sanders (1982), Sanders and Dadds (1982), and Sanders and Plant (1989) found that while some parents generalized their implementation of behavioral procedures in a situation in the home, others did not and required extra generalization enhancement intervention to produce consistent implementation across settings. These findings highlight the need for careful attention to the multiple settings within which parenting takes place and to the issue of generalization and maintenance of treatment effects.

Applications with New Populations

The versatility of a behavioral family intervention model has become more apparent with the expansion of the technology to new clinical problems. This expansion has involved more active involvement and preparation of parents in the individual treatment of children for problems such as obesity (Graves, Meyers, & Clark, 1988), chronic pain, and the management of chronic diseases such as cystic fibrosis (Sanders, Gravestock, & Wanstall, 1990). For example, Sanders, Rebgetz et al. (1989) trained children to employ self-coping strategies such as relaxation and distraction in managing episodes of recurrent abdominal pain. In addition, however, parents were trained to prompt and reinforce self-coping behavior and the absence of pain complaints. Other expansions have involved the direct application of parent-training procedures to new problem areas. These additional areas of application include teaching parents to become remedial tutors for children with severe reading difficulties (McNaughton et al., 1987; Scott & Ballard, 1986) and teaching parents of depressed children more effective child management skills (Sanders, Dadds, Johnston et al., 1989).

SUMMARY

Behavioral family intervention is effective in many families seeking assistance for their child because of behavioral and emotional problems. Graziano (1977) argued that the approach has revolutionized clinical services for children and is now widely used in many clinical settings. Training which combines instructions, modeling, and feedback is useful in teaching parenting skills.

Behavioral family intervention can be used with a wide variety of clinical problems. Parental involvement is often important in child-oriented therapy (e.g., pediatric pain management programs), in which parents often influence whether a child takes the process of therapy seriously, completes homework tasks, and so on. The broader social context within which the family operates is an important determinant of whether parents and children implement agreed-on solutions. Most of the problems that come to the clinicians' attention concern social interaction. Furthermore, it is through daily interactions with family members that children learn maladaptive behaviors which may bring them into conflict with siblings, their peer group, school authorities, neighbors, and law enforcement agencies.

Children referred to mental health services for psychological or adjustment problems present with a variety of complex, interrelated problems in areas of social, emotional, language, cognitive, and academic functioning. For example, children referred for acting-out behavior problems such as aggression, noncompliance, tantrums, and destructiveness often have problems of impulse control as well as anxiety, depression, and poor school performance. They may also be engaged in secretive or covert behaviors such as stealing, truanting, or lying that bring them into conflict with school authorities, the police, and their parents. Such children can be markedly lacking in social skills and have few friends. Other children who may benefit from a behavioral family intervention approach include shy, withdrawn children whose behavior is more a problem to themselves than to others in their social environment.

Behavioral family intervention allows therapists to tailor solutions to family problems according to the complexity of the presenting problems and their maintaining conditions. The interventions may be brief or may last many months or years in difficult cases.

Part II
Clinical Assessment of Family Interaction

Chapter 3
Intake Interview

The next three chapters deal with the clinical assessment of children with behavioral and emotional problems. The assessment process plays an important role in behavioral family intervention. First, it involves the formulation of a child's problem into a behavioral diagnosis wherein presenting problems are conceptualized as excesses, deficits, or problems of inappropriate or inadequate stimulus control (Kanfer & Saslow, 1969). Second, it helps defines the type of intervention a child and family should receive. Third, it allows for the continuous monitoring and evaluation of the effectiveness of treatment. Fourth, assessment clarifies the obstacles (e.g., poverty, parental motivation) and resources (e.g., cooperative classroom teacher) in the child's environment which may either hinder or facilitate achieving therapeutic objectives. Finally, assessment enables the selection of therapeutic procedures that are compatible with the family's current life situation.

Assessment comprises four main elements: the intake interview, the use of observational and self-report measures, the completion of a functional analysis of behavior, and the communication of assessment results to relevant family members and in some cases others involved in the care, supervision, or education of the child (e.g., a child's teacher). In this chapter we discuss strategies for conducting an intake evaluation of a child's problem and the difficulties clinicians can experience in this phase of the consultation process. Chapter 4 discusses behavioral observation and self-report measures which can be employed in the initial assessment and the completion of a functional analysis. Chapter 5 discusses the communication of assessment information to parents and others.

INTAKE INTERVIEW: AN
OVERVIEW

The intake interview serves an important function in the clinical assessment of children. It is usually the family's first point of contact with a clinical service and can determine whether parents return for further assistance. Most parents who are concerned about their children's welfare or behavior and have made the effort to consult a professional to discuss the problem, approach the initial contact with some trepidation. Parents' anxiety can be due to uncertainty about the process of therapy, concerns about their own role in contributing to the problem, or uncertainty about whether taking the child to see a professional is the right way to handle the problem. Such anxieties are compounded if the child's parents or relatives disagree over the issue of seeking professional help or if a parent has had to coerce a reluctant child or spouse into attending the initial appointment. Parents may have received inaccurate information from a referral agency about the kind of help a clinic can provide, and thus they may need an explanation of the therapy process.

During the intake interview, the clinician must formulate hypotheses about the nature of the presenting problem and its maintaining conditions, and determine the type of therapeutic approach that is indicated and whether the problem is likely to benefit from the type of help the therapist can offer. The intake interview has several additional functions. These include establishing rapport with the parents and child, identifying factors within the broader social and cultural context in which the child lives that might affect the child's development, determining the parents' capacity to carry out a treatment program, and establishing mutually acceptable goals for treatment and a contract for the provision of professional services.

Preparations for an Initial Appointment

Depending on how the referral was received, a great deal or almost nothing may be known about the case prior to a first contact. It is often useful to make certain preparations prior to the initial session to ensure that the parents attend the appointment on time and that the first session gets off to a good start. These preparations can include the following steps:

1. *Check clinic files.* This should be done routinely to determine whether the child has been referred previously or has been seen by another therapist in the same clinic. Check on the outcome of the previous contact. What services were received? What was the referral problem at that time? Who was involved in the case? What was the outcome of the contact according to case notes? For cases seen for the first time, check on the date of initial referral. Have the parents had to wait for a long time before

receiving an appointment? If so, what explanation for the wait has been provided?

2. *Arrange the initial appointment at a time that allows both parents (where appropriate) to attend.* Arrange the first appointment for the parents only. Several steps can be taken to ensure that both of the child's parents in an intact, two-parent family can attend. These include requesting that both parents attend the initial meeting and scheduling appointments at a time when both parents' attendance is more likely (after normal working hours). Another useful strategy is to call each parent personally and invite them to come in, explaining that their presence will facilitate proper assessment of the child's problem. This issue is considered in more depth in chapter 9. Check that the parent can make alternative childcare arrangements, where possible.

3. *Give the parents clear directions to the clinic.* Send them a map to the clinic if necessary to decrease the likelihood that the parents will get lost and arrive late or miss the first session.

4. *Check whether the family has any special needs.* This includes needs of either the child or parents which would hinder or promote regular attendance (e.g., access for wheelchairs, transportation problems due to physical disability).

5. *Give a reminder.* Considerable time can be wasted due to parental nonattendance at initial appointments. Three days prior to the scheduled appointment, ask the clinic receptionist (if available) to call the family to confirm attendance.

6. *Reinforce the parents for prompt attendance.* This can involve thanking the parents for arriving on time or for finding the clinic if it is difficult to find.

INTERVIEW WITH PARENTS

During the intake interview with the parents, the clinician must complete a thorough psychological and developmental history. This is best conducted without the child present. The intake procedure is organized into two sections: an interview with the parents and an interview with the child. The main areas to be explored and examples of appropriate questions follow. However, skillful clinical interviewing is more than covering a predetermined list of potentially relevant questions or topics. It is a fluid process of hypothesis generation and testing in which the interviewer, after an initial description of the presenting problem, generates hypotheses about the nature of the problem and its maintenance. Questioning and other interviewing tools (e.g., paraphrasing, summarizing) are used to formulate and test hypotheses generated, and the interviewer is constantly on the alert for both confirmatory and contradictory information which will lead to refinement of the hypotheses about the child's or family's problems. Answers should influence what subsequent questions are asked. The clinician should try to eliminate unnecessary repetition or digression, to structure the interview appropriately, and to manage time efficiently. At the same time, the interviewer must communicate concern for and understanding of the parents' difficulties with their child.

Clinical Guidelines

The clinical interview with the child's parents can usually be accomplished in an hour, although on some occasions it may take up to 90 minutes.

Obtain Identifying Information. Basic biographical information is important in every case; however, it is not necessary to begin an interview in this way.

Establish Source of Referral. Clarify how the referral came about. Who referred the child? Did the parents bring a referral letter? If so, quickly read the letter before proceeding.

Discuss Parents' Main Concerns About Their Child (Presenting Complaint). Begin with open-ended questions that give the parents an opportunity to describe what the child is doing that causes concern. "How can I help you? What's the problem your having with John . . . ?"

Use follow-up questions to encourage parents to elaborate on the nature of the presenting complaint. "Apart from his bad temper, is there anything else that Brad does that is concerning you at the moment?"

Use exemplification probes to place the problem described in a specific situational context. "Can you think of a recent example where he became violent and tell me exactly what happened?"

Establish the approximate frequency, intensity, duration, and context within which each of the problems occurs. Clarify approximately when the problem first began.

Clarify Other Difficulties the Child May Have (Associated Problems). The parents' description of the presenting problem provides a reasonable idea of the major problems that concern the parents. At this stage, hypotheses about the nature of the presenting problem will emerge (is this child anxious, depressed, enuretic, having conduct problems at school? and so on). Explore the occurrence of problems that covary frequently with the main presenting complaint. Knowledge of clinical psychopathology in children is needed to do this. Summarize the main complaints, and then ask about associated or related symptoms. For example, "Let me sum up. So you're mainly concerned about his bad temper at home, his disobedience, and his poor grades in math. Is that right? OK. Can you tell me whether he has any of the following problems? Have you had any problems with stealing or lying?"

Explore the presence or absence of other problems which may be logically related to the pattern of presenting complaints.

Establish the History of the Presenting Complaint.
1. *Date of onset:* Establish when the problem first began. If the problem has been episodic, date the commencement of the most recent episode. "When did this problem first begin?" "How long has Jimmy been crying in his sleep?"
2. *Chronological development of symptoms:* Clarify how the problem has changed from the time it first began to the present. Note whether there have been any periods of remission since the date of onset.

Establish Topography of Presenting Problems. Clarify the dimensions of the problem behavior by getting a best estimate of the frequency, duration, or intensity of each behavior of interest.
1. *Establish frequency:* It is important to determine whether you are dealing with a high- or low-frequency behavior, as this will influence the selection of specific assessment and intervention techniques.
2. *Estimated duration:* Ask the parents to estimate how long a behavior lasts from commencement to termination. Establish the highest, lowest, and average duration of the behavior.

Previous History of Psychological or Psychiatric Help.
1. *Type of problem:* Have the parents sought the help of any psychiatric, psychological, or other mental health services for the child in the past?
2. *Previous help sought:* What kind of help was sought, who was seen, how frequently, what was advised, and what was the outcome?

Family History and Circumstances. Determine the main characteristics of the child's family unit, and identify any circumstances which may create obstacles for therapeutic change.
1. *Family structure:* List the names, sex, and age of all members of the child's family, from eldest to youngest. Draw a family tree or genogram if appropriate, noting all family members deceased or living.
2. *People in the home:* List all people who live in the child's home on a regular basis.
3. *Contact with grandparents:* Are the child's grandparents alive? What kind of contact is maintained? Is there any interference by grandparents or other relatives? What kind of support is received?
4. *Family history of psychiatric disturbance:* Is there any history of psychiatric disturbance in the mother or father's family? If so, note the type of problem.
5. *Living arrangements:* Where does the child live? Do the parents own their own home or rent or lease accommodations? How long has the family lived in the current residence? Has the child been subjected to frequent changes of residence?

6. *Childcare arrangements:* Determine what kind of childcare arrangements the family has. Who is responsible for the child after school if both parents work? If there are multiple caregivers, list the childcare arrangements for each day of the week. Note whether other caregivers experience difficulty with the child.

7. *Financial problems:* Is the family experiencing any major financial troubles (e.g., unemployment, recent loss of job or bankruptcy) that constitute a source of family stress?

8. *Neighborhood:* What are the parents' perceptions of their neighborhood? Is the neighborhood a high crime area?

Family Relationships and Interaction. Explore the nature of the child's relationships with family members.

1. *Relationships between parents:* Determine the nature and degree of marital conflict that may exist in the family. Inquiry into this area must be handled tactfully. A statement such as the following can be helpful in discussing this issue: "Sometimes children who are having problems place a strain on the parents themselves. For example, there may be disagreements or arguments about how to deal with the child's behavior. How has [name of child] problem affected the way you get along with each other?"

Once the general topic is opened up, inquiry into other aspects of marital relationships is easier. The main issue to determine is whether the degree of marital conflict is sufficient to create a serious obstacle to developing alternative child management techniques. Is family dissolution a possibility? If there has been a marital break-up, obtain precise information about custody and access arrangements. In a reconstituted family, determine the child's relationship with the stepparent or de facto partner. (Chapter 9 discusses the assessment of marital conflict in more depth.)

2. *Parent-child interaction:* Obtain a verbatim account of how parents see their own and each other's relationship with the child. "How would you describe your relationship with [name of child]?" or "How does [spouse's name] generally get along with [name of child]?"

3. *Parents' expectations and family rules:* Determine the kinds of rules and expectations the parents have of the child. Clarify regular and occasional chores required of the child, what pocket money, or allowance system (if any) the family operates on, as well as the child's involvement in daily household tasks or supervision of younger siblings.

4. *Child's involvement in family decision making:* Clarify how the family arrives at decisions that directly affect the child such as what clothing a child wears, where the family spends holidays, family outings on weekends, out-of-school sporting activities, participation in music lessons.

5. *Child's relationship with siblings and significant others:* In the parents' view,

how does the child get along with brothers and sisters (if any) or significant others such as aunts, uncles, cousins, grandparents, and stepparents with whom the child has regular contact?

Developmental History. The developmental history provides information about the nature and circumstances of the child's development. It is used to identify any significant deviations from normal in the rate of development, as well as any adverse environmental conditions which may have affected the course of the child's development.

1. *Pregnancy, delivery, and neonatal period:* Was the pregnancy planned? Were there any complications or difficulties during the pregnancy or delivery?

2. *Infancy:* Were there any problems with feeding, sleeping, fussing, or crying during infancy? Were developmental milestones for physical and social development (e.g., sitting unsupported, walking unaided, first words, two-word utterances) attained within normal limits?

3. *Toddler years:* Have there been any problems with elimination or toilet training? List significant immunizations, allergies, illnesses, and periods of separation. Was the child active or placid? Were there any problems with attachment or reunion with the mother after separation?

4. *Preschool age:* What kind of preschool experiences has the child had (playgroups, kindergarten, preschool)? Were there any difficulties with any of these? How did the child cope with separation and interacting with other children?

5. *Middle childhood:* How did the child cope with beginning school? Does the child like school? How does the child get along with teachers and classmates? Does the child exhibit any disruptive behavior or other difficulties at school (teasing, bullying, being bullied)? Are there any problems with academic performance or completing homework? Does the child make friends easily?

6. *Early adolescence:* What level of physical maturation has been attained? Are there any problems with menstrual periods or other changes associated with puberty? How has the child coped with the transition to high school? Is the child short for his or her age?

Educational History.

1. *Schools attended:* List the schools the child has attended and dates. This is important to determine to what extent the child's school experience has been disrupted by changes of schools or teachers.

2. *Academic progress:* Inquire about the child's academic progress, including grades earned in the previous 2 years. A copy of recent report cards is often helpful.

3. *Behavior and peer relationships at school:* Ask the parents about the child's behavior in the classroom and relationships with other children. "How

does he get along with the other children? Does he have any difficulty making friends with other children?"

Child's General Health. Does the child have any current major health problems, handicaps, or disabilities? Has the child had any significant medical problems in the past? Have there been any operations or hospitalizations? Ask the same questions regarding the health of both parents.

Therapeutic Expectations. Determine the parents' expectations regarding the process and outcome of therapy. Some parents have clear ideas about the kind of help they would like; others are unsure about the usefulness of treatment. Clarify with the parents what specific changes they would like to see in their child's behavior or adjustment.

INTERVIEW WITH THE CHILD

Some therapists design intervention programs without actually having spoken to the child about the problem, preferring to use either direct observation of parent-child interaction or simply relying on parental reports. We believe such an approach is a mistake for the following reasons. First, children themselves (particularly those over the age of 6 or 7) often have important ideas regarding the nature of the presenting problem. Second, the child's or family's problem can be inaccurately formulated if parental report is relied on exclusively. For example, the parent may be unaware of the child's subjective experiences (e.g., thoughts about death, running away, suicide, expectations, hopes, fantasies, fears, or worries), particularly if communication is poor. However, a child's level of involvement in formulating the solution to a problem depends on the type of problem, the child's developmental level, and the parents' competencies in handling the problem themselves. For example, with anxious and depressed older children, children themselves are the best informants regarding their feelings, suicidal ideation, and so on. With disruptive, aggressive, oppositional children or developmentally disabled, psychotic, or autistic children, parental and teacher interviews and direct observation often provide more useful assessment information.

Clinical Guidelines

Children's capacity to discuss a personal problem or their view of the family situation depends on the therapist's ability to help the child relax and feel comfortable with an unfamiliar assessment environment.

Set the Child at Ease by Discussing Some General Issues First. Begin by greeting the child by name and introducing yourself: "Hello Brian, I'm Dr. . . . ." Next, discuss some general issues or nonthreatening factual questions that will help the child get started. For example, find out the child's full name, age, school, grade, teacher's name, and names of brothers and sisters, if any.

Establish the Child's View of the Reason For Attendance. After the initial greeting, it is often useful to ask children if they know why their parents brought them to the clinic today. For example, "Do you know why mom brought you in here today?" If the child says yes, find out the child's view of the reason. If the child says that he or she does not know, give a general explanation of what you understand to be the reason, and then establish a time frame for the interview and get the child's consent to proceed.

> Your mom mentioned to me on the phone that you were having a few problems at school with your teachers this year and getting into fights with your brother at home. I'm interested in how you see things. I would like to talk to you for about 15 minutes; then I will speak to your parents again and decide what to do from there. OK?

Establish the Presenting Complaint from the Child's Perspective. Ask questions as follows:

> What do you see as your main problem?
> Why do you think your folks brought you in here?
> What do you see as the problem here?
> Can you guess why your parents brought you here?

If the child refuses to acknowledge that there is a problem or accuses the parents or a sibling of having the problem, then ask the child to describe the most recent incident mentioned by the parent as having caused problems.

"Your father mentioned that you became quite upset on Tuesday after getting home from Boy Scouts. Can you tell me some more about that? What happened?" If the child expresses the problem entirely in terms of the reactions of parents, ask for a specific description of what the parent was doing that was annoying.

"When you say Dad's always hassling you, what specifically does he say that gets to you? Can you remember a time when this last happened?"

Clarify Specific Problem Behaviors. Once a child begins talking about the problem, use active listening, elaboration, clarification, and exemplification probes to explore specific problems fully.

> Can you tell me more about that? *(Elaboration)*
> Keep going. *(Elaboration)*
> How did you feel when you found out that Mary had been in your room? *(Clarification)*
> Can you give me an example of that? *(Exemplification)*
> What happened next? *(Elaboration)*

Clarify Associated Problems. Check whether the child has any other problems or symptoms that might covary with the main presenting complaint.

"Do you have any other worries? [alternatively hassles, difficulties, or concerns] Is anything else troubling you? Is there anything else you would like help with?"

Clarify the Child's Social and Friendship Network. Who are the salient figures in the child's social network who may have some impact on the child's behavior?

> How do you generally get along with other kids?
> Do you find it easy to make friends?
> Who's your best friend?
> Who do you spend lunchtimes with at school?
> Do you ever have friends from school over to play or visit?

Questioning a child further about friends may reveal inconsistencies. For example, a best friend at the same school who the child never plays with at school during lunchtime, who never calls or visits, and who the child's parents know nothing about may be an imaginary playmate. This child may be lonely and have few friends.

Mental Status Assessment. A formal mental state assessment of the child can be a useful format summarizing observations about the child's behavior during the interview situation. However, such observations are based on a sample of the child's behavior in a strange clinical situation. Determine whether similar behavior occurs in other situations and to what extent. Table 3.1 summarizes the main areas of the mental status assessment.

Interview Problems

Most children who attend outpatient appointments are reasonably co-operative during intake interviews. However, there are a number of problems that can arise. Some of these problems involve enactment of behavior that constitutes the child's problem behavior at home. The parental intake interview can reveal how the child may handle the interview situation.

The Child Who Is Disruptive, Demanding or Throws Tantrums. Children should not be permitted to engage in disruptive behavior in the clinical setting. The key to managing disruption during an intake interview is to arrange the environment so the child has appropriate engaging activities to participate in. Disruptive children must be supervised at all times. Secretarial staff may need specific advice on what to do if a child becomes disruptive or agitated.

The Child Who Refuses to Separate from the Parent. Some preschool children become distressed, cling, and cry when the clinician tries to interview the

Table 3.1. Outline of Mental Status Assessment

Appearance and Behavior:

Start with a brief description of what the child looks like (size for age, dress, grooming, prevailing facial expression, posture, cleanliness). Comment on how the child separated from the parents. How did the child react to your attempts to interact?

Affect:

1. Emotional expressiveness and range (laughs? smiles?)
2. Happiness
3. Anxiety and specific phobias
4. Panic attacks
5. Observable tension
6. Signs of autonomic disturbance
7. Tearfulness
8. Sadness, despair, apathy
9. Depressed or suicidal feelings
10. Shame, embarrassment, perplexity
11. Anger, aggressiveness
12. Irritability

Motor activity:

1. General level
   (a) Restlessness: inability to remain in seat
   (b) Fidgeting: squirming in seat, movement of parts of the body while stationary
2. Coordination
3. Involuntary movements
4. Tics
5. Stereotypies
6. Mannerisms
7. Posturing
8. Rituals
9. Hyperventilation

Language:

1. Hearing
2. Comprehension
3. Speech, vocalization, babble
4. Gesture: imitation, comprehension, use

Social responses to interviewer:

1. Social use of language and gesture
2. Social modulation and responsiveness to topics (e.g., praise, reward)
3. Humor
4. Rapport (e.g., odd, aloof)
5. Eye contact: quality, quantity
6. Reciprocity
7. Empathy
8. Cooperation and compliance
9. Social style (e.g., reserved, expansive, disinhibited, cheeky, teasing, negativistic, shy)

Thought content:

1. Worries, fears
2. Preoccupations, obsessions, suspicions
3. Hopelessness, guilt

Continued

Table 3.1. *Continued*

---

4. Low self-esteem, self-hatred
5. Fantasies or wishes
    (a) Spontaneously mentioned
    (b) Evoked (three wishes)
6. Quality or ideation and play

Abnormal beliefs and experiences:
Cognition:

1. Attention span and distractibility
2. Tasks
    (a) Draw a person (note handedness)
    (b) Write name
    (c) Give days of the week
    (d) Months of the year
    (e) Counting
    (f) Addition
    (g) Serial 3's from 20
    (h) Serial 7's from 100
3. Persistence
4. Curiosity
5. Orientation in time and place
6. Academic attainments

Note: Adapted from mental state assessment guidelines for children developed by the Department of Psychiatry and Child Psychiatry, Institute of Psychiatry (1987), *Psychiatric Examination: Notes on Eliciting and Recording Clinical Information in Psychiatric Patients*. Oxford, England: Oxford University Press.

parents or tries to engage the child in an activity. Determine in advance whether the parents expect the child to become upset during a separation situation. If the parents report persistent problems with separation, the parents should be interviewed with the child present (at least initially). If it is necessary to speak to the parents for an extended period of time, alternative childcare arrangements should be made.

The Sullen, Uncommunicative, or Angry Child. Some depressed or aggressive children may meet almost all attempts to initiate conversation with a stony silence or absolutely minimal responding. They may use monosyllabic answers and fail to elaborate on any comment unless specifically asked to do so. Even then, answers may be uninformative. In such instances, the child should be gently confronted.

> You don't seem too happy about being here today. Didn't you want to come in?
> What was it about coming here today that upset you the most?
> I know you're feeling pretty unhappy about talking to me right now about this; however, I can't help you unless I know what's troubling you.

Sometimes when upset children realize that someone is aware of how they feel and will not subject them to criticism, they will talk about their problem, although perhaps reluctantly at first. If a child is completely nonresponsive or mute, this is diagnostically important and often signals severe disturbance, particularly when it occurs in other situations as well.

INTEGRATING ASSESSMENT INFORMATION

In the process of conducting an intake interview, the clinician begins to formulate hypotheses about the nature of the child's problem and the role of family interactional factors in the development and maintenance of the problem. The clinical interview provides a rich source of potentially testable hypotheses. The clinician, on the basis of the intake interview, prepares a list of the main problems mentioned by either the parents or the child. These problems can be assigned a priority rating based on considerations such as the perceived importance of the problem to the parents or child, the interrelatedness of different problems, the dangerousness of the behavior in question, or the risks to the client or others associated with a continuation of the problem. Based on this list the therapist plans a second assessment session and selects assessment measures and tasks that will enhance the database available on each problem. Chapter 4 discusses the types of assessment measures that we employ in our program.

Determining Whether a Family-Based Approach is Warranted

One of the reasons for conducting a comprehensive intake evaluation is to determine the suitability of the referral for behaviorally oriented family therapy. Information from the intake interview is helpful in deciding whether to take the case or to refer the child elsewhere.

The main indications for behavioral family therapy include the following:

1. The presenting problem(s) can be described in behavioral terms as excesses and deficits in the child's behavioral repertoire.
2. At least one but preferably both parents agree that they are experiencing a problem and are prepared to enter therapy.
3. There is reasonably clear evidence from the history or other assessments of significant social learning influences within the family contributing to the development or maintenance of the problem.

PRINCIPLES OF EFFECTIVE
PARENT CONSULTATION

Behavioral family intervention involves learning to work with both parents and children. In addition to general interviewing, there are several other important consultative skills that are involved in working effectively with parents. Being an effective consultant to a parent about a child-rearing issue is a complex process. In part it involves learning how to communicate effectively with parents so they become actively involved in contributing to the solution of the problem. It also involves dealing with many of the complexities of the therapeutic relationship including dependency, hostility, resentment, and parental attempts to blame others (e.g., spouse, interfering relatives) as these problems arise. Throughout the therapy process the therapist must balance acting as a child advocate, on the one hand, and a parent advocate, on the other. Suggestions for creating an effective consultative relationship with parents are as follows.

1. *Attend to emotional responses of parents.* It is not uncommon for material discussed in the intake interview to generate emotional upset in parents, particularly when there is evidence of a severe marital problem or domestic violence, a history of depression in either or both parents, spouse abuse, or other parental psychopathology. However, parents can also become upset if the therapist is insensitive to their strong feelings toward the child or opinions about the nature of the problem and its causes. Recognize signs of emotional upset and respond appropriately to the expression of affect. A variety of interviewing and counseling skills can be used. These include the use of reflection, summarization, paraphrasing, using clarification questions or probes, and confrontation.

2. *Demonstrate an interest in parents as people.* Parents are more likely to respond to questions and feedback if they see the therapist as genuinely interested in them as people, not just as the mother or father of James.

3. *Demonstrate competence, caring, and interest in the child.* Avoid talking to the parents about the child in the child's presence, and ensure that the child is appropriately engaged (i.e., has something to do) while you are busy with the parents. Occasionally prompt the parents to check on the child if he or she is in another room.

4. *Validate parents' existing attempts to solve the problem.* Assume that parents have already tried to solve the problem before seeking help. Asking them, "What have you tried so far in dealing with this problem?" conveys your expectation that they are active problem solvers. Acknowledge their previous attempts to solve the problem and the difficulties inherent in making such attempts. The solution may have been only partially successful, but at least the parents tried.

5. *Avoid criticizing or blaming parents.* Many parents become defensive and guarded if they are made to feel inadequate or incompetent. This can occur

when the therapist asks a seemingly innocuous question such as, "Why did you wait so long before deciding to seek help?" (implies the parents should have acted more quickly), or alternatively when the therapist makes an authoritative but unsupported statement such as, "I think you've been too overprotective [lenient or worried]." Both imply that the parents have handled the situation incorrectly.

6. *Give constructive feedback without blaming.* Successful parent consultants develop skills of conveying information without accusing or blaming. Examples of how to do this are discussed in chapter 5. However, until the assessment is complete, it is ill advised to give parents specific advice about how to handle problems, even if they ask for it.

7. *Use humor appropriately.* Successful therapists often use humor effectively. They can see the funny side of some of the dilemmas children create for their parents, and vice versa. Effective use of humor involves recognizing parents' attempts to lighten a sensitive issue by laughing or joking. It also involves being able to convey amusing anecdotes about parenting and child rearing without belittling children in the process.

8. *Use self-disclosure appropriately.* One of the main advantages of being a parent as well as a family therapist is enhanced credibility. Therapists can use self-disclosure to convey examples or anecdotes directly relevant and interesting to the parents.

9. *Solicit parents' ideas about the causes of the problem and what can be done to solve it.* Effective parent consultation involves creating conditions for independent future problem solving. One way of promoting increasingly independent problem solving is to prompt and reinforce the parents for successive approximations of this objective. Ask the parents to express their ideas about the nature, causes, and possible solutions to the problem. For example, "Can you think of any other possible reasons why this problem developed? How might John's problem of whining while you're traveling in the car be dealt with? Do you see any similarities between this situation and the one you worked on last session?"

10. *Focus on the developmental competence of the child as well as resolution of problem behaviors.* It is easy to become too problem focused and thereby pay insufficient attention to the overall developmental competence of the child. For example, a successful behavioral program to reduce whining, tantrums, and aggression may have little direct impact on the child's ability to make new friends, to read and write competently, or to learn to express ideas without boasting. Time in therapy should be directed to encouraging parents to create opportunities within a child's home life that encourage well-rounded development. Parents can promote development by taking an interest in the child's range of hobbies and leisure pursuits, academic performance, language proficiency, and musical, sporting, and artistic pursuits.

11. *Link intervention goals to future developmental tasks for both parents and child.* Whenever possible, explain to parents how current goals relate to future

competencies. For example, being polite and cooperative with parents is preparation for similar interactions with other adults.

12. *Use expert knowledge to provide information.* Therapists have expert knowledge relating to children's behavior, development, diagnosis, and the types of assessment and treatment available. This expert knowledge must be conveyed to parents in ways that are comprehensible and practical. However, there must be a balance between advice and information and the teaching of parental self-management skills. During the assessment phase, avoid giving treatment advice.

13. *Avoid overloading parents with homework tasks.* Assessment and treatment progresses more smoothly if homework tasks are kept to an essential minimum. All tasks, including records to keep and questionnaires to complete, should only be set after considering the context of existing demands on parents' time.

14. *Keep parents informed by providing a rationale for tasks and advice.* Compliance with homework tasks increases if parents understand why the task should be completed and how completion of the task helps the course of subsequent therapy.

15. *Be an advocate for the child.* Parents often appreciate it when therapists act as an advocate for their child. This can be achieved in a number of subtle ways such as explaining a child's seemingly incomprehensible actions from the child's perspective. For example, some parents find it difficult to understand why children repeat behavior that gets them in trouble. Explaining to a parent the principle of reinforcement through attention, even negative attention, from a child's perspective makes sense of a seemingly incomprehensible action.

SUMMARY

Effective behavioral family intervention depends on laying the groundwork at each stage for the next phase of the intervention process. During the assessment, care must be taken to ensure that the appropriate psychological conditions are created so a collaborative approach to solving family problems is possible. Attentiveness to the nature of the communication process between the therapist, parents, and child is necessary to ensure that the family's problem can be properly assessed. Many interviewing problems can be avoided or dealt with through the effective use of appropriate communication skills during the initial information-gathering phase. In most cases, the intake interview should enable the clinician to formulate and test specific hypotheses about the nature of the presenting problem. The interviewer guides the selection of appropriate observational and self-report measures, which allow more rigorous validation of the initial formulation.

Chapter 4

Observational and Self-Report Measures

Once the intake interview has been completed and it is decided that a family-based intervention is indicated, the clinician should move to a more detailed assessment of the child's and family's problems. This involves the use of direct observation, self-report, and self-monitoring procedures. For common child behavior problems, a comprehensive assessment will usually involve the following stages prior to the intervention: (a) completion of selected self-report checklists, (b) direct observation of parent-child or family interaction, (c) design and implementation of self-monitoring procedures, (d) information gathering from other clinicians and institutions who have contact with the child and family (e.g., school, medical practitioners), and (e) sharing assessment results and treatment plans with the family. It is essential that the assessment process is clearly explained to the parents. After an initial interview, parents are often eager to receive advice on how best to manage the child's problem and may become frustrated and uncooperative if they do not fully understand the assessment process or do not have clear expectations about when treatment will begin. Throughout the assessment process, the clinician should involve the family members as active and fully informed participants. This may include actively encouraging parents to express their opinions about the nature of their problems and incorporating their views into the overall assessment strategy.

The type of information derived from the assessment of the behavior problems depends on the method by which the information is collected. When assessing children, information may come from parental report, teacher report, child self-report, and the therapist's observations of the child or family interaction. Each type of information illuminates different and important facets of the problem. A comprehensive assessment should be multimodal and employ a range of assessment modes and independent informants. In this chapter, we present a number of assessment strategies including direct observation, parental monitoring, and self-report measures. These are complementary systems, each adding to the overall assessment strategy.

OBSERVATION OF FAMILY INTERACTION

A cornerstone of the behavioral and social interactional approaches to assessment is the use of reliable direct observations of the behavior as it occurs in its natural social context. The degree to which such observations can be used successfully depends on the observation system employed, the nature of the behaviors and the context in which they occur, and the resources available to the clinician. While the goals of direct observation will vary, in general they are to (a) assess the frequency, duration, and intensity of problem behaviors; (b) identify the immediate antecedents and consequences of the problem behaviors; and (c) assess the broader ecological context of the behaviors (e.g., the physical environment, family routines and activities, noise level, and so on).

The following steps can be used in deciding an appropriate observation strategy.

1. *Generate hypotheses.* Information collected from the intake interview and referral sources should be used to generate hypotheses about the nature of the family's problem. These hypotheses should be formulated in terms of directly observable patterns of behavior so further assessment can either support or refute them. For example, assume it is hypothesized that fighting between siblings is being maintained in part by the pattern of parental consequences it produces. The clinician could operationalize this hypothesis as follows: At times when the siblings are together, unsupervised, and parents are occupied elsewhere, the siblings engage in screaming, hitting, and whining, which produces an immediate increase in attention from parents (move to vicinity of children, negotiate problem, and so on). Note that the hypothesis includes elements pertaining to the target behavior (fighting), the consequences it produces (parental engagement), and the situation in which it is likely to occur. These hypotheses will be stated more comprehensively later in the assessment phase using a SORCK analysis (see Table 4.7). At this point, however, tentative hypotheses are generated to guide the selection of observational and self-report strategies.

2. *Select target behaviors.* Target behaviors may include the child's problems that prompted the referral, as well as other child, parent, or sibling

behaviors that are hypothesized to maintain the problem. Targets can be expressed as interactional sequences as well as discrete behaviors. These should be stated in concrete terms that can be observed directly.

Research into the nature of parent-child interactions that are characteristic of distressed families and children has led to the development of a number of methods for categorizing parent and child behaviors. One such method is the Family Observation Schedule (FOS), (Sanders, Dadds, & Bor, 1989). The frequencies of these behaviors, in particular the aversive categories of parent and child behavior, have been shown to discriminate between distressed and nondistressed families. Table 4.1 lists definitions of behavioral categories used in the FOS.

Behaviors vary greatly in their amenability to direct observation. Oppositional behavior in young children (e.g., crying, noncompliance, aggression) can be readily observed in the family home or clinic if the setting is selected appropriately. In the home, such behavior tends to escalate at times in which parents attempt to engage young children in routine activities such as bathing, bedtime, getting ready to leave on outings, and mealtimes (Sanders, Dadds, & Bor, 1989). In clinic settings, oppositional behavior will similarly tend to occur when the parent tries to engage the child in structured teaching tasks or when compliance is enforced (e.g., cleaning up toys).

Many problem behaviors, however, cannot be so readily observed. For example, stealing and firesetting tend to be secretive and relatively infrequent behaviors. Similarly, anxious or depressed behaviors may not occur in the presence of the clinician. Further, clinicians are often unable to make observations in the home due to resource limitations. A number of strategies have been developed for approximating naturally occurring parent-child interactions in clinic settings. A prerequisite is the availability of a room equipped with toys suitable for children at various developmental levels, chairs and tables, and video or audiotaping equipment or viewing mirrors. A useful design consists of three adjoining rooms: an interview room large enough for interviewing families; a child's play room which is visually accessible from the interview room (allowing parents to monitor their child while working with a therapist and the child to feel secure that his or her parents are nearby); and a video control and observation room, visually accessible to the two other rooms.

3. *Select an observation procedure.* This includes deciding on the task to be given to the family members, the means of instructing the family to engage in this task, and the activities of the therapist throughout the process. Ideally, the procedure is designed to elicit the problem behaviors and observe the family interaction patterns in which such behaviors are embedded (Patterson & Reid, 1984). This must be done in a way that best approximates the natural occurrence of these patterns and yet provides

Table 4.1. Summary of Observed Parent and Child Behavior Categories

Category	Symbol	Definition
Parent		
Praise	P	Any nonaversive comment of approval offered to the child by the parent; it may be descriptive or global.
Contact	C	Any contact deemed to be nonaversive (i.e., not causing or having the potential to cause pain or discomfort).
Aversive contact	C−	Any contact causing or having the potential to cause pain or discomfort in the child.
Question	Q	Any nonaversive request for information from the child.
Aversive question	Q−	Any request for information deemed aversive due to content or tone of voice.
Instruction (alpha)	IA	Any verbal command that is clear, has a specific behavioral referent, and is presented nonaversively.
Aversive alpha instruction	IA−	Any verbal command that is clear, has a specific behavioral referrent, but is presented aversively.
Instruction (beta)	IB	Any verbal command that is unclear, lacks a specific behavioral referent, and is presented calmly.
Aversive beta instruction	IB−	Any verbal command that is unclear, lacks a specific behavioral referent, and is presented aversively.
Social attention	S+	Any nonaversive attention, verbal or nonverbal, that cannot be scored under other categories, whether it was parent-initiated or in response to the child.
Aversive social attention	S−	As above, except deemed to be aversive due to content or voice presentation.
Child		
Noncompliance	NC	Refusal to initiate compliance with an instruction within 5 seconds.
Complaint	C	Verbal complaints involving whining, screaming, vocal protests, or temper outbursts.
Aversive demands	M−	Instructions directed to another person by the child scored as aversive or unpleasant (e.g., "Give me my truck back.").
Aggression	PN	Actual or threatened attacks or damage to another person or destruction of an object or materials (e.g., punching, biting).
Oppositional	O	Other inappropriate behaviors that are not included above (e.g., breaking family rules, teasing).
Noninteraction	S	Absence of interactions with persons or play objects, repetitive object manipulation, or self-stimulation (e.g., face slapping).
Appropriate Verbal	AV	Intelligible verbalizations by the child in the absence of any deviant behavior.
Engaged Activity	AE	Any nondeviant behavior that does not include intelligible verbalizations, such as complying with instructions, toy playing, or attending to others.

sufficient procedural structure to prevent conflict or aggression from escalating to a level that may be distressing for participants.

For young children, a structured parent-child interaction task is useful for sampling a range of parent-child interactions. Table 4.2 summarizes a procedure in which parents are requested to encourage the child to engage in free, independent play and then lead the child through a number of structured activities. The clinician can make qualitative observations of both the parents' and child's behavior as well as use more formal procedures such as the FOS for coding parent-child interactions in such settings. When the goal is to sample the immediate antecedents and consequences of child behavior in a short period of time, such structure is warranted in that it directs the parent to interact with the child. When the clinician is more interested in the natural topography of parent-child interaction, less structure can be useful in providing data on the extent to which the parent structures activities for the child, provides routine, and gives attention.

As children approach middle childhood and adolescence, they become far more conscious of an observer's presence in the home and are less likely to engage in open conflict with parents and siblings. With older children it is more important to provide structured guidelines or select settings that tend to prompt family interaction. Examples of such settings are family mealtimes and family meetings in which current problems are opened up for general discussion and potential problem solving. Similarly, when problems behaviors are secretive (stealing, truancy, sexual problems) or low in frequency, direct observation of natural interactions is less likely to provide any useful data, and clinic-based family tasks or sole use of self-report may be necessary.

Table 4.2. A Structured Parent-Child Task Procedure

Task	Details
Free play	Show the family to a room equipped with age-appropriate toys and chairs. Ask the parents to engage the child in free play for approximately 5 minutes. Watch for the extent to which the parents interact with the child, prompt play and suggest activities, are child centered while the child plays, and use praise and encouragement. Observe the extent to which the child plays independently and creatively and explores the environment. Observe parental response to child initiations (e.g., questions).
Structured task	Ask the parents and the child to try to complete a jigsaw puzzle or some other goal-directed activity that is appropriate to the child's developmental level. Observe the parents' use of instructions and prompts, praise and encouragement, and their ability to be child centered. Observe the child's responses to parental instructions.
Clean-up	Ask the parents to supervise the cleaning up of the toys. Observe the use of and response to instructions, and the use of praise and other encouragement.

A useful procedure which is now common in clinical research into marital distress, parent-adolescent conflict, and family factors in severe psychopathology is the family problem-solving discussion (Miklowitz, Goldstein, Falloon, & Doane, 1984). Such discussions are appropriate for children age 7 and older. Table 4.3 summarizes the procedure we use for holding these discussions in a clinic setting. A number of authors, notably Blechman and McEnroe (1985), emphasize the role of problem-solving competence in protecting a family against conflict and breakdown. The major points for observation are the extent to which family members actively listen to each other, take time to agree on a problem definition, generate solutions and action strategies, or conversely interrupt each other, criticize, talk tangentially, and prevent problem solving through vagueness and expression of hopelessness and despair.

Family problem-solving discussion can be stressful for family members. Clinicians must guard against the discussion degenerating into the parent lecturing or criticizing an overwhelmed child. While this provides an insight into an obvious parent-child problem, it should be terminated as quickly as possible. The likelihood of this occurring is reduced if the clinician gives clear, simple instructions to the family about the importance of trying to find solutions to the problems, keeping the discussions to between 5 and 10 minutes, and using problems nominated by the child as well as by the parents. The Issues Checklist (Robin, 1981) can be used to generate problems for discussion and is filled out by both parents and child. We use 5 to 10 minutes for discussion of the child's nominated problem and a similar period for that of the parents.

The use of observational procedures is limited only by the imagination and resources of the clinician or researcher, and the aforementioned proce-

Table 4.3. Family Problem-Solving Discussion

Task	Details
Select Problem	Ask parents and child to complete the Problem Issues Checklist. Make note of the problems selected by parents and the problems selected by the child.
Establish Setting	Seat the family in a comfortable room with video or two-way mirror facilities, with chairs facing each other in an equidistant circular formation.
Present Instructions	Ask the family to discuss and attempt to find solutions to the nominated problems. Spend 5 minutes on the child's problem and 5 minutes on the parents' problem. Ask the family to begin discussing the problem as soon as the therapist leaves the room and continue until he or she returns.
Debrief	Discuss the attempts to find solutions with the family and deal with any distress that has arisen. Inform the family that the results of this assessment will be used for treatment planning and that they will be fully informed of the results. Thank the family.

dures are just a sample. Depending on the presenting problem, clinic-based observations can be used for a diversity of problems. Children with anxiety problems can be assessed in vivo using approach and behavioral avoidance tests (Strauss, 1987), and a range of situations can be structured in the clinic setting to assess social skills problems (Christoff & Myatt, 1987). Recent work in behavioral pediatrics has successfully utilized observations of clinic-based feeding routines as part of an assessment package for children who fail to thrive (Sanders, Patel, Le Gris, & Shepherd, 1991).

4. *Select a data collection method.* Methods for collecting and analyzing data range from qualitative observations made by the clinician to elaborate coding systems that can specify the frequency, intensity, and duration of a set of predefined behaviors. A recent innovation in behavioral assessment has been the development of computerized observation and analysis systems that allow the clinician to test hypotheses about conditional probabilities of interrelated sequences of family behavior (e.g., Dumas, 1989). When quantitative methods are used, the main problem is how to represent complex and often fast-moving sequences of behavior as useful, meaningful data.

As mentioned, the first step is to operationalize the behavior of interest. The second step is to devise a system of recording the occurrence, sequence, intensity, or duration of the behavior. Table 4.4 shows a range of observation strategies that provide an estimate of the strength of the target behavior prior to treatment, and gives examples of appropriate uses of each procedure.

5. *Evaluate the hypotheses.* The data derived from direct observation should be used, in conjunction with interview and other data, to continue the ongoing process of hypothesis testing about the nature of the child's and family's problems and their maintaining factors. The data should be summarized in written form, in tables or figures that are self-explanatory and can be used to help the family understand the nature of the problem. These data summaries will be used in the next phase of treatment, communicating assessment findings (see chapter 5).

SELF-MONITORING

The use of parental and/or child self-monitoring procedures serves several functions. First, self-monitoring introduces family members to the idea that they are active participants in the treatment process, that their perceptions are important, and that treatment is to be implemented and evaluated in a shared way. Second, self-monitoring tests a client's adherence to treatment instructions prior to therapy. If parents or children consistently avoid self-monitoring, it is probably a sign that treatment instructions will not be implemented properly. In this case, a shared analy-

Table 4.4. Observation Procedures Used to Obtain Estimates of Target Behaviors

Procedure	Definitions and Examples
Event Record	Each occurrence of a behavior is recorded. Most usefully used for behaviors that are low frequency and have a clear beginning and end. Examples: swearing, out of seat in classroom, pants soiling, smoking cigarette.
Permanent Product	Records the specific outcome of a behavior or series of behaviors. Examples: number of exams passed, windows broken, chores completed, wet beds, items of clothing left in bathroom.
Momentary Time Sample	Records the occurrence of a behavior if it is occurring at the moment a given time interval ends. Useful for long-duration or high-frequency behaviors. Examples: number of inpatients who are lying on bed at the end of each 10-minute interval, rocking in an autistic child, on task behavior in the classroom.
Partial Interval Time Sampling	Records the presence or absence of a behavior if it occurs once or more in a specified time interval. Useful for high-frequency, brief behaviors that do not have a clear beginning or ending. The final measure is the percentage of intervals observed in which any instance of the behavior occurred. Examples: A parent records "yes" to each consecutive, 10-minute interval in which any crying by child has occurred, noncompliance, fighting, complaining.

sis of any obstacles to homework completion can be undertaken prior to the important phase in which treatment plans begin.

Third, self-monitoring of target behaviors provides a validity check of the reported nature, frequency, duration, and intensity of selected problem behaviors. It is not uncommon for parents to report during intake interviews that child behaviors such as noncompliance happen all the time. However, when structured self-monitoring is undertaken, behavior may be limited to selected situations such as homework or bedtime. Fourth, accurate self-monitoring requires a number of skills including the ability to observe behavior and classify it into various predefined categories. Much evidence indicates that deficits in tracking and classification skills are associated with parent-child problems (Wahler & Dumas, 1984), and thus self-monitoring can be an important vehicle for the assessment and modification of tracking, discrimination, and labeling skills.

Finally, the most obvious purpose of self-monitoring is to collect data. When problem behaviors are of low intensity, are secretive, or cannot be directly observed (cognitions, affective states), self-monitoring may be the only method of data collection available. Alternatively, it may represent a means of validating data collected by interview, checklists, or brief direct observations. Thus, the design of self-monitoring procedures is crucial. In our experience, the ability to design a self-monitoring procedure that is simple to use and generates useful, reliable data is not easily achieved. Self-monitoring strategies are often rejected by parents, teachers, nursing staff, and other agents because they are too cumbersome and time-consuming. It is better to design a simple procedure that provides limited but reliable data than a more comprehensive measure that assesses all aspects of a problem but in reality produces little of value due to practical problems with its use.

In designing a self-monitoring procedure, the following points must be considered. First, the form must be designed to be simple and easy to complete in a short time. Instructions should be clear and openly displayed, and simple definitions of target behaviors must be specific, clear, and easily visible to the client. Second, the procedure for completing the form must be designed with the ongoing activities of the individual in mind. A teacher cannot stop every 2 minutes in class to fill out a form. A parent with young children cannot be expected to cease all activity for a few minutes during the rush hour that usually occurs prior to dinner each night. Adherence to self-monitoring can usually be maximized by ensuring that times set aside for completion of the form concur with naturally occurring breaks in the individual's ongoing activities.

Third, the choice of time-sampling units is crucial to the application of the previous two points. Time sampling is used to break down observation periods into a series of shorter intervals. For example, a parent may note whether or not a tantrum has occurred within each consecutive 30 minute period. Similarly, a nurse could obtain an estimate of activity level in inpatients by counting how many are lying on their beds at the end of each hour. A range of observation strategies is available and should be selected according to the nature of the problem behavior and the availability of the observer. Table 4.4 lists useful observation strategies ranging from event records, in which every occurrence of a behavior is recorded, to partial interval strategies, in which only the presence or absence of a behavior is recorded, regardless of its frequency, if it occurs within a specified time interval. Figures 4.1, 4.2, and 4.3 show examples of some self-monitoring forms for use by parents.

SELF-REPORT INVENTORIES

In this section we describe self-report inventories that have documented reliability and validity and that can be used to assess a broad range of child, parent, and family characteristics. Self-report inventories produce results that are affected by a range of factors over and above the phenomena they seek to describe. For example, a mother's report of her child's behavioral adjustment will be reflective of her personal and social adjustment and the

Date	Behavior(s)	How often did they occur?	Total

FIGURE 4.1. A sample event record.

Successive episodes

Date	1	2	3	4	5	6	7	8	9	10	11	12	13	14	15	16	17	18	19	20	Totals

FIGURE 4.2. A sample duration record.

Dates								
Times	Fighting	Swearing	Teasing	Non-Complies	Arguing	Stealing	Other	Total
Daily total								
Weekly total:								

FIGURE 4.3. A time-sampling record.

demand characteristics of the assessment setting, as well as her child's actual adjustment. It is thus crucial that whenever possible, self-report assessments are supplemented with other forms of assessment or other informants, such as teachers.

General Measures of Child Dysfunction

A number of checklists are available that provide a measure of behavioral disturbance across a number of empirically derived dimensions. Checklists developed by Achenbach and colleagues can be completed by parents (Child Behavior Checklist, Achenbach & Edelbrock, 1983), teachers (Teacher Rating Form, Achenbach & Edelbrock, 1986), and children between 11 and 18 years (Youth Self-Report Form, Achenbach & Edelbrock, 1983). The checklists each contain approximately 118 items, each scored on a scale from 0 to 2. Each item contributes to a specific dimension of dysfunction (e.g., depression, hyperactivity), two global dimensions of disturbance (internalizing versus externalizing), and a total behavior problem score. The range and composition of the dimensions of dysfunction differ according to the age and sex of a child and the informant providing the information. The Revised Behavior Problem Checklist (Quay & Peterson, 1983) is a similar checklist which is designed for completion by parents.

Specific Measures of Child Dysfunction

Depression in children can be measured using the Child Depression Inventory (Kovacs, 1980), which can be completed by children age 7 or older, or the Bellevue Index of Depression (Petti, 1978), which is completed by parents. The Child Depression Inventory consists of 27 items scored on a scale from 0 to 2 and is similar in structure and content to the Beck Depression Inventory for adults. Much literature is available on the structure and interpretation of the Child Depression Inventory (Kolko, 1987). The Bellevue Index of Depression consists of 26 items scored for both severity and duration.

The measurement of hyperactivity as a unique construct is a problem because the disorder shares many elements with conduct and oppositional disorders. Thus, most self-report measures of hyperactivity load heavily on conduct disturbance. The most well-known measures of hyperactivity are the Conners Parent and Teacher Rating Scales (Conners, 1969, 1970; Goyette, Conners, & Ulrich, 1978). The parent scale consists of 48 items that load on five dimensions of dysfunction and has been normed on children age 3 to 17. The teacher version consists of 28 items that load on three dimensions, and similar norms are available (Goyette et al., 1978).

Poor concordance between child and parental reports is typical in the measurement of childhood anxiety disorders (Strauss, 1987), and obtaining accurate self-reports from children is critical in this area. General levels of anxiety can be assessed using the Children's Manifest Anxiety Scale— Revised (Reynolds & Richmond, 1978) a checklist that has well-documented reliability and validity (Strauss, 1987). Specific fears can be assessed using the Fear Survey Schedule for Children (Scherer & Nakamura, 1968), an 80-item checklist on which children rate their fears on five-point scales. A modified version of this checklist appears to have the best psychometric properties and has been normed in various countries (King et al., 1989; Ollendick & Francis, 1988).

Measures of Parental Dysfunction

Measures of individual parent psychopathology can be obtained on a number of general and specific self-report checklists. Depression can be measured on the Beck Depression Inventory (Beck, Ward, Mendelson, Mock, & Erbaugh, 1961), a widely used and researched checklist that can be used with adolescents (Kolko, 1987). The most commonly used and researched measures of anxiety are the adult counterparts of the measures of childhood anxiety described earlier: the State-Trait Anxiety Inventory (Spielberger, Gorsuch, & Lushene, 1970) and the Fear Survey Schedule (Wolpe & Lang, 1964). Recently, Spielberger developed and demonstrated the psychometric and clinical utility of a measure of anger problems in adults (Spielberger, Jacobs, Russell, & Crane, 1983).

Estimates of general psychological functioning in adults can be assessed using the General Health Questionnaire (Goldberg, 1972) or the Brief Symptom Inventory (Derogatis & Melisaratos, 1983). Both of these forms list items describing a range of dimensions of distress, and parents rate themselves on Likert scales. Good self-report measures of social support have proven difficult to develop due to problems with the definition and operationalization of social support as a unidimensional concept (Winefield, 1984). The Perceived Social Support Scales (Procidiano & Heller, 1983) appear to have reasonable validity and reliability and have separate forms for perceived support from family and friends. A self-report measure of parenting efficiency and satisfaction has recently been developed by Johnston and Mash (1989). While in need of further examination, preliminary data indicate good psychometric properties for this measure, which taps a relatively unexplored dimension of parenting. Finally, the Child Abuse Potential Inventory (Milner, 1980) is a well-researched self-report checklist which provides a total score and scores on a number of dimensions that are associated with risk for child abuse and neglect.

Measures of Marital and Family Functioning

While a number of self-report measures have recently been developed for assessing more global aspects of family functioning, most are based on systemic concepts and do not have well-documented reliability and validity. However, the Family Environment Scale (Moos, 1974) is a commonly used and well-researched instrument that can be completed by both parents and children. Scores on a number of empirically derived dimensions of family functioning are produced. Marital functioning can be assessed in terms of global marital satisfaction as measured by the Dyadic Adjustment Scale (Spanier, 1976), a useful revision of the widely used Marital Adjustment Test (Locke & Wallace, 1959). Other measures are available that focus on more specific aspects of the marital relationship such as open conflict (Porter & O'Leary, 1980). The Parenting Problems Checklist (Dadds & Powell, in press) is a 16-item checklist that provides a measure of interparental disagreements over child rearing. The Parenting Problems Checklist has high internal consistency ($\alpha = .7$), test-retest reliability ($r = .9$), and correlates with both global marital satisfaction and behavioral disturbance in children. The Parenting Problems Checklist is shown in Table 4.5.

FUNCTIONAL ANALYSIS OF PROBLEM BEHAVIORS

At this point in the assessment, it is assumed that information on the presenting problem has been collected from various combinations of interviews, self-monitoring, direct observation, and checklists. One hallmark of behavioral assessment is that assessment is an ongoing process that is fully integrated with treatment. Thus, the attempt to conceptualize the presenting problem is seen as the generation of hypotheses that are subject to continuous scrutiny by ongoing assessment and treatment data.

In this section we draw heavily on the conceptual model developed by Kanfer and Saslow (1969). This model emphasizes the classification of a client's behavior in excesses, deficits, inappropriate stimulus control and assets, and the use of a SORCK model to analyze the patterns of antecedent and consequent events which maintain problem behaviors.

There has been a growing tendency within family systems models of child and family psychopathology to reject the aforementioned approaches because of their assumption of undirectional causality. We believe that no such assumption is inherent in these models. Rather, to the extent that family members' behavior is causally interrelated, each member's behavior

Table 4.5. Parenting Problems Checklist

Check each item that has been a problem for you and your spouse over the last month.

1. Disagreements about household rules (e.g., bedtime, play areas) ☐
2. Disagreements about type of discipline (e.g., smacking children) ☐
3. Disagreements about who should discipline children ☐
4. Fighting in front of children ☐
5. Inconsistency between parents ☐
6. Children preventing parents from being alone ☐
7. Disagreements about sharing childcare workloads ☐
8. Inability to resolve disagreements about child care ☐
9. Discussions about child care turning into arguments ☐
10. Parents undermining each other (i.e., not backing up each other) ☐
11. Parents favoring one child over another ☐
12. Lack of discussion between parents about child care ☐
13. Lack of discussion about anything ☐
14. One parent is "soft," one parent is "tough" with children ☐
15. Child(ren) behave(s) worse with one parent than the other ☐
16. Disagreements about what is undesirable behavior ☐

is seen as being reciprocally (rather than undirectionally) determined. A behavioral analysis does attempt to freeze this reciprocal interaction in time, thus arbitrarily assigning one person's behavior as an antecedent, another's as a response.

Classifying Behavior

On the basis of data collected, each relevant person's behaviors are classified according to the definitions presented in Table 4.6. Specific behaviors should be listed in clearly stated terms that allow them to be reliably observed by independent observers. Vague, overinclusive terms such as *aggression* or *hyperactivity* should be more clearly operationalized into discrete behaviors such as hitting, biting, name calling, or failing to complete a task. Once a comprehensive classification of problem behaviors has been generated to the satisfaction of both therapist and clients, the list should be prioritized for intervention. Selecting which behaviors should be targeted in what order is a process involving a number of criteria: (a) the expressed concerns of the family; (b) the importance of the behavior in terms of its adverse consequences for the child and family; (c) the likelihood of success in changing the behavior; (d) the interrelationships between the target behaviors (Are particular behaviors dependent on other behaviors such that they can be expected to decrease if the behaviors they are dependent on are targeted? For example, it may be unnecessary to target swearing if it only occurs during tantrums that result from the ineffective management of noncompliance.); and (e) the ability of the parents to implement strategies for a particular behavior.

Conducting a Functional Analysis

Once a tentative prioritization of behaviors has occurred, the behavioral conceptualization should be formalized using one or more SORCK analyses. Table 4.7 lists definitions of the type of information to be included in each section of a SORCK analysis. This can be done using the following steps. First, the target behavior (response) is selected and clearly defined to the satisfaction of therapist, parents, and the child (when appropriate). Second, the immediate antecedents to the behavior are listed. These antecedents are limited to events occurring immediately prior to the target behavior (a few minutes or less). Again, these events should be listed in clearly observable terms. Third, contextual events that are associated with the occurrence of the target are listed. (A detailed discussion of contextual events can be found in Wahler and Graves, 1983). Contextual events do not directly elicit the occurrence of the target behavior, but they either increase the probability that an antecedent will occur or increase the probability that the target behavior will follow the relevant antecedent stimuli. For example, the arrival home of an irritable father may increase the

Table 4.6. Categories of Target Behaviors

Category	Definition
Excesses	Behaviors that occur at such a high frequency, intensity, or duration that they are problematic in the setting in which they occur (e.g., hitting, kicking, thoughts of self-worthlessness, crying, obsessive checking).
Deficits	Behaviors that occur at such a low frequency, intensity, or duration that they are problematic in the setting in which they occur (e.g., eye contact, task engagement, independent play, self-praise).
Inappropriate Stimulus Control	Behaviors that occur at a reasonable frequency, intensity, or duration and are adaptive, but are elicited by inappropriate stimuli (e.g., sexual arousal to objects, voiding urine when anxious, social interaction during homework time).
Assets	Behaviors that are developmentally and socially appropriate and constructive (e.g., hobbies, language and problem-solving skills, social support).

Table 4.7. Information to Be Included in the SORCK Analysis Definition

Stimuli (S)

☐ Historical   Antecedent stimuli that historically precede the target behavior, increase the likelihood that it will occur, but do not elicit the behavior directly. For example, a disagreement between mother and father over breakfast may increase the likelihood that the mother and child will engage in conflict later that morning.

☐ Contextual   Contextual stimuli that do not directly elicit the target behavior, but occur concurrently with it and increase the likelihood of it occurring.

☐ Immediate   Stimuli that occur immediately prior to the target behavior and directly elicit its occurrence. May be either a conditioned stimulus (CS) which elicits a response (e.g., fear) or a discriminative stimulus (S^D) that signals the availability of reinforcement or punishment. The same stimulus may function as both a CS and S^D: for example, the parent gives a vague, angry instruction to the child, which elicits crying and complaining.

Organismic Variables (O)

Variables that moderate the relationship between antecedent stimuli and target behavior and are characteristic of the current state of the organism; for example, illness, psychophysiological state, cognitions, affect, drugs.

Target Behavior (R)

The behavior of interest; the subject of the analysis.

Consequences (C)

☐ Immediate   Stimuli that occur immediately after the target behavior that alter the likelihood of recurrence of the behavior; the effects or changes in the environment produced by the target behavior.

☐ Long-term or Delayed   Changes produced by the target behavior that are not immediate, do not directly effect the likelihood of its recurrence, but influence contextual variables that may be indirectly related to the recurrence of the behavior. For example, fighting between siblings may produce parental attention, which reinforces the fighting (immediate consequence), and cause parents to become less involved in the siblings' play on future occasions (delayed consequences). Both increase the likelihood that the siblings will fight.

Contingencies (K)

Hypotheses about the relationships between the antecedent and consequential stimuli and the target behavior of interest.

likelihood that a mother will speak aggressively to her child, or may increase the likelihood that the child will refuse to go to bed when instructed to do so.

Fourth, historical factors that may have led to the emergence of the behavior but are no longer in operation can be listed in the historical section of the first column. While these data may have little bearing on intervention selection, they are useful in helping parents to understand the origins of their current problems. Fifth, factors intrinsic to the person that may be functionally related to the occurrence of the behavior are listed. These may include medical illnesses, handicaps, and temporary states such as tiredness, hunger, drug use, diet, and physiological arousal. When cognitions or attitudes are hypothesized to be important, they can be included to describe their role in the mediation of stimulus events and behavioral responses. Cognitions may also be listed as stimulus events.

Sixth, the consequences column lists those stimuli that occur immediately following the problem behavior. These reinforcing or punishing stimuli are often hypothesized to be associated with maintenance of the problem behavior. Delayed consequences of the problem behavior are also recorded. The latter are often not directly related to the performance, but operate indirectly by feeding back into antecedent conditions and organismic states. For example, aggression is often followed by compliance or counteraggression in the short term, and these consequences will reinforce the likelihood of further aggression (Patterson, 1982). In the long term, the aggression may lead to social rejection. However, the social rejection will feed back as a contextual antecedent (e.g., the person is ignored by others and so has to act aggressively to get others' attention) or as an intrinsic state (e.g., the person feels angry and vengeful and thus is more likely to act aggressively in a similar situation). Finally, the contingencies (K) column summarizes the functional links, or contingencies, that connect the previous four columns.

The following example shows how to use the system to design a treatment program for a young boy with a common behavior problem. The results of the assessment and conceptualization are shown in Tables 4.8 through 4.11.

Andrew, 6 years old, was referred for help by his mother due to her inability to manage his behavior and following reports from his preschool that he would have to leave if his behavior did not improve. Andrew's mother reported that problems in both settings included noncompliance with instructions, physical aggression to parents and other children, swearing and name calling, overactivity, and inability to play independently and concentrate on activities. Andrew was assessed using interviews with both parents, a clinic-based observation of structured and unstructured activities with Andrew and both parents, a telephone conver-

Table 4.8. Classification of Each Family Member's Behavioral Repertoire

Andrew	Mother	Father
Excesses		
Noncompliance with instructions	Vague instructions presented in an aggressive voice tone	Criticizing mother for Andrew's behavior
Hitting, kicking, biting	Labeling Andrew as naughty, unpleasant	Vague instructions to Andrew
Swearing, calling parents names	Screaming, smacking Andrew	
Whining, crying voice		
Deficits		
Compliance with instructions	Consequences applied to misbehavior	Contribution to management of Andrew
Independent play and activities	Pleasurable activities away from Andrew	Consequences applied to misbehavior
Speaking nicely to parents	Positive feelings for husband	Praise skills
Independent self-care activities (bathroom, eating)		Acknowledgment of need for change in own behavior
Inappropriate Stimulus Control (ISC)	Ignores Andrew's appropriate behavior	Gives affection to Andrew when he misbehaves
	Responds to misbehavior with anger, threats, or love withdrawal	Ignores appropriate behavior
Assets		
Normal intelligence	Normal intelligence	Affection for wife and Andrew
Physically coordinated	Positive feelings for Andrew	Normal intelligence
Affectionate to parents	Accepts need for change in own behavior	

Table 4.9. Functional Analysis of Andrew's Excesses

S	O	R	C	K
Historical	No frank psychopathology detected.	Noncompliance: Says "no." Ignores request.	Immediate Parent either (a) withdraws instructions, or (b) repeats instructions with escalating emotion in voice, repetition of name, and physical contact.	(a) Negative reinforcement, or (b) positive reinforcement in context of low rates of parental attention for good behavior. OR Increasing aversive stimulus that Andrew will seek to terminate.
Father has stayed long hours at work, leaving mother alone feeling unsupported.	Primary diagnosis of oppositional-defiant disorder.			
Family has shifted house, resulting in loss of child care and other supports.				
History of chronic ear infections in Andrew leading to incidences of extending screaming and preschool refusal.				

Continued

85

Table 4.9. *Continued*

S	O	R	C	K
Contextual-Concurrent		Andrew screams, swears, hits, and kicks. Refuses to comply.	Immediate	
Father absent.			(a) Parent withdraws instructions but smacks Andrew and talks emotionally about his naughty behavior.	Negative reinforcement
Mother overwhelmed with competing demands to run the household.				Positive reinforcement
Communication problems between parents. Excesses of criticism, deficits in support.			THEN	
Disagreement over child-rearing practices.			(b) Sits and cuddles Andrew to calm him down, talks gently, and arranges a shared activity for them to "feel better about each other."	Positive reinforcement
Immediate				
Parent gives instruction to Andrew. Often vague, emotionally laden, or in pleading, questioning tones.			Long Term	
			Parents find Andrew a burden; ignore him unless problem occurring.	
Parent demands compliance, yells, smacks.				

sation with his preschool teacher, and parental completion of a number of self-report forms. On the basis of these data, Andrew was diagnosed as having an oppositional-defiant disorder (DSM-IIIR) in the context of poor marital adjustment (Dyadic Adjustment Scale scores < 80 for both parents) in an otherwise well-adjusted and financially secure family.

Table 4.8 shows our behavioral classification for each family member's behavior. For Andrew, the behaviors conform closely to his parents' description with the notable addition of whining and crying. This behavior is common in oppositional children and is often the first step in an escalation into aggression and tantrums. However, parents often fail to report it as a problem, having seemingly habituated to its occurrence and not realizing its role in the problem. For the mother, excesses centered around the use of vague instructions and aversives, the most common form being to repeat her son's name over and over in increasingly aggressive tones. Deficits and inappropriate stimulus control problems consisted of inattention to appropriate behavior and responding with emotion to misbehavior.

For the father, parenting behaviors were observed to be similar to the mother except that he had no praise skills in his repertoire and offered little contribution to the management of Andrew or day-to-day chores around the home. He would often criticize his wife for Andrew's behavior and her inability to handle him, rather than offering to help. Thus, Andrew's behavior had become a major source of tension in the marital relationship, causing the mother to become increasingly burdened with the care of Andrew, the father to withdraw more and more into work and other activities outside the home, and little positive engagement between the parents except for aversive discussions about Andrew's problems.

Behaviors necessary for successful treatment can also be included in this analysis. While the mother perceives that a change in her behavior is needed, the father stated that he did not see that he was to blame for the problem, and thus only his wife and Andrew needed to change. This is listed as a deficit that must be targeted as part of a comprehensive treatment strategy; otherwise we would predict that the father's attendance at sessions and implementation of treatment suggestions may be less than optimal.

The next step is to decide on priorities and goals for treatment and to conduct a functional analysis of the selected target behaviors. In this case, the parents' priorities for change focused on Andrew's excesses — noncompliance, hitting, kicking, swearing, and tantrums. Our data indicated that these behaviors were interrelated in that they occurred in a cluster. Parental attempts to direct Andrew's behavior would result in noncompliance, and the ensuring battle would escalate to include the hitting, kicking, swearing, and tantrums. We thus felt that these behaviors could be targeted with one compliance management routine that was well within the

Table 4.10. Functional Analysis of Andrew's Deficits

S	O	R	C	K
Historical Same as Table 4.9	Same as Table 4.9	Plays appropriately and independently from mother	Mother stays away from Andrew due to following assumptions:	Behavior is extinguished. Setting serves as a discriminative stimulus signaling the unavailability of parental reinforcement.
Contextual Same as Table 4.9			(1) While he is quiet she should count her blessings and not disturb him.	
Immediate Mother engaged in housework			(2) This independent play represents one of the few opportunities to get some housework done.	

Table 4.11. Functional Analysis of Parental Conflict

S	O	R	C	K
Historical Role models of father as executive decision maker responsible for finances; mother responsible for home and child management. No training in problem solving, communication. **Contextual** Little extended family or community support. Father works long hours. Mother receiving negative feedback from preschool about Andrew's behavior.	Mother: chronically tired, feeling ineffective as a parent and unsupported. Father: feeling nagged by his wife because of her problems coping with Andrew.	Mother: speaks calmly or not at all about her day at home. Mother: demands help, complains about parenting difficulties. Escalates emotion.	Father ignores mother and does not ask about her day. **Short Term** Father ignores until behavior escalates to distressing level. Responds with perfunctory solutions that she should pursue. Sometimes offers help. **Long Term** Avoids coming home early from work and other situations where wife's complaints may occur.	Escalation of mother's behavior; calm talking is extinguished. Intermittent schedule of positive reinforcement.

Continued

Table 4.11. *Continued*

S	O	R	C	K
Immediate Father home from work.		Father: attempts to get involved in parenting, comes home early.	Andrew is unmanageable, noncompliant. Wife complains.	Punishment of father's behavior.
		Father: criticizes wife about her management of Andrew.	Wife defends herself by increasing her independent management of Andrew, decreases demands of husband (which to her constitutes evidence she is a failure).	Negative reinforcement (decreases wife's demands, decreases own feelings of failure).
		Father: Increasingly seeks activities outside of home.	Avoids complaints, conflict. Pleasant activities.	Negative reinforcement Positive reinforcement

capacity of the parents to implement. The second group of problems consisted of deficits in independent play and self-care. Again, we felt that the implementation of procedures to increase these behaviors was well within the capacity of the parents, and they were eager to target these deficits as well.

The third group of problems centered around deficits in the parents' ability to work as an effective team, to avoid criticizing each other, and to encourage and support each other's role in the family. These problems were openly discussed with the parents, and agreement was achieved to target this area for change. However, both therapist and parents felt the first priority was to target change in parent-child interactions and then follow with a marital focus. Our rationale for this approach and the process by which it is implemented is detailed in chapter 9.

Given the foregoing rationale, we conducted three functional analyses, one for each of the problem clusters. These are shown in Tables 4.9, 4.10, and 4.11. The SORCK sequence allows simultaneous analysis of multiple factors that are hypothesized to interact to produce the target behavior. Further, the SORCK lists multiple factors that can be targeted for change, including contextual and immediate stimulus conditions, organismic variables, and consequences.

SUMMARY

Observational and self-report measures are used to test hypotheses about the nature of the presenting problem and its maintaining conditions. They can also be used to refine existing hypotheses or to generate further hypotheses, which can be tested with further data collection. Each observation measure has its advantages and limitations. However, practical constraints often mean reaching a compromise between selecting a measure which might be ideal and one which a parent can use consistently throughout the assessment and treatment phase. Chapter 5 discusses the next step in working with the family: the sharing of assessment information and the formulation of treatment goals.

Chapter 5

Communicating Assessment Findings

EFFECTIVE COMMUNICATION OF ASSESSMENT INFORMATION

Treatment cannot begin until relevant assessment information has been discussed with the family. This is an important but neglected area of behavioral family intervention. Communicating assessment findings can be difficult because the data may implicate the parents either directly or indirectly in the genesis or maintenance of the child's problem. Parents may feel that they are personally responsible and are to blame for their child's problem. They may feel inadequate and react defensively. This phase of the assessment process requires the ability to communicate clearly and with sensitivity to the emotional impact of the data.

There is a substantial body of research in the area of physician-patient relationships which shows that patients' adherence to medical advice is a complex social process influenced not only by the nature of the treatment regimen (e.g., number of medications) but by other factors as well (Haynes, Taylor, & Sackett, 1979; Masur, 1981). These factors include the nature of the physician-patient communication, the type of disease, the patient's memory and understanding of the advice given, and the complexity of the regimen. Much of the aforementioned research has examined medication taking, a relatively simple behavior when compared to the complex behavioral changes that are typically involved in altering dysfunctional patterns of family interaction. There are many opportunities in family intervention for misunderstandings and noncooperation with therapy tasks. To achieve high levels of parent involvement in therapy, particular attention must be directed to developing effective methods of conveying information and advice about child rearing and parenting.

As we saw in chapters 3 and 4, several types of data can be collected during a clinical assessment. These data include information gathered from interviews with the parent, child, teacher, or staff member; the results of direct observations of child behavior or family interaction conducted by parents or trained observers; the results of self-report inventories; and occasionally, psychological tests of ability or attainment. This assessment information is potentially threatening, as it may question the effectiveness of a parent's current management practices. For example, if parents report that they punish their child for fighting by using the wooden spoon, and the parents' baseline monitoring of the child's behavior shows a stable rate of both fights and parental hits, this suggests threatening to use the spoon is not effective in reducing the child's fighting. These same parents may believe that this method of disciplining their child works because it stops the fighting at the time.

Other assessment data may reveal a problem of a more serious nature than the parent anticipated. For example, a parent may report only occasional temper tantrums, but baseline observations reveal that this behavior occurs at a rate of 5 to 10 times per day. From a scientific point of view, these data are neutral; from a parent's perspective the results of the assessment are personally significant. An anxious parent may have been trying to minimize the significance of the child's problem. In some cases assessment findings may suggest continuing difficulties in the future (e.g., when a child is diagnosed as being clinically depressed, autistic, or developmentally disabled).

Faced with these challenges, beginning therapists may find it difficult to discuss diagnostic and assessment information with parents. Several problems can occur. The parents may become defensive, failing to "own" the data or to comprehend the information or explanation given by the therapist. Poor handling of this phase of the consultation can lead to premature termination of therapy and consumer dissatisfaction. In addition, therapists must be able to handle parents questioning or challenging their judgment.

The approach we recommend for conveying information to family members about the child is based on four fundamental assumptions.

1.   Parents are more likely to comply with treatment suggestions and recommendations when they are in broad agreement with the therapist concerning the nature of the problem. This means that the therapist must develop a shared perspective with the parents in defining the problem.

2.   Parents more readily commit themselves to the goals of therapy and implement recommended changes (particularly changes in parent behavior) if they understand and agree with the causes or explanations of the problems they confront and the relationship between their own actions and their child's behavior.

3.   Parental cooperation and understanding is increased if parents have access to the clinician's reasoning. The inferences a therapist derives from the assessment data should be made explicit and shared with the clients. This allows the parents to test the validity of the inferences drawn about their family. This process of sharing hypotheses and inferences with clients promotes better, more open, informed participation and collaborative problem solving.

4.   Parents' subsequent use of recommended strategies (e.g., new parenting strategies) is a function of the environmental antecedents and consequences of the parents' own behavior. Subsequent reinforcement of parental behavior change is required to produce enduring changes in the way parents interact with their children.

Selection of Shared Information

The discussion of assessment findings creates a rational basis for the introduction of specific intervention strategies. Information is more useful and therapeutic when the salient points (particularly conclusions about the nature and etiology of the problem) are understood, remembered, or easily retrieved by the parents. The presentation of assessment data should be clear, logically sequenced, and comprehensible. It should point out what the data say and what they mean (particularly how they relate to the parents' or child's current method of dealing with the problem). The discussion should provide an opportunity for the parents to ask questions or seek clarification about the nature of the problem, its causes, prognosis, recommended treatment, and any other issues relating to any subsequent therapy proposed.

The information the clinician conveys should be derived from reliable and valid data and not based exclusively on interview information. There are several important clinical tasks that must be accomplished during this final phase of the assessment process to lay the foundation for the actual intervention.

The most important of these tasks is the integration of all available assessment information into a coherent, empirically derived formulation (set of propositions or hypotheses) about the nature of the problem and its causes (controlling conditions). This formulation, when appropriate, should also include hypotheses the parents have generated on the basis of their experience with their child. Second, this clinical formulation must be translated into a language that is comprehensible to the parents and, when appropriate, the child. Third, the therapist must be sensitive to the possible emotional impact of the data and use the data to introduce treatment goals and procedures. This involves attending to family members' nonverbal cues.

Guidelines for Communicating Assessment Results with Parents

We usually devote a substantial part of the third session (30–50 minutes) to discussing assessment information. The following procedure, known as a *guided participation model of information giving,* can be useful in preparing, organizing, and discussing information with parents. This strategy provides descriptive, factual information in a sequenced manner, as well as opportunities for parents to process, react to, question, and challenge the clinician's reasoning. It is essential that the parents derive their own understanding of the data.

Prepare for the Session. Review all available assessment data and decide what information to convey to the family and how. Audiovisual aids such as diagrams, overhead transparencies, tables, or charts can be useful to illustrate key points. Be willing to discuss the following: your viewpoint regarding the nature of the child's or family's problem, the likely causes of the problem, the possible options in resolving the problem, the proposed goals of an intervention, and the estimated time and cost for the family.

At the previous contact, discuss the goals of the session, how long it will take, what information, if any, you would like the parents to bring (e.g., report cards), and who should be present at the session (it is desirable to have both parents attend this session). Generally, it is better not to have the child attend this session. Older children may attend, but we recommend holding a feedback session separately with them. Make sure all tests, questionnaires, and observation records have been scored and graphed, when appropriate.

Negotiate an Agenda. Following initial greetings, introduce the goals of the session briefly and clearly and review the agenda with the parents.

> Let's start by discussing what we will be doing today. What I'd like to do during this session is to review what we found out so far about Damian's problems from the assessment — in other words, what the assessment shows. Then we will discuss some possible causes of the problems, and finally what options we have for dealing with them. The main idea is that by the end of the session we should reach agreement about what the problems are, what's causing them, and how we proceed from here. Is that OK with you? If there's anything else you'd like to discuss, we can deal with it after these three issues.

Summarize the Presenting Problem. Summarize the major problems the parents have mentioned in previous contacts. Ask the parents to indicate whether these problems are still current. For example, "Last week when you were here, we discussed three main problems you were concerned about. These were Damian's stealing, his lying to you, and his disobedience. Are these still the main problems as you see it?" If the situation has changed, ask the parents to describe how.

Present Descriptive Information Relating to the Problem. Make sure this information incorporates any changes the parents have mentioned.

1. Describe the types of information gathered: "You will recall last week we did three things to assess the problem. I spoke to John and called his teacher about his progress at school, I observed John here in the observation room with you, and you filled out some questionnaires for me about his behavior and other aspects of how your family members get along with each other."

2. Present the data on each type one at a time: "My discussion with John suggested a couple of interesting things about how he gets along with other kids at school. He says he feels he has no friends and he doesn't know what to do to make friends."

3. Monitor the parents' understanding and reactions to each type of information. In particular, be on the lookout for nonverbal cues suggesting confusion, misunderstanding, or disagreement. You may ask, "Does that make sense to you? What's your reaction to that? You look surprised."

4. Proceed to the next category of information: "You remember that record you have been keeping of times John swore or hit his brother at home? I have put all that information on this graph. Let me explain how to read the graph so it makes sense to you." Explain the axes and what the data points mean. Keep the graph and explanation simple and within the parents' grasp. Most parents can understand a simple line or bar graph. Continue until all major information has been discussed. When using handouts (e.g., graphs), ensure that copies are available for each parent. Be attentive to signs of disinterest and lack of attention or concentration. However, parents are usually interested in hearing the results of any assessment of their child.

5. Provide a concise, integrating summary of the problem: "So from our assessment, John's whining, demanding, and tantrums are causing the most concern at home, but things are OK at school. There is also some disagreement between the two of you about how best to deal with John's behavior at home, and both of you are concerned that Andrew [the younger brother] is starting to copy John's behavior."

This summary draws together the major conclusions about the nature of the problem. At this point, decide whether to convey a formal DSM-IIIR diagnosis to the parents. In our experience, using a diagnostic label is anxiety provoking for many parents and keeps them from focusing on the child's predominant behavior pattern.

6. Check the accuracy of your summary: For example, you can ask the parents, "Does that sum up the problem as you see it, or are there other problems I have not mentioned?"

Review Possible Causes of the Child's Problem. The next step is to provide an explanation for why the problem has developed. On a chalkboard or poster board, write a heading such as, "Possible causes." Then say, "I'd like now to discuss some of the possible reasons for Damian's behavior." Then explain what you are about to do and develop a personalized list of possible causes that are relevant to the child's or family's circumstances.

> I thought it might be helpful if we write down on this board the possible causes so you can think about each one as we proceed. You know Damian better than anyone else. As I write down each cause, ask yourself whether this might apply to Damian or rings true for you. OK. After I have written some general ideas first, then we will add to the list anything else you think might be important in understanding Damian's problem. The basic idea is for us to arrive at a shared view of the problem and its causes. This will provide the best basis for planning a treatment plan suited to both you and your child's needs.

The list of possible causes should include factors that have been clearly identified from the research literature as contributing to the problem. In addition, however, there may be specific causal factors identified through history taking or observation that can be included. We often recommend a handout called "Causes of Common Behavior Problems in Children" for take-home reading after this session (See Table 5.1). Briefly discuss each one and give an example of each, drawing on interactions the parents have mentioned to you or that you have observed directly.

After discussing each point, ask the parents for their opinion on which of the listed possibilities apply to their child. "Let's review the list we have generated. Which of the points on the list do you think apply to Damian?" Ask the parents to add any factors they feel are important but which have not been covered. "Is there anything else that you feel is important in understanding how this problem developed that we have not covered so far?"

Summarize the agreed-upon factors. "Let's draw this together. So you feel that the escalation trap, ignoring desirable behavior, inconsistency, and his starting a new school are important. OK, this suggests that we need to look at each of these areas in planning where to go from here."

When appropriate (particularly with parents who appear defensive or

Table 5.1. Possible Causes of Children's Behavior Problems

---

1. Genetic and biological factors
     Your child's temperament
     Your child's health
2. Day-to-day interactions (learning and experience)
     Accidental rewards for misbehavior
     Escalation traps (from child's and parents' point of view)
     Learning through watching (parents, siblings, peers)
     Ignoring desirable behavior
     How parents give instructions or make rules (too many, too few, too hard, too
     vague, rapid fire, poorly timed, body language)
     Using emotional messages (angry messages, guilt-inducing messages, character
     assassinations)
     Ineffective use of punishment or discipline
3. Things that affect us as parents
     Parents' level of stress and other personal problems
     Marital conflict
     Social support
     Financial stress
4. Any other factors

---

anxious), acknowledge the tentativeness of your interpretation. Use sentences with words such as *seems* or *appears* rather than *obviously* or *clearly*, which convey a higher degree of certainty than is usually warranted. When there are disagreements about which factors are important, refer to existing and future data collection. Solicit descriptive examples when parents suggest disconfirming evidence. "When you say he's just being pigheaded and does it deliberately to annoy you, what specifically does he say and do at these times? Can you recall a recent example when this happened?"

Present Options for Future Action. Present your recommendation for the course of action that has the best chance of succeeding. "I suggest we follow option 1. This would involve us meeting regularly over the next 5 weeks, to help you develop some alternative ways of handling Andrew's behavior at home." Seek the parents' views on their preferred option. Ask the parents about their expectations for treatment (i.e., what outcomes they would like to achieve in therapy).

Plan a Schedule for Future Contact. Work out the details for further appointments, who should be present, and a time for the next appointment. Explain how you see your own role (e.g., to help parents help themselves).

Assign Any Homework. Assign parents a further data collection task or other relevant homework assignment to be completed prior to the next appointment. This can include asking parents to continue baseline recording of the targeted behavior. Provide a written summary of what was decided during the session, and highlight any specific action to be completed by both the therapist and parents.

Difficulties in Discussing Assessment Findings

Several difficulties can arise when discussing assessment findings with parents. Most, however, can be avoided using the following suggestions.

1. *Establish session goals clearly.* A lack of clearly stated goals can result in excessively long appointments, with little achieved beyond a rehashing of material already covered in previous meetings. This can be avoided by thinking carefully about the session goals in advance, negotiating an agenda, and establishing an approximate time frame for the session and sticking to it.

2. *Avoid getting sidetracked by tangential issues.* This leads to redundancy of information gathering and to frustration for both parents and therapist. Try to follow an agenda, be alert to irrelevant or extraneous material, and reschedule discussion of irrelevant topics for later in the session. Use clarification probes (e.g., "You were saying earlier that Kevin came home in a grumpy mood last Tuesday. What specifically happened when he first entered the door after school?") and transition probes (e.g., "OK. I've got a fair idea about his difficulties at school with Mrs. Jameson. Could you tell me about how he gets along with other children in the neighborhood?").

3. *Avoid offering premature interpretations of the child's behavior or motivation.* This can occur when you use diagnostic jargon such as, "I think James has an attention deficit disorder" or vague descriptions ("He seems to be lazy and lacks motivation") to explain a behavior (e.g., low grades in math). Possible solutions to this problem involve presenting relevant descriptive data one at a time, before offering interpretations of their meaning, and selecting relevant examples that are meaningful to the parents. Seek the parents' views of your interpretations.

4. *Avoid being vague and overgeneralizing.* This leads to confusion and increases the chances that parents will disagree with your interpretation. Be specific and use concrete examples.

5. *Avoid being too definitive based on an inadequate database.* Acknowledge possible alternative interpretations, and look to future data collection tasks to test alternative parent-generated hypotheses.

6. *Do not ignore parents' views or become defensive when your own views are challenged.* Encourage parents to present their own views of the problem. Reinforce parents for expressing their own ideas by paraphrasing or summarizing their viewpoint. Avoid becoming defensive when challenged. Ask parents to be more specific, concrete, and to exemplify the challenging or critical statements they make. In some instances it is possible to point to future or existing data or assessments to clarify any disagreements. For example, if a parent referred for a feeding problem is concerned about

some allergic reaction or undiagnosed medical problem, a referral back to a medical specialist may be appropriate.

7. *Deal empathically with defensive or upset parents.* Use focused inquiry, which combines open-ended and probe questioning with summarizing, paraphrasing, and reflection skills, to identify the source of the parents' concern. Be supportive. Challenge irrational assumptions by presenting alternative ways of conceptualizing the problem. Occasionally parents will become distressed when they realize they have been handling a situation poorly. If you remain supportive, encouraging, optimistic, and acknowledge the parents' feelings, the distress may be short-lived and the treatment may continue.

8. *Avoid using jargon.* Use everyday language. If you wish to introduce a new concept, explain it clearly, exemplify it, and use it consistently. Use straightforward examples and vocabulary. Role-play examples as required. Probe to determine parents' understanding of what you have said.

9. *Use focused inquiry with overtalkative parents.* This is a common problem, especially when parents are anxious about their child's behavior. Use interview strategies to guide the parents back to the session agenda. Such strategies include brief summaries which close the topic ("So you feel that last year was a difficult one for you both. How are you feeling at the moment?"); transition probes ("OK. I think I've got a clear idea about his behavior over the last few months. I'd like to ask you some questions now about his progress at school."); retrospective probes (taking the parents off the current irrelevant topic and back to an earlier issue that is immediately relevant); interrupting the parents; and rescheduling the current topic to a later time.

10. *Prompt participation from the nonengaged parent.* Occasionally one parent appears to be disengaged (e.g., yawns, slouches in chair, does not participate in the discussion). When one parent appears to be dominant in the relationship, the less talkative parent can switch off. Disengagement may signal marital problems or disagreements between the partners over seeking professional help. Possible strategies for dealing with this include asking for the disengaged parent's view or opinion on the issue at hand. Reinforce the parent for making contributions to the discussion by showing increased interest and attention, by summarizing his or her point of view, and by asking clarification questions.

SUMMARY

Parents are more likely to cooperate and become actively involved in the process of changing family interaction if they have a clear understanding of the nature of the problem and its causes. Such an understanding should provide a rationale for the proposed treatment plan that is acceptable to the parents. In the behavioral approach to working with families, assessment data should be used to justify treatment options. However, these data must be explained in a way that leads to shared understanding of the problem. In doing so, therapists must be alert to parents' emotional reactions and must deal with them effectively so treatment may continue.

Part III
Details of Family Intervention Procedures

Chapter 6

Training Parents in Positive Parenting and Child Management Skills

Parenting is primarily concerned with the care and education of children. Many parents of behaviorally disturbed children have difficulty managing their children because they lack the skills required to promote prosocial behavior and to manage problem behaviors in children. This chapter describes an intervention process for teaching parents of disturbed, preadolescent children a variety of positive family interaction and child management skills. Effective family intervention involves using assessment data to derive an intervention strategy suited to a family's individual requirements. The need for flexible tailoring is simplified by the availability of a fairly robust child management training intervention which can be applied to a variety of clinical problems and family circumstances with only slight modifications.

The intervention procedures described in this chapter were originally developed to treat oppositional and conduct-disordered children to the age of 9. We have used variations of these procedures in treating children with other problems including attention deficit disorders, depression and conduct disorders, feeding disorders, anxiety disorders, and behavior disorders in developmentally disabled children. These children have ranged in age from infancy to 10 years old. This chapter describes (a) the skills training process we employ in helping parents develop new ways of relating to their children, and (b) examples of the written materials we employ in the process. The material that follows describes the intervention processes that are most suitable for dealing with conduct-disordered children to the age of 10. For older children, the intervention must be modified to reflect their increasing developmental competence. This may entail greater involvement of the children in all aspects of treatment planning and implementation. In some instances it may be necessary to train family members in negotiation and problem-solving skills, or the child may benefit from cognitive coping skills to supplement skill-based training for parents. (Chapter 7 discusses cognitive coping skills.)

The program discussed in this chapter teaches parents how to foster desirable behavior and to deal constructively with a range of common behavior problems. The target behaviors described were selected because they are commonly encountered among children referred to mental health specialists for behavioral and emotional disturbances, particularly those with oppositional behavior problems. These problems include demanding, whining, aggression, teasing, temper tantrums, noncompliance with parents' requests, and interrupting.

Our child management program is divided into two discrete phases: a training phase (parents alone), and a practice plus feedback phase (parents plus children). The core training procedure involves an active teaching process which combines giving parents guidance (verbal and written information) about how to handle specific problems and situations; the modeling of behavior change techniques (e.g., praise, use of time out); behavioral rehearsal involving therapist modeling, prompting, and feedback; in vivo feedback following direct observation of parent-child interaction in the home or clinic; and structured between-session homework assignments. The program was originally designed for use with individual families (Sanders, 1982; Sanders & Glynn, 1981) but has also been used in a group training format (Dadds & McHugh, in press; McFarland & Sanders, 1990; Sanders, 1982). The basic program involves approximately 8 to 10 hours of clinical contact after an initial assessment. However, in routine clinical practice this training time can be shortened or extended depending on the entry skills and progress of parents. The two initial training sessions introduce parents to basic parenting strategies. Parents rehearse these skills while the therapist provides coaching and feedback as necessary. In vivo feedback training, either in the home or clinic, involves a further three to six sessions and helps parents implement the child management program.

During the initial two sessions, parents are introduced to a broad range of techniques and are given examples of their application to a variety of common problems of family life. These skills are applied initially to several specific problem behaviors which are the focus of the parents' concerns. The emphasis of these early sessions is on the parents learning general principles and techniques, the factors that influence their effectiveness (e.g., immediacy, consistency, decisiveness), and their application to several different problems rather than to isolated individual problem behaviors. This strategy is adopted to encourage parents to view the skills as having broad applicability to many different parenting situations beyond the immediate problems their child is experiencing.

SKILLS TAUGHT DURING CHILD MANAGEMENT TRAINING

The program involves teaching parents to use up to 17 specific behavior change strategies, which are divided into two groups. The first group includes strategies which encourage positive interactions between parent and child and which help children learn socially appropriate behaviors, self-care and independence skills, and other prosocial behaviors. The second group introduces parents to strategies for managing problem behavior. Table 6.1 provides an overview of the training process, and Table 6.2 provides a definition of each intervention strategy and includes the age range for which different techniques are useful. The parenting skills described below are adapted from the literature on behavior modification with children, developmental psychology, and examples of childcare advice by Risley and colleagues (e.g., Hart & Risley, 1972; O'Brien, Porterfield, Herbert-Jackson, & Risley, 1979) and others (e.g., Forehand & McMahon, 1981). The specific skills parents are taught can be determined from an analysis of the parents' behavior repertoire, the child's age, and the type of problem behavior the child displays.

The intervention was designed to promote the generalization of parents' newly acquired skills to different settings. A diverse range of exemplars are used to illustrate the potential application of these skills with different family members (not just the referred child). Parents receive training in the actual settings in which they must cope with the child (either in the home or in specially planned clinic sessions). Finally, parents learn self-management skills in an effort to promote the generalization and maintenance of parent behavior changes. The skills include self-observation, self-selection of goals for behavior change, and self-evaluation.

The next section provides detailed session outlines of the intervention process for teaching parents to use the aforementioned skills in their daily interactions with the child.

Overview of Session 1

Session 1 introduces parents to skills for encouraging appropriate behavior by providing instructions in the use of contingent positive attention and contingent consequences for dealing with problem behaviors. The session begins by briefly reviewing the child's presenting problem and its

Table 6.1. Overview of Child Management Training

Session	Duration of Session	Skills Taught	Training Methods Used
1	1½ to 2 hours	Strategies for encouraging desirable behavior: Do's for encouraging Do's for discouraging Use of instructions Use of quiet time Use of time out Behavior correction routine for dealing with noncompliance	Information giving, modeling, rehearsal, feedback, reading assignment
2	1½ to 2 hours	Use of good behavior charts; procedures for dealing with aggression, tantrums, interrupting, and whining	Instructions, modeling, rehearsal, feedback, reading assignment
3 through 6	1 hour	Self-monitoring of treatment implementation; goal setting	Prompting self-selection of goals, in vivo feedback regarding treatment implementation

causes (as discussed in the previous session) and then introduces parents (via behavioral rehearsal) to positive attending and the use of contingent consequences for managing problem behavior. The parent is requested not to implement any of the new strategies for dealing with problem behavior until after the next session.

Prepare for the Session. Have on hand copies of handout materials in Tables 6.4 and 6.5, for each parent attending the session. In clinical practice we normally present the handout information in these tables on 6" × 8" color coded cards. The therapist chooses those cards that are most relevant for the family's problem.

Negotiate an Agenda. Introduce the proposed goals for the session. For example, "During this session I thought we might try to do two things. First, to get a brief update on whether there have been any changes in Damian's behavior since we last met, and second, to discuss in some detail strategies for encouraging desirable behavior and for discouraging misbehavior. At the end of the session we hopefully will have worked out a clear plan that you feel comfortable with for dealing with the problems. OK?"

Review Progress Since Previous Session. Ask the parents whether there have been any changes in the child's behavior since your last contact. Some parents

Table 6.2. Strategies Taught in Child Management Training

Type of Strategy	Description	Recommended Age	Applications
Increasing Desired Behavior or Teaching a New Skill:			
Spending quality time with children	Involves spending frequent, brief (30 sec. to 3 minutes) uninterrupted time involved in child-preferred activities	All ages	Conveying interest and caring for the child: provides opportunities for children to self-disclose and practice conversational skills
Tuning in to desirable behavior	Providing contingent positive attention following prosocial or other appropriate behavior	All ages	Speaking in a pleasant voice; playing cooperatively, sharing, drawing pictures, reading, compliance
Giving plenty of physical affection	Providing contingent positive physical contact following desired child behavior	All ages	Hugging, touching, cuddling, tickling, patting
Conversing with children	Having brief conversations with children about an activity or interest of the child	All ages	Vocabulary, conversational and social skills
Using incidental teaching	Using a series of graded prompts to respond to child-initiated language interactions	1 to 5 years	Language utterances, problem solving, cognitive ability
Setting a good example through modeling	Providing the child a demonstration of desirable behavior through the use of parental modeling	3 to 12 years	Using bathroom, washing hands, tying shoelaces, solving problems
Encouraging independence through *ask, say, do*	Using verbal, gestural, and manual prompts to teach self-care skills	3 to 7 years	Self-care skills (brushing teeth, making bed, tidying up)
Providing engaging activities for children	Involves arranging the child's physical and social environment with persons, objects, materials, and age-appropriate toys	All ages	Board games, felt, paper, paints, pens, tapes, books, construction toys, balls

Continued

Table 6.2. *Continued*

Type of Strategy	Description	Recommended Age	Applications
Weakening or Reducing Problem Behavior:			
Establishing ground rules	Involves negotiating in advance a set of fair, specific, and enforceable rules which apply in particular situations	4 to 12 years	Rules for watching TV, shopping trips, visiting relatives, going out in the car
Directed discussion	The repeated rehearsal of the correct behavior contingent on rule breaking	4 to 10 years	Leaving school bag on floor in kitchen, leaving a mess on the table
Good-behavior charts	A simple token economy involving the provision of social attention and back-up rewards contingent on the absence of undesired behavior or following the performance of desired alternative behavior	3 to 9 years	Doing homework, not swearing, lying, stealing, or having temper tantrums, playing cooperatively, speaking pleasantly when making requests
Terminating instructions	A form of verbal reprimand involving a description of the incorrect and correct alternative behavior	2 to 8 years	Touching electrical outlets, dangerous play (e.g., pulling cat's tail), hitting baby, pulling another child's hair
Logical consequences	The provision of a specific consequence which involves either the removal of an activity from the child or the child from an activity	4 to 12 years	Leaving a bike or toys in the hall, leaving the computer turned on
Quiet time	Placing a child in chair or bean bag in the same environment as other family members for a specified time	1 to 5 years	Squealing, temper outbursts, whining, demanding, hitting, noncompliance

Table 6.2. *Continued*

Type of Strategy	Description	Recommended Age	Applications
Time out	The removal of a child to an area away from other family members for a specified time period contingent on a problem behavior	1 to 9 years	Swearing, stealing, aggressive behavior, tantrums
Planned ignoring	Extinction. The withdrawal of attention while the problem behavior continues	1 to 7 years	Answering back, protesting after providing a punishing consequence, crying and whining
Planned activities	Providing engaging activities in specific high-risk situations	All ages	Out-of-home disruptions (e.g., shopping trips, visiting, traveling in a car, bus, train)

will spontaneously report that the child seems to have improved, perhaps because they feel more optimistic about the possibility of change. However, usually these reports of dramatic change are a result of wishful thinking rather than stable behavior change. Keep this discussion relatively brief (between 2 and 3 minutes). Do not encourage the parents just to give more examples of the same kinds of problems raised in the previous week. Summarize key changes and then move to the next agenda item.

Introduce Strategies for Encouraging Desirable Behavior. Provide an initial orienting statement such as, "What I'd like to do now is to discuss some possible ways of helping Damian overcome his problem by encouraging him to behave in a more appropriate manner." Hand out a copy of "Do's for Encouraging Desirable Behavior" (see Table 6.3), which details nine alternative strategies for promoting desirable behavior. The initial approach we use is to introduce parents to a variety of options to consider. More detailed information on each technique appears in Table 6.4.

Mention to the parents that they may already use some of these strategies. This conveys the idea that the parents are probably already doing many things competently with their child. Briefly explain and give examples of each strategy, answering any queries the parents may have. Parents will sometimes mention that they unsuccessfully used a particular technique in the past (e.g., praise). Some may express doubts or reservations about other techniques (e.g., using rewards to motivate improved behavior

Table 6.3. Strategies for Changing Children's Behavior

Some Do's for Encouraging Desirable Behavior Misbehavior	Some Do's for Discouraging
1. Do spend time with your child individually, doing things he or she likes to do.	1. Do set limits to your child's behavior.
2. Do talk to your child, ask questions, take an interest in his or her play, games, and friends.	2. Do praise your child enthusiastically for behaving appropriately.
3. Do praise your child enthusiastically for accomplishments and appropriate behavior.	3. Do respond to misbehavior immediately, consistently, and decisively.
4. Do cuddle, touch, tickle, laugh, and have fun with your child often.	4. Do respond to misbehavior by describing what the child has done wrong.
5. Do encourage independence by using *ask, say, do* and allowing your child to do things to help you.	5. Do respond to misbehavior by telling the child what would have been more acceptable.
6. Do listen and respond to your child when he or she asks for your help, information, advice, or opinion, or wants to tell you something.	6. Do back up your instructions or your reasonable requests by using natural or logical consequences, quiet time, or time out.
7. Do provide a good language model for your child (i.e., don't baby talk).	7. Do remain calm when speaking to a child who is upset or has misbehaved.
8. Do provide lots of interesting and stimulating toys, games, or objects to encourage play, talking, and intellectual stimulation.	8. Do speak calmly but firmly to your child when he or she misbehaves.
9. Do model behaviors yourself which you want to encourage in your child (e.g., helping others, being a good listener, taking care of your belongings, being friendly, cheerful, and interested in others).	9. Do act quickly; don't threaten to act.
	10. Do deal with the problem yourself rather than threatening someone else's action.
	11. Do try to prevent problems by ensuring that your child has plenty of interesting and engaging things to do.
	12. Do discuss rules with your child, and give him or her a chance to be involved in deciding on rules.

Table 6.4. Strategies for Encouraging Desirable Behavior

Strategy	Specific Guidelines
Spending quality time with children	Involves spending frequent, brief (30 seconds to 3 minutes) uninterrupted time doing activities your child likes. Taking an interest in your child's activities conveys that you care.
Tuning in to desirable behavior	Involves catching your child doing the right thing by providing contingent positive attention following desirable behavior.
	1. Observe your child's behavior closely. Identify what he or she is doing that you would like to occur more often.
	2. Praise your child enthusiastically by describing the behavior you like. "That's terrific, Andy. You went to the bathroom all by yourself."
	3. Initially attend immediately and often.
	4. Take an interest in what your child is doing. If a child knows you are watching their game or activity, it can serve as a powerful motivator.
	5. Comment enthusiastically on your child's game or activity. "Did you build that block tower all by yourself?"
	6. Comment on your child's toy. "Hasn't dolly got beautiful yellow hair?"
	7. Offer help to a child having difficulties with a toy and games. "If you turn the nut the other way, it will go on."
	8. Positive attention can include nonverbal behavior. Sitting or standing nearby, touching, smiling, or joining in a game all convey that you are pleased with what is going on.
	9. Share your own positive feelings. Use "I" statements occasionally when you praise. "I am really pleased you stayed close today when we went shopping."
	10. Attend to small improvements in behavior.
Giving plenty of physical affection	Involves giving positive physical contact during or immediately following desirable child behavior.
	1. Have plenty of physical contact. Holding, touching, cuddling, tickling, kissing, hugging, patting.
	2. Vary your contact. Children enjoy variety.
	3. Avoid being rough. Accidents can easily happen when children become overexcited.

Continued

Table 6.4. *Continued*

Strategy	Specific Guidelines
	4. Avoid giving physical contact when the child is misbehaving to calm down an agitated, disruptive child. 5. Combine touch with caring words. Tell your child you care. 6. Do not force physical affection.
Conversing with children	Involves having brief conversations with children about an activity or interest of the child.
	1. Wait until the child is engaged in an activity; then approach and move to within conversational range. 2. Pause and observe the child's activity. Try to figure out the purpose of the child's activity or play. 3. Respond to the child's requests, questions, or comments about the activity. 4. Withdraw if there is a negative reaction or the child seems uncomfortable with your presence. 5. Give a brief, interested comment about the child's activity. "You've nearly finished that puzzle." 6. If the child responds or asks you a further question, continue the conversation by making further comments. 7. Share information. Volunteer information about your experiences, highlights of your day, ideas, opinions, and feelings. 8. Keep the interactions relatively brief (30 to 60 seconds). Children often converse better in short bursts.
Using incidental teaching	Involves using interactions that children initiate (i.e., when they approach an adult) as an opportunity to teach a new skill.
	1. Set the scene. Incidental teaching works in any situation where there are interesting and engaging things for children to touch, explore, or experience. 2. Be accessible and wait for the child to initiate conversation or an interaction. 3. Respond to the child's initiation by directing your full attention to the child. Look at the child, smile, and listen. 4. Check that you understand what the child is trying to say. "Do you mean the fire engine?"

Table 6.4. *Continued*

Strategy	Specific Guidelines
	5. Request that the child elaborate, expand, explain, or clarify. "What do you want me to do with this carriage?" or "What color is the car?"
	6. If necessary, prompt a better response. If the child cannot or does not answer, prompt the child by giving a clue. "Remember how we made the pattern last time? One piece goes here and this piece goes . . . ?"
	7. Provide a model. If the child does not answer or answers incorrectly, tell the child the answer and ask her to repeat it. "Six times 3 equals 18. What does it equal?"
	8. Give positive feedback. This involves confirming the answer given by the child so he or she knows the answer is correct. "Blue, that's right. The color of your shirt is blue, the same color as your bike."
	9. Keep the interaction brief and enjoyable for both parent and child. Stop incidental teaching as soon as the child has lost interest.
Setting a good example through modeling	Involves creating opportunities for children to learn desired behaviors by observing their parents.
	1. Identify behaviors you wish to encourage and which you can model for your child.
	2. Let your child watch you perform these behaviors or actions.
	3. Describe what you are doing as your child watches.
	4. Answers your child's questions.
	5. Let your child imitate your actions.
	6. Help your child when necessary.
	7. Give positive feedback for correct performance.
Encouraging independence through *Ask, Say, Do*	Involves using verbal, gestural, and manual prompts to teach children self-care skills.
	1. Get all items you need ready in advance (e.g., utensils, materials, objects, equipment).
	2. Gain your child's attention.
	3. *Ask* your child what is the first thing to do.
	4. Repeat aloud your child's correct answer.

Continued

Table 6.4. *Continued*

Strategy	Specific Guidelines
	5. *Say.* Tell your child the correct answer cheerfully. 6. If child complies, praise your child for completing the task. 7. *Do.* Manually guide the child through the motions. 8. Give positive feedback for accomplishments. 9. Repeat steps 3 through 8 for each part of the task until it is completed. 10. Phase out your help once the child has mastered all the steps involved.
Providing engaging activities for children	Involves arranging the child's physical and social environment with persons, objects, materials, and age-appropriate activities or toys to create opportunities for children to develop manual, language and social skills.

or time out). Encourage the parents to express these reservations by asking questions about the basis of their concern. For example, "What is it about the idea of using incentives with Damian that concerns you? What specifically did you do when you used a star chart?" Do not challenge or confront the parents directly. Simply summarize their viewpoint nonjudgmentally; then suggest that sometimes using several strategies in combination works or that there may be other strategies they will find helpful.

Model the Use of Positive Attending. Demonstrate the strategy for tuning in to desirable behavior (see Table 6.4) by conducting the following role-play. The scenario selected should be appropriate for the age of the child. Play the role of the parent; the parent should play the role of the child. For a young child, arrange the setting so that there are toys available. Set up the child (parent) in an activity such as building a block tower; then attend positively to the child's play. "That's a lovely tower you're building. Where does the red block go?" or "This looks like fun, Andrea. You've been playing so nicely this morning. I'll come back in a minute to see how your tower is going."

Give parents a copy of "Tuning in to Desirable Behavior" (see Table 6.4) and explain how positive attending strategies can be used to encourage desirable behavior. Answer any queries the parents may have. Repeat the role-play, reversing roles. Using behavioral rehearsal procedures, get each parent to practice the skills until a satisfactory level of performance is achieved. This rehearsal may involve reinforcing those elements of the parents' behavior that were performed appropriately, giving feedback about elements that need further practice, modeling or prompting the parents to perform those components again, and then getting the parents to practice the entire sequence of behaviors. Some parents may have difficulty generating a descriptive praise comment and may need considerable coaching before they can demonstrate the behavior with appropriate voice tone.

Introduce Strategies for Dealing with Misbehavior. Hand out copies of "Do's for Discouraging Misbehavior" (see Table 6.3). Mention to the parents that they may have already tried some of the strategies. Explain and exemplify each strategy. Hand out and explain the routine for improving compliance with parental instructions (see Figure 6.1, p. 118). Emphasize the importance of using the procedure every time the behavior occurs. Give the parents handouts which explain the use of each of the following consequences: terminating instructions, logical consequences, quiet time, and time out (see Table 6.5). Emphasize the importance of consistency and predictability.

Practice Using Behavior Correction Routines for Dealing with Noncompliance. Role-play a situation in which the parent wants the child to complete some task or activity (e.g., get dressed, undressed, brush teeth). Assume (for the purpose of the role-play) that the child has the necessary skills to carry out the instruction but is simply refusing to do so. In the first role-play, model the procedure with the parent playing the child. In the second role-play, reverse roles. Prompt, model, and give feedback until the parent can demonstrate accurate implementation of the skill. Discuss any difficulties the parent envisages in using the strategy.

Assign Homework. Write down all the training materials the parents should read before the next session. These include the strategies for encouraging desirable behavior and for dealing with difficult behavior. Ask the parents not to implement the new strategies until after the next session. Explain what will be covered in the next session. Deal with any uncertainties the parents may have, and emphasize the importance of completing the homework tasks.

Overview of Session 2

This session continues the initial training of the parents in basic child management skills. During the session, review homework from the previ-

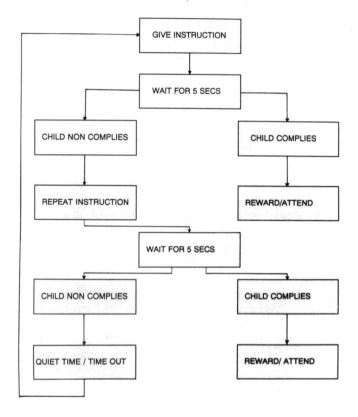

FIGURE 6.1. Procedure for promoting compliance.

ous session and then introduce the use of good behavior charts (a simple token economy) and procedures for managing other problem behavior.

Negotiate an Agenda. Introduce the proposed session goals and give an estimate of the time involved: to review reading tasks; discuss the use of behavior charts; discuss procedures for dealing with aggression, tantrums, interrupting, whining, and noncompliance; and plan subsequent home feedback sessions. Review this agenda with the parents.

Review Homework. Inquire whether the parents had any difficulties with the assigned homework (i.e., the reading tasks). Answer parents' questions about the readings. Thank the parents for completing the tasks.

Introduce the Behavior Chart as a Behavior Change Strategy. Explain to parents that one useful way of encouraging more acceptable behavior patterns is to use a happy-faces or good-behavior chart. Provide a brief rationale for the

DAY: _____   DATE:_____

Times	Faces	Times	Faces
7.00 – 7.30		1.00 – 1.30	
7.30 – 8.00		1.30 – 2.00	
8.00 – 8.30		2.00 – 2.30	
8.30 – 9.00		2.30 – 3.00	
9.00 – 9.30		3.00 – 3.30	
9.30 – 10.00		3.30 – 4.00	
10.00 – 10.30		4.00 – 4.30	
10.30 – 11.00		4.30 – 5.00	
11.00 – 11.30		5.00 – 5.30	
11.30 – 12.00		5.30 – 6.00	
12.00 – 12.30		6.00 – 6.30	
12.30 – 1.00		6.30 – 7.00	

FIGURE 6.2. Behavior chart.

procedure. "The behavior chart is a useful way of encouraging more acceptable behavior because it gives children a sense of achievement and recognition for their efforts in changing their behavior. The happy-faces chart is only used as a temporary measure to help children get started. However, it gives children feedback on their progress and how well they are doing. It will need to be phased out once the new behavior is established."

A sample chart appears in Figure 6.2. Ask the parents to nominate one or two additional behaviors that occur at home that are problems (e.g., getting the child to stay in his or her own bed). Do not include a large number of problem behaviors. Keep the system as simple as possible. Some parents may wish to use the charts with siblings as well. This should be encouraged to promote the generalization of parenting skills. Refer parents to the handout entitled "Guidelines for Using Behavior Correction Routines" (see Table 6.5) and discuss each step. Select an appropriate reinforcement schedule — either a differential reinforcement of zero rate (DRO) or a fixed ratio (FR) schedule. Select and explain the procedure to be used for dealing with the misbehavior (e.g., logical consequences, quiet time, or time out). Hand out blank happy-faces charts. Summarize the main steps in setting up the behavior chart.

Table 6.5. Guidelines for Using Behavior Correction Routines

Routine	Specific Guidelines
Establishing ground rules	Involves negotiating in advance a set of fair, specific, enforceable rules which apply in particular situations. 1. Have a small number of rules. 2. Rules should be fair (i.e., apply to all children in the family). 3. Rules should be easy to follow. 4. Rules should be enforceable. 5. Rules should be positively stated (i.e., describe what the child can do, rather than cannot do). 6. Have ground rules for particular situations (e.g., shopping, visiting).
Introducing new rules	1. Set the scene (call a family meeting, TV off, eliminate distractions). 2. State the reason for calling the meeting. 3. State clearly each rule you would like observed. 4. Seek your child's opinion on the rule. 5. Ask the child to repeat the rule. 6. Repeat steps 4 and 5 for each additional rule. 7. Summarize the rules and, if necessary, write them down. 8. Decide on specific consequences for complying with and breaking the rule. 9. Wind up the discussion.
Dealing with rule breaking with directed discussion	The repeated rehearsal of the correct behavior contingent on rule breaking. 1. Gain your child's attention. 2. State what the problem is briefly, simply, and calmly. 3. Explain why the behavior is a problem. 4. Describe or get the child to suggest a correct alternative behavior. 5. Rehearse the correct alternative behavior. 6. End the discussion by praising the child for the correct behavior.
Good behavior charts	A simple token economy involving the provision of social attention and back-up rewards contingent on the absence of undesired behavior or following the performance of desired alternative behavior. *Before you start* 1. Get everything you need ready (chart, stickers, gold stars).

Table 6.5. *Continued*

Routine	Specific Guidelines
Good behavior charts (*Continued*)	2. Hold a discussion with your child, explaining the system. 3. Prepare your child by describing the problem simply, briefly, and calmly. 4. Give a reason why the behavior concerns you. 5. Describe how the behavior chart works. 6. Describe how often the child can earn the stars, happy faces, or stickers. 7. Describe what back-up rewards can be earned for a specific number of stars. 8. Ask the child to state the rules for earning stars and back-up rewards. 9. Decide on a procedure to follow if the child breaks the rules. 10. Explain to your child the consequence for breaking the rules. 11. When possible, have a practice run to prepare the child for the consequences. *Managing the program* 1. Watch your child's behavior closely. 2. Catch your child being good by praising desirable behavior. 3. Describe the problem behavior and the consequence. 4. Fill in the chart at the required time. 5. Give the back-up reward as agreed.
Giving clear, calm instructions	A clear, specific instruction to the child to engage in a specific behavior or to carry out some task or activity. 1. Get physically close (within arm's length). 2. Gain the child's attention. 3. Use good body language (turn body toward child, get down on child's eye level, look into child's eyes). 4. State what you would like the child to do. 5. Give the child time to comply (5 seconds). 6. Give positive feedback if the child complies. 7. Repeat the instruction if the child noncomplies. 8. Wait another 5 seconds. 9. Praise the child for complying. 10. If the child still doesn't comply, back up your request with an appropriate consequence (e.g., time out).

Continued

Table 6.5. *Continued*

Routine	Specific Guidelines
	11. After the time-out period, return the child to the place where the problem arose and repeat the instruction.
Terminating instructions	A special type of request that involves describing the child's incorrect and another correct alternative behavior.
	1. As soon as the problem behavior occurs, stop what you are doing and gain the child's attention. 2. Clearly and firmly tell the child to immediately cease what he or she is doing. "Richard, stop that rough play immediately." 3. Describe or explain the correct alternative behavior in a calm manner. "You should touch the baby softly." 4. Terminating instructions should be used immediately, as soon as you see the behavior occurring. Don't wait until it has happened three or four times.
Logical consequences	The provision of a specific consequence which involves either the removal of an activity from the child or the child from an activity.
	1. When you observe the undesired behavior occurring, gain the child's attention and clearly describe the nature of the problems. 2. Remove the activities from the child (e.g., remove a troublesome toy) or the child from the activities (e.g., turn off the TV). 3. Give an explanation. Tell the child why you are doing this and for how long the activity will be withdrawn. 4. Keep to the conditions and allow the child access to the activity once the time is up. 5. Be reasonable in the amount of time the activity is withdrawn. 6. When the problem occurs, be decisive and act immediately. Don't debate or argue the point.
Quiet time	Involves placing the child in a chair or bean bag in the same environment as other family members for a specific time following an undesired behavior.

Table 6.5. *Continued*

Routine	Specific Guidelines
Quiet time (*continued*)	1. Before you begin, explain to your child how quiet time works. Tell your child what behaviors will earn quiet time and explain calmly why you will be using it. Show your child exactly what will happen the next time the disturbing behavior occurs (i.e., rehearse the procedure).
	2. When the problem occurs, gain the child's attention and calmly but firmly tell the child what's wrong by giving a terminating instruction. "Peter, stop pushing your sister right now." Act quickly whenever you see the behavior occurring.
	3. If the behavior stops, thank the child for doing as told and suggest another activity the child can do.
	4. If the behavior continues or occurs again in the next hour, back up your instruction with quiet time. Tell the child what he or she has done wrong and the consequence of disobeying. "Now go to quiet time."
	5. Do not lecture, nag, or threaten quiet time.
	6. Act; don't threaten to act. Make sure the child is taken to the quiet time area. Protests should be ignored. If the child protests or refuses, firmly but calmly guide the child to the quiet time area.
	7. Before you leave, let your child know the rule. "After you have sat here quietly for 3 minutes, you can come out."
	8. Deal with disruptions (e.g., struggling, screaming, or getting out of the seat) in quiet time with time out for a further 3 minutes.
	9. Do not speak to your child, and ensure that the child receives no attention from others while in quiet time.
	10. When quiet time is over, engage your child in an activity. Don't mention the incident. Look for an opportunity to "catch" him or her being good.
Time out	The removal of a child to an area away from other family members for a specified time period contingent on a problem behavior.

Continued

Table 6.5. *Continued*

Routine	Specific Guidelines
	1. Same as for quiet time, except that the child is removed from the setting where the problem behavior occurred. Used as a back-up (e.g., bathroom)
Planned ignoring	Extinction. The withdrawal of parental attention while the problem behavior continues.
	1. When you observe the undesired behavior, decide whether you should ignore it. If you decide to ignore a behavior, make sure you ignore it every time.
	2. Withdraw all attention. Avoid eye contact, turn away, and if necessary walk away.
	3. Continue to ignore if behavior worsens.
	4. Attend to your child when the problem behavior ceases.
	5. If the problem starts again, once again remove all attention while the behavior continues.
	6. As soon as your child is busy and engaged in an activity, speak up and praise.
Planned activities	Providing engaging activities in specific high-risk situations.
	1. Pinpoint high-risk situations where children have been bored or disruptive because there was little for them to do (e.g., traveling in the car).
	2. Identify suitable activities for each situation.
	3. Discuss the ground rules for the situation with your child in advance and ask child to select something he or she would like to take with them.
	4. Generate an activities list for school holidays, weekends, and other free time.
	5. Help your child get started, if necessary.
	6. Give your child attention periodically while he or she is busy.

Managing fighting, tormenting, or teasing other children									
Instructions: Whenever this situation occurs, record yes, no, or NA (not applicable) for each of the steps below.									
Steps to be followed:	Date:								
	Time:								
1. Gain child's attention.									
2. Give a terminating instruction.									
3. Describe the correct behavior (what child should do).									
4. Speak up and praise if the child obeys your request.									
5. If problem continues, describe what is wrong and introduce an immediate natural consequence (e.g., remove the troublesome toy); say why you are doing it.									
6. If child disobeys or throws a tantrum, describe what he or she has done wrong again and take child immediately to quiet time.									
7. If problem continues, put child in time out immediately with a brief explanation.									
Number of steps completed correctly:									

FIGURE 6.3. Parental self-monitoring procedure.

Introduce Procedures for Dealing with Aggression, Tantrums, Interrupting, and Minor Whining. Refer parents to handouts dealing with each of these behaviors (Table 6.6, Figure 6.3). Figure 6.3 is an example of a self-monitoring card parents can use in tracking their implementation of treatment procedures during initial phases of training. Explain each procedure that is relevant to the parents, step by step, highlighting the common points in each routine. Answer queries and check for parent understanding of the steps involved.

Plan Feedback Sessions. Negotiate with the parents for home visits or clinic feedback sessions twice weekly. Provide a rationale for these sessions. "The main idea of the home visit is to give you some support during the

Table 6.6. Procedures for Managing Aggression, Tantrums, Minor Whining, and Interrupting

Fighting, Tormenting, or Teasing Other Children	Temper Outbursts (Loud Screaming, Uncontrollable Shrieking, Crying, or Stamping Feet)	Minor Whining Not Directed at Anyone Else, Whining or Complaining That Results from Being Refused Something	Interrupting Parents' Conversation or Phone Call
1. Gain child's attention.	1. Gain child's attention as best you can.	1. Remove all attention from child while the unpleasant behavior continues. Turn away from the child and, if necessary, walk away.	1. Gain child's attention.
2. Give a terminating instruction.	2. Give a terminating instruction that this screaming must stop or the child will have to go to time out.	2. When the whining stops, wait a few seconds and then attend to the child. Suggest something else to do.	2. Tell child that you don't like it when he or she interrupts. Ask child to say "Excuse me" and to wait until you are free.
3. Describe the correct behavior (what the child should do).	3. Do not argue the point. If the tantrum continues, describe the problem ("You have not done as I asked") and use the back-up immediately ("Now go to quiet time").	3. As soon as the child is busy and engaged in play, speak up and praise.	3. Speak up and praise the child for waiting.
4. Speak up and praise if the child obeys your request.	4. If tantrum continues, take the child to time out, explain what is wrong and what the rules of time out are.		4. If child demands or protests, give a terminating instruction (describe the behavior).
5. If problem continues, describe what is wrong and introduce an immediate natural consequence (e.g., remove the troublesome toy); say why you are doing it.			5. Follow up immediately with a natural consequence with a brief explanation.
6. If child disobeys or throws a tantrum, describe what he or she has done wrong again and take child immediately to quiet time.			6. If the child disobeys or displays aggression or a tantrum results, put child in quiet time immediately.
7. If a problem continues, put child into time out immediately with a brief explanation.			7. If tantrum continues, put child in time out immediately, with a brief explanation.

early stages when you are trying out the new way of handling Damian's behavior. It will also give me a chance to discuss any difficulties you may be having and to answer any queries."

Assign Homework. Ask the parents to implement the happy-faces or behavior chart for the selected target behavior, begin using the management routines for demanding and noncompliance, and reread handouts dealing with specific problem behaviors. Emphasize the importance of discussing the procedures with their spouse. Summarize main points. Deal with any uncertainties the parents may have.

Overview of Sessions 3 Through 6

Sessions 3 through 6 involve active in vivo skill training with the parents and child. This training can take place either in the child's home (which in many ways is the preferred location, particularly for preschool children) or in a structured clinic situation. The aim of the in vivo training sessions is to provide parents with clear, specific, and helpful information about their interaction with the target child and siblings. Parents are encouraged to take personal responsibility for changing their own behavior, and the therapist's role is to prompt and support the parents' use of skills such as self-tracking, self-identification of strengths and weaknesses, and self-selection of future goals.

At each session the parents and therapist set goals for further improvement. Sessions begin with the therapist prompting the parents to recall the goals worked out at the preceding session. A 15- to 20-minute observation is then conducted in which the parents attempt to implement the program. Following the observation, the therapist provides feedback to the parents. This general process involves a gradual shaping of the parents' behavior and their problem-solving skills.

Home feedback sessions are conducted preferably twice per week for 3 consecutive weeks during child management training. Sessions should be scheduled at any agreed-upon time, as long as the target child is present and the visit will not cause any serious disruption to the family's normal routine. These feedback sessions can be spread out over a longer period of time, if necessary. However, we favor frequent contact, particularly in the first few weeks of treatment. During home visits the TV should be turned off, the children should be confined to family living areas, and no outgoing telephone calls should be made.

Review Session Goals. Arrive at the scheduled time. Ask the parents to describe the goals worked out at the previous home feedback session. If no goals were established, suggest that the parents deal with any problems that might arise using the behavior correction routines introduced in the last session. On subsequent occasions specific goals might include rewarding the child for being good by praising at least five times during the session; remaining calm when the child demands parental attention; speaking calmly but matter of factly; rereading the handout on using time out.

Introduce the Parents to Self-Monitoring Their Use of Treatment Procedures. Tell parents how to self-monitor their implementation of the targeted treatment procedures during the home observation, using monitoring cards shown in Figure 6.4. Treatment steps can be written on the card as required.

Begin the Observation Session. Inform the parents when the observation is ready to begin, making sure that the conditions for the observation are appropriate. Begin a 20-minute observation, taking note of interaction in which the parents correctly and incorrectly follow the management protocol. The observation protocol shown in Figure 6.5 illustrates the observation schedule. Keep track of the frequency of general or specific praise comments as well as clear and vague instructions to the child. At the end of the observation, complete the parents' feedback sheet in duplicate (see Table 6.7).

Instructions: Whenever this situation occurs record yes, no, or NA (not applicable) for each of the steps below.						
Steps to be followed:	Date and time:					
1.						
2.						
3.						
4.						
5.						
6.						
7.						
8.						
Number of steps completed correctly:						

FIGURE 6.4. A blank self-monitoring card.

	Episodes									
Demanding	1	2	3	4	5	6	7	8	9	10
1. Gains child's attention										
2. Prompts										
3. Further prompts										
4. Speaks up and praises										
5. Terminating instruction										
6. Quiet time										
7. Time out										
Number of steps correct										

	Episodes									
Interrupting	1	2	3	4	5	6	7	8	9	10
1. Gains child's attention										
2. Describes correct behavior										
3. Prompts correct behavior										
4. Speaks up and praises										
5. Terminating instruction										
6. Natural consequence										
7. Quiet time										
8. Time out										
Number of steps correct										

	Episodes									
Minor whining	1	2	3	4	5	6	7	8	9	10
1. Ignores										
2. Prompts engagement										
3. Speaks up and praises										
Number of steps correct										

FIGURE 6.5. Home observation and feedback sheet.

Conduct Feedback. Before starting the feedback session, prompt the parents to set up the child in an activity. Parents should explain to the child or children that they will be busy for a few minutes talking to the therapist and that they do not want to be interrupted. Periodically during the feedback session, the parents should praise the child for not interrupting.

Aggression	Episodes									
	1	2	3	4	5	6	7	8	9	10
1. Gains child's attention										
2. Terminating instruction										
3. Describes correct behavior										
4. Speaks up and praises										
5. Natural consequence										
6. Quiet time										
7. Time out										
Number of steps correct										

Noncompliance	Episodes									
	1	2	3	4	5	6	7	8	9	10
1. Gains child's attention										
2. Repeats instruction (once)										
3. Speaks up and praises										
4. Natural consequence										
5. Quiet time										
6. Time out										
Number of steps correct										

Tantrums	Episodes									
	1	2	3	4	5	6	7	8	9	10
1. Terminating instruction										
2. Quiet time										
3. Time out										
Number of steps correct										

FIGURE 6.5. *Continued.*

If interruption occurs, the parents should prompt the child to wait and then respond to the child when there is an appropriate pause in the conversation. If disruptive behavior occurs, the parents should be encouraged to deal with the problem using the appropriate behavior correction routine.

Table 6.7. Parents' Feedback Sheet

Parents' names _____ Date _____ Session no. _____
1. Amount of problem behavior _____

2. Amount of time correction routines were accurately carried out:
   Demanding/whining _____
   Fighting/teasing   _____
   Tantrums   _____
   Interrupting   _____
   Minor whining   _____
   Noncompliance   _____
   Average overall   _____

3. Number of praise comments
   General   _____
   Specific   _____
   Total   _____

4. Number of instructions
   Clear   _____
   Vague   _____
   Total   _____

5. The way you spoke to your child

   _____
   _____
   _____

6. Goals for next session
   (a) _____
   (b) _____
   (c) _____
   (d) _____

Prompt the parents to review the session as a whole. "How do you feel the session went today?" Reinforce the parents for identifying any specific positive or negative behaviors they engaged in. For example, "I thought I kept my cool much better today when Andrew started demanding his afternoon snack." Use praise comments, reflections, summaries, or clarification probe questions as appropriate to help the parents identify relevant behavior. If the parents make fairly vague or nonspecific comments, ask them to identify two things they felt they handled well today. Reinforce the parents for accurate self-identification of positive behavior. If these prompts do not produce the desired response, describe two situations that the parents handled appropriately or that had improved from previous occasions.

Prompt the parents to identify two things they think they could have done differently. "Is there anything you would like to have changed about the way you handled Jim's behavior this morning?" Prompt the parents to generate some alternative ways of dealing with the problem. "What options do you have in this situation?" Prompt the parents to set some specific goals to work on in subsequent sessions. Summarize the main points covered, and prompt the parents to write down these goals on the home feedback sheet shown in Table 6.7. Confirm the date of the next appointment, and close the session.

Assessing Parents' Competencies. During each observation session, one of the key clinical tasks is to monitor the level of the parents' proficiency in implementing targeted skills. Unless parents are directly observed interacting with their children in situations where problem behavior occurs, it is difficult to gauge the extent to which the parents have acquired the necessary skills. Some parents can give a misleading impression of how well their child is doing. Rely on direct observation rather than just on what the parents tell you. When possible, parenting advice should be written, in clear, comprehensible language that lends itself to easy assessment of whether it has been followed or not.

Terminate Training. Training sessions should continue until the parents are observed to implement positive attending and behavior correction routines in the home. Some parents will spontaneously report generalizing the use of skills with children in out-of-home situations, and this should be encouraged. However, other parents may require additional training to produce reliable generalization (see chapter 7).

TROUBLESHOOTING GUIDE

In most cases, child management training proceeds relatively smoothly without major disruption. However, there are several problems that can arise during child management training that can be either prevented or remedied. Some parents are initially concerned that using a reward system is a form of bribing their child. Parents are sometimes concerned that their child will become dependent on rewards and will refuse to do anything unless there is a payoff. In most instances it is best to acknowledge the validity of the parents' concern (and to assure them that these problems can be overcome when child management techniques are used appropriately). It is rare that praise and other rewards decrease the intrinsic value of completing a task or activity. Unfortunately, many behaviorally disturbed children do not obtain a great deal of intrinsic pleasure from activities that are developmentally important.

Table 6.8 lists other problems that can be encountered during child management training and possible solutions to these difficulties. Problems which require special adjunctive treatments, such as marital difficulties, maternal depression, or social insularity, are discussed in chapters 7 and 9.

ADAPTATIONS OF THE BASIC
TRAINING PROCESS

The core elements of the intervention process can be adapted to a variety of clinical situations that involve training parents to alter their current ways of dealing with problems. These core elements include (a) the preparation of written materials which detail in a sequential, behaviorally specific fashion the steps parents should follow to deal with particular situations or problems; and (b) the modeling, rehearsal, and implementation of the skills in situations where the family can be observed interacting and feedback and support can be provided. We have used these core elements in developing parent advice for the management of complaints in children with recurrent abdominal pain and headaches (Sanders, Rebgetz et al., 1989), a feeding disorders management guide for parents (Sanders, Le Gris, Shephard, & Turner, 1990), a parent management protocol for

Table 6.8. Troubleshooting Guide for Child Management Training

Problem	Possible Solution
1. Parent fails to implement the correct procedure at the right time.	When child's disruptive behavior occurs, prompt parent to implement.
2. Parent complains about stressful events which affect capacity to implement procedures.	Determine whether stressful events can be resolved by simple changes (e.g., altering early-morning routine) or require more complex interventions (stress management, relaxation training).
3. Parent complains that spouse is not implementing or does not agree with some of the procedures.	Reassess nature and extent of marital conflict. Consider using partner support training.
4. Parent reports feeling distressed by child's upset behavior during time out.	Remind parent of the importance of ignoring the child in time out until the protesting stops. Make sure there is support available to the parent during early attempts at implementing time out.
5. Parent reports being able to implement procedures at home but reports continuing difficulties in certain out-of-home situations (e.g., visiting, dropping child off at daycare or preschool).	Consider using planned activities and training procedures to promote generalization of implementation to community settings.
6. Parent reports difficulties in transitional situations (e.g., getting ready to go out).	Devise organizational strategies to reduce the amount of time the child waits during transitions.

dealing with depressive behavior in children (Sanders, Dadds, Johnston et al., 1989), and in enhancing the adherence of children with cystic fibrosis to their medical regimen (Sanders, Gravestock, & Wanstall, 1990). In each of these examples, while the target behaviors of the child and the specific advice given vary somewhat depending on the situation, the training process for equipping caregivers is similar.

For children above age 9, home visits can be replaced by asking the parents to audiotape home interactions at high-risk times (e.g., mealtimes). These tapes can be reviewed with the parents at clinic visits during the treatment phase. The child and parents can rehearse the proposed management routine together in the clinic. The therapist can explain the procedure to the child and prompt and reinforce correct implementation of the strategy. For children with persistent feeding problems, we videotape family interactions in the clinic during mealtimes.

It is worthwhile to observe family members interacting with each other in meaningful observation situations. This is necessary to determine whether skills being taught have actually been mastered. We favor spending relatively less time on instructing and advising and more on providing practice and feedback in situations when children are present. It is not uncommon to find parents who can tell you exactly what they should do (after receiving instructions) but cannot put the procedure into effect correctly with their own child until the practice and feedback sessions.

SUMMARY

This chapter provides an overview of an intervention process for developing parents' competencies in implementing a range of behavior change techniques to deal with a variety of common problem behaviors in children. The techniques include strategies to increase desirable behavior, teach new skills, and reduce problem behaviors. Parents are taught to apply these strategies in multiple situations with classes of problematic behavior rather than with isolated individual target behaviors. While many parents benefit from the discussion and provision of reading material which describes techniques, in many ways the focus of the intervention is the provision of home-based training and feedback. There is frequently little correspondence between what parents say they do and what they actually do. Home-based training is the context in which parents learn to implement techniques in their moment-to-moment interactions with their children in a supportive, noncritical environment. Parents' implementation of specific techniques often must be developed gradually through a combination of parental self-evaluation and reflection, and therapist feedback and suggestion. Some parents will acquire basic child management skills quickly, show strong generalization of treatment effects across settings, and maintain their use of skills over time (Sanders & Plant, 1989). Other parents will require additional interventions before clinical improvement is apparent.

Chapter 7

Strategies to Improve Generalization and Maintenance of Treatment Effects

One hallmark of behavioral intervention is its commitment to developing procedures for effecting the generalization and maintenance of therapeutic change across different settings, behaviors, individuals, and over time (Baer et al., 1968; Stokes & Baer, 1977). While behavioral family intervention has been repeatedly demonstrated to be effective in changing child behavior, the generalization and maintenance effects of treatment have been less rigorously investigated (Edelstein, 1989; Sanders & James, 1983). Relatively little attention has been given to the study of variables that influence the extent to which parents generalize the application of their skills.

IMPORTANCE OF GENERALIZATION

The generalization of parent behavior is important for several reasons. First, parents presenting with behavior problem children often experience management problems in multiple settings (e.g., at home and in community settings such as shopping malls). Unless parents apply behavior change strategies consistently across different situations, children can easily discriminate between settings where contingencies operate and those where they do not. This can result in improved behavior in one setting but no change or even deterioration in another. Second, because the siblings of referred children often experience similar behavior problems, it would be advantageous if parents acquired skills which generalize to all relevant family members. Third, the durability of treatment effects is a major concern with all psychosocial interventions. Effective treatments of parent-child problems must produce sustained change in a child's behavior to be judged clinically efficacious. Since parental behavior seems to be an important determinant of durable child behavior change, detailed attention must be given to identifying variables associated with generalized and durable changes in parental behavior.

While there continues to be some disagreement in the literature regarding terminology, Stokes and Baer (1977) proposed a useful definition of the phenomenon. They defined generalization as "the occurrence of relevant behavior under different, non-training conditions (i.e. across subjects, settings, people, behaviors and/or time without the scheduling of the same events in those conditions as had been scheduled in the training conditions)" (1977, p. 350). They also argued that generalization occurs when additional training manipulations are used to produce change in extra training settings, provided the cost or extent is clearly less than that of the initial intervention.

Drabman, Hammer, and Rosenbaum (1979), however, pointed out that the distinction between generalization and training settings is essentially an arbitrary one which depends on the identification of certain salient discriminative stimuli which are present in the training setting but absent from the generalization setting. For example, if modeling procedures were used to teach parents to use time out in the clinic, and assessment indicated that time out was being used in the home, then generalization would have been demonstrated. If, however, modeling had to be used later in the home to get the parents to implement time out, the example would not be one of generalization but would merely be an extension of the same procedure to a new setting. This is also known as the sequential modification of behavior (Stokes & Baer, 1977). This chapter deals primarily with how to promote the generalization of parent behavior. However, many of the principles can be used to promote the generalization of child behavior changes.

When Does Generalization Become a Therapeutic Goal?

Generalized treatment effects are not always desirable. In many situations the therapeutic goal is more appropriately one of discrimination rather than generalization. For example, the indiscriminate and overgeneralized use of punishment procedures, even when applied correctly (e.g., response cost, time out), would be countertherapeutic and probably render parents less effective in promoting prosocial behavior. Hence, therapists attempting to program for generalization should identify the stimulus conditions (behaviors, settings) under which the generalization is therapeutic.

Contingent positive attending, clear instructions, and back-up consequences are skills that have broad applicability to a variety of parenting situations and children of different ages; however, treatment should attempt to equip parents to recognize situations and problems where application of particular skills is inappropriate (e.g., use of time out with teenagers).

The tasks encountered in designing effective generalization procedures are similar to those involved in designing any behavior change program. That is, the therapist should define the type of generalization effect to be sought (target change), identify the contingencies or variables that may facilitate or obstruct the desired generalization effect, and assess whether the desired generalization goal has been achieved. Finally, the therapist must ensure that an initial generalization effect (e.g., across settings) maintains over time.

Obstacles to Generalization

The development of generalization techniques in behavioral family intervention has been hampered by inadequate knowledge of variables that effect parent behavior in different contexts. Parents' behavior (including their capacity to implement or generalize their use of skills) may be influenced by affective, cognitive, social, and parenting task variables, the physical ecology (architecture, activities, materials, furniture) of the setting within which parenting takes place, as well as reinforcement contingencies.

The mechanisms by which different components of an ecosystem interact are not well understood. In particular, the interrelationships between marital, affective, cognitive, and other family factors and treatment variables have not been clearly documented. For example, while it is generally believed that marital factors affect parenting, the conditions under which specific types of marital interchange influence parents' behavior (e.g., coerciveness) with a child are unclear. When a husband criticizes his wife's handling of their child's behavior, this may constitute a high-risk setting event for the mother failing to carry out parenting advice. However, the actual impact of the criticism on the mother's behavior may vary depending on factors such as the mother's affective state prior to the comments, whether there are concurrent or competing demands on the parent from other siblings, and so on. Whether the parent acts coercively (fails to implement treatment) following a critical comment from a spouse may depend on the simultaneous presence or absence of additional demands. However, few studies have addressed the relationship between ecological variables and parenting.

Parents' Affective State

Several studies have shown that a parent's psychological state can affect the outcome of parent training (Griest & Wells, 1983; Miller & Prinz, 1990; Webster-Stratton, 1985; Wolfe, Fairbank, Kelly, & Bradlyn, 1983). Depressed parents seem to have difficulty implementing treatment procedures, drop out from treatment prematurely, fail to maintain changes in behavior over time (McMahon et al., 1981), and are less satisfied with treatment (Furey & Basili, 1988).

Behavioral family intervention encourages parents to respond consistently and contingently to both appropriate and inappropriate child behavior. Fundamental to such responding is the parents' ability to monitor and evaluate their child's moment-to-moment behavior accurately and to formulate and enact appropriate parental responses which take into account the context within which the problem occurs and the child's developmental level. Several authors have hypothesized that depressed parents have difficulty acquiring evaluative and monitoring skills — the skills taught in behavioral family intervention programs. When parents are depressed, they may be less discriminating in their interactions with their children. Some evidence shows they fail to monitor or supervise their child's behavior and hence miss many opportunities either to reinforce or correct the behavior. Such nondiscriminative parenting creates contingencies for the child, which once again give rise to problem behavior. A vicious cycle is set in motion whereby a deterioration of the child's behavior may heighten a parent's feelings of hopelessness and further intensify depression.

A wide variety of psychiatric conditions alter affective state and may influence a parent's interaction with the child. Hence, it is important to determine the degree of parental psychological distress and to provide or refer the parents for appropriate treatment. Some studies have shown that when parents have emotional problems themselves, the effect of parent training can be improved by providing adjunctive treatment focusing on parents' psychological adjustment (Miller & Prinz, 1990). For example, Griest et al. (1982) provided parents with parent enhancement therapy, which focused on the parents' affective state, perceptions of child behavior, marital problems, and problems in extrafamilial relationships. This combined child management and parent enhancement treatment produced maintenance of treatment effects at 2 months follow-up, superior to parent training alone. Other studies have combined parent training with anger control techniques, problem-solving skills, and self-management techniques (Sanders & Glynn, 1981). However, none of these studies has examined the effects of adjunctive treatments with parents who have clinically diagnosed affective disorders.

Another study by Wolfe et al. (1983) showed that abusive parents had a greater physiological arousal to stressful videotaped scenes of parent-child interactions than nonabusive parents. These authors argued that parents experiencing anger and rage in response to child aversive behaviors need specific training to decrease their emotional overreactivity. Such treatment might include relaxation skills, coping skills, or cognitive restructuring (Ambrose, Hazzard, & Hayworth, 1980).

Cognitive Variables

Sometimes failure to generalize parenting skills appropriately may be related to cognitive variables such as parents' expectations and beliefs about parenthood or child development, the goals of treatment, their global evaluations of their child, attentional factors, and parents' understanding of treatment procedures. The role of cognitive factors in the treatment process has received little attention. However, parents' attributions, expectations, and perceptions of their children's behavior are important issues to consider if a treatment plan is to be accepted, implemented, and subsequently generalized to settings in which there is minimal therapist surveillance (Griest & Wells, 1983).

Several studies have shown that parents' global evaluations or ratings of their children change in a positive direction following parent training (Forehand & McMahon, 1981). Other studies suggest that some parents fail to alter their verbal descriptions of their child's behavior following parent training.

Many parents present in therapy with vague, overgeneralized, and nonspecific evaluations of their child. For example, the child may be described as headstrong, irritable, impatient, out of control, and so on. Behavioral family intervention encourages parents to be more discriminating and specific in their descriptions of the child. A variety of tasks (e.g., record keeping) also discourage parents from sustaining overgeneralized subjective views of their children. Despite these efforts, some parents continue to label their child as being a problem even though objective observational data show steady improvement in the child's behavior (Wahler & Afton, 1980). These parents may have distorted observational tracking styles that bias their perceptions and summary reports of their children.

Wahler and Graves (1983) proposed that multidistressed mothers' summary reports covary with the occurrence of aversive parent behavior. Furthermore, these summary reports are part of a response class that consists of both an overly aversive behavior and verbal descriptions ("I am furious"). Since the summary reports covary with aversive behavior, occurrences of the report increase the probability of aversive responding. In this model, the verbal report exerts indirect stimulus control over subsequent coercive interchange. Setting events, such as an argument with a spouse earlier in the day, may exert direct stimulus control over parental coercion.

Wahler proposed a strategy to alter the impact of both setting events and summary reports and to increase generalization effects in parent training. In this process, mothers are encouraged to report on sources of coercion in their lives, in addition to child behavior problems, and are reinforced for more elaborate and specific descriptions of these problems. Presumably, this process enables the parent to become more aware of the relationship between setting events, verbal descriptions or summary evaluations, and parenting, and to develop alternative adaptive ways of coping with extrafamilial stresses. However, there are few data available documenting the efficacy of this strategy.

When a parent's cognitive construction of a parenting situation is obstructing desired generalization, a variety of strategies may be considered. For example, cognitive restructuring may be useful and permit exploration of the parent's rationale for not using a procedure in a particular situation. This may reveal as yet unexpressed concerns the parent has about using procedures in certain situations.

Attentional variables are relevant to understanding several categories of generalization. Some parents may fail to apply a procedure in a generalization setting (e.g., at play group) because the parents' attention is engaged in another activity (e.g., talking to another parent). Alternatively, the parents may construe the child's behavior as tolerable though inappropriate because using time out might prompt negative evaluations from other parents, particularly if the child protests. The parents may attribute the child's behavior to organismic variables — for example, being tired, hungry, physically ill (i.e., "state" variables) — and hence warrant a different approach. The parents may justify nonintervention by rationalizing the behavior on such grounds. Parents may fail to generalize their skills due to competing or incompatible constructions, expectancies, or attentional factors that are specific to particular settings. As a result, parents may fail to discriminate that the setting is an appropriate one to generalize their skills.

Marital Variables

Marital factors are widely believed to influence the effects of treatment and can be related to poor generalization and maintenance effects (Cole & Morrow, 1976; Dadds, Schwartz, & Sanders, 1987; Reisinger, Frangia, &

Hoffman, 1976). When both parents participate in treatment, agree on specific targets for change, and support and give corrective feedback to each other, they find it easier to generalize their skills across settings and over time. However, work commitments, inflexible clinic hours, and lack of motivation of fathers often mean mothers are the primary recipients of parent-training efforts. Moreover, in families where there is severe marital dysfunction, the trained parent may fail to generalize skills because the spouse undermines such efforts through direct criticism, passive resistance, indifference, or lack of reinforcement for spouse behavior.

Nevertheless, it is inaccurate to assume that all parents from discordant marriages are at risk for treatment failure. Many parents can perform well despite what seems insurmountable marital discord. For other couples, marital therapy, or at least focused spouse support training, may be necessary before significant generalization occurs.

Parenting Task Variables

When parents are taught how to implement behavioral procedures in a clinic setting, they are usually able to attend to the therapist's instructions relatively free from interruptions or distractions. This permits parents to track their children's behavior and their responses to it closely. However, in the home environment parenting involves a variety of competing parenting tasks (e.g., getting ready for work, household chores, cooking, answering the telephone, dealing with one or more demands from other children in the family, and so on). In many ways, family life involves frequent shifts in parent attention as the parents move from one activity to the next. Each activity has its own task requirements.

The social ecology of parenting may create obstacles for program implementation, particularly where parents have multiple demands on their time and attention. For example, two siblings may be fighting in the yard. The therapist has suggested that the parent intervene early, give a terminating instruction, and back up with time out as a consequence for both children. However, if the parent is bathing or diapering a baby, following the training instruction involves terminating an ongoing reinforcing activity (the parent would have to leave the baby, and even then the parent's response is likely to be delayed). If at the same time the telephone rings, a pot on the stove boils over, and the baby starts crying, parents experience these events as stressful. This combination of task and setting variables can therefore constitute a high-risk generalization setting. In many households such occurrences may typify daily interchanges. The physical setting and competing task requirements on the parents may create contingencies that are incompatible with implementation of parenting skills. Unless parents are taught to reorganize their time, to set priorities, or in some other way rearrange the antecedents of fighting, it may be physically impossible for them to generalize. Unfortunately, no studies have been located which have focused on teaching parents to reorganize domestic routines as a strategy to enhance generalization.

Social Factors

As mentioned previously, Wahler and his colleagues (e.g., Panaccione & Wahler, 1986; Wahler, 1980; Wahler & Graves, 1983) showed that social factors, particularly low socioeconomic status and interactions with relatives, neighbors, and social agencies, can affect parents' ability to implement and generalize parenting skills. Wahler found that low-income, single parents who are poorly educated and live in poverty conditions frequently lack a support network. Moreover, these families' interactions with their social environment are frequently coercive. In one study, on days when parents had arguments with relatives or neighbors, they also failed to implement training procedures at home on the same day and subsequently failed to maintain treatment effects over time (Wahler, 1980). Other studies show that socioeconomically disadvantaged families with antisocial children are less likely to persist with treatment than more advantaged families (Kazdin, 1990b; Dumas & Wahler, 1983).

CLINICAL STRATEGIES FOR ENHANCING GENERALIZATION EFFECTS

Setting Generalization

Once the precise conditions under which generalization is sought are determined, a variety of strategies can be used to facilitate the generalized implementation of parenting skills. It is important to identify potential ecological obstacles that may prevent or preclude parents from applying their skills in particular situations. Some evidence suggests that certain childcare activities or times may make it more difficult for parents to implement procedures than at other times. For example, Sanders and Christensen (1985) found that prior to treatment parents of oppositional children distribute their levels of coercive interactions in accordance with particular childcare activities. In an observational study, families were observed during each of five childcare activities (breakfast, leaving for preschool, structured play time, bathtime, and bedtime). Parents engaged in significantly higher levels of coercive interaction during bathtime and mealtime.

Many parents of young children report difficulties implementing procedures when visitors arrive or in social situations where back-up contingencies are lacking — for example, a time-out area is not available (Sanders & Glynn, 1981). There are considerable differences among parents in what constitutes a high-risk parenting environment. For example, despite being able to use a particular parenting strategy, some parents may be unable to implement the skill when there are increased demands on their time or attention, when children in addition to the target child are simultaneously engaging in disruptive behavior, or when there are concurrent coercive interchanges between the marital partners.

Generalization across settings cannot be expected in situations where the prevailing social ecology of the setting is not conducive to the implementation of skills. At least two options become available under such circumstances. First, therapists can alert parents' attention to the obstacles and help them develop strategies for coping with them. Second, the ecological obstacles themselves may need to be removed. In either case, high-risk generalization settings need to be identified on the basis of careful, ongoing assessment of the ecological milieu within which a family lives. A variety of strategies have been suggested in the literature for enhancing generalization across settings. Most of these suggestions must be viewed as hypotheses awaiting empirical confirmation. These are summarized in Table 7.1.

Generalization Across Behaviors

Behavior generalization involves a change in the nontarget behavior of a parent in the treatment setting during an intervention phase. Essentially, behavior generalization relevant to parent training involves examining whether parents who are trained to alter one behavior (e.g., praising) generalize to other behaviors (e.g., aversive question asking or yelling). However, most successful programs attempt to teach parents all relevant component skills instead of programming for behavior generalization. It is probably better to provide direct instruction for parents in the range of skills they require to deal with specific problems (e.g., use of prompts, instructions, praise, response cost, extinction, exclusion and nonexclusion time out, and verbal reprimands or terminating instructions) than to train only a subset of these skills. Such training makes it unnecessary to demonstrate behavior generalization.

Generalization Across Individuals

It is now generally recognized that it is desirable to train both parents in parenting skills. If this ideal situation can be realized, there may be little need to consider generalization across individuals. However, this strategy

Table 7.1. Clinical Strategies for Enhancing Generalization Across Settings

1. Provide direct instruction to parents to use specific skills or behaviors practiced in the training setting in all relevant settings with all relevant individuals.
2. Give graded homework assignments in the nontraining setting.
3. Emphasize common elements in the training and nontraining setting. Highlight similarities between tasks attempted in the clinic (e.g., having to deal with demanding behavior) and those to be attempted in the home.
4. Provide initial training in an environment that simulates a natural environment as closely as possible (include discriminative stimuli in the training setting that are present in the nontraining setting). Examples include using mock apartments, or play rooms with one-way screens.
5. Train the desired behavior under a variety of stimulus conditions (e.g., multiple settings or multiple therapists). This strategy involves loosening the stimulus control over parent behavior so parents do not associate implementation of skills with a narrow range of therapy stimuli.
6. Arrange for the desired behavior to be reinforced in the nontraining setting. Select parent behaviors that are likely to meet with success and reinforcement when used in the natural environment.
7. Teach parents to self-monitor and self-evaluate the performance of skills in the nontraining settings. Ask parents to self-record whether they implement a target procedure in a variety of settings.
8. Teach individual skills or behaviors that have an opportunity to be performed in the nontraining condition and are likely to be reinforced. Behaviors can be selected because they are likely to recruit naturally available sources of reinforcement.
9. Fade out artificial prompts introduced in the training setting that are not present in the nontraining setting. Fade the intrusiveness of therapy prompts so parents' implementation in nontraining settings is under the control of stimuli in that setting.
10. Verbally reinforce accurate self-reports of behavior in a different setting. Probe to check the accuracy of self-reports. Reinforce reports of spontaneous and appropriate generalization.
11. Apply contingencies to response classes (e.g., coping in the face of resistance) rather than discrete behaviors. Prompt and reinforce parents for behavior that is part of a class of behaviors (e.g., planning ahead, advance preparation).
12. During training, extract general principles from specific examples (i.e., teach rules). Draw out general principles and commonalities between situations, tasks, behaviors, and settings and reinforce rule-governed behavior.
13. Reinforce adaptive changes in nontargeted behaviors that occur in nontraining settings. Reinforce parents for spontaneous generalization of nontarget behavior changes that occur in different settings.
14. Train the parents to perform all the relevant behaviors or components to increase the likelihood of generalization to diverse settings.

involves demonstrating a change in the target behavior of a nontarget subject in the treatment or training setting while the target subject's target behavior changes in the therapeutic direction. This would involve observing the target parent (e.g., a mother) and the untrained spouse (e.g., the father) in the training setting (e.g., the home). Therapists would then provide training for the mother but not for the father and note whether the father's behavior changes. Under such circumstances, modeling influences would presumably account for observed changes in the father's behavior. However, other possibilities also exist (e.g., as the mother becomes more skillful in dealing with a difficult child, there are fewer opportunities for the father to engage in coercive interactions with the target child). In this situation, the opportunity to be coercive would be removed. However, the parent concerned may still lack the relevant parenting behaviors.

Generalization Over Time

Time generalization refers to the durability of a target behavior change of a parent in the treatment setting following the withdrawal of training contingencies. This class of generalization is demonstrated when, during follow-up periods, no formal retraining or booster sessions are scheduled. Table 7.2 summarizes various strategies that can be incorporated into initial training to enhance generalization over time.

Maintenance

Maintenance of treatment effects occurs when a change in parents' target behavior endures during follow-up periods. In addition, however, treatment is considered to be ongoing. Maintenance is distinguished from generalization over time primarily because therapists continue to apply posttraining contingencies to the parents' behavior. In generalization over time, the posttraining contingencies are absent. Table 7.3 summarizes possible clinical strategies that can be used to program for maintenance effects.

Table 7.2. Clinical Strategies for Enhancing Generalization over Time

1. Alert the parents to the importance of continued application of skills.
2. During therapy, schedule a specific period of training to program the generalization over time.
3. As part of initial training, fade out artificial prompts introduced as part of the training, so at the termination of therapy the training environment approximates as closely as possible the stimulus conditions the parents encounter following therapy.
4. Train the parents to recruit naturally available sources of reinforcement (behavior trapping). Teach the parents entry behaviors into natural communities of reinforcement (e.g., social skills, communication skills).
5. Teach self-management skills such as goal setting, self-monitoring, self-reinforcement, self-punishment. Prompt and reinforce self-directed learning, and encourage parents to take active responsibility for resolving family problems. Avoid reinforcing dependent behavior.
6. Teach problem-solving skills that can be applied to future problems.
7. Train individuals in spouse and peer support techniques. Coach couples in supportive behaviors (e.g., how to have casual discussions about the primary caregivers' parenting day, what to do when one spouse is dealing with a problem, how to schedule problem-solving discussions).
8. Train other family members to cue and reinforce desired parenting behavior. Cue and reinforce parents or siblings for responding favorably to effective use of parenting skills.
9. Teach stress management techniques (e.g., relaxation skills, cognitive restructuring, time management) that can be used to eliminate or reduce the impact of setting events or other ecological obstacles to parenting.

Table 7.3. Clinical Strategies for Enhancing Maintenance Effects

1. Schedule booster, periodic retraining or relapse prevention sessions in the posttraining period to keep setbacks from turning into relapses.
2. Devise a self-management maintenance plan which can be applied in the posttraining period under reduced therapist surveillance.
3. Switch to a leaner schedule of intermittent reinforcement. During contacts with parents, make social reinforcers less predictable.
4. Train parents who have been through the training program or who went through the program simultaneously to provide continuing support for each other (eg., set up "buddy" systems of support for families who have few social contacts).
5. Specify contingencies for a return to the clinic (e.g., try out maintenance plan or problem-solving skills, collect further data on the problem before contacting the therapist).
6. Reprogram the social environment to facilitate the continued performance of the desired behavior. Design parenting environments so they are more conducive to the continued application of skills. Consider and lobby for organization changes that are helpful to families (e.g., community recreational facilities, redesigning supermarkets).

PLANNED ACTIVITIES TRAINING

This section introduces a clinical strategy known as *planned activities training* that is useful in helping parents learn to generalize their parenting skills to a variety of childcare situations. Planned activities training teaches parents a generalized set of problem-solving skills which can be used to prevent behavior problems in specific high-risk parenting situations. The essence of the approach is to teach the parents how to arrange activities for children in situations where they might otherwise be bored and disruptive. Many parenting situations, particularly out of the home, pose problems because the environment is not designed for children and hence few activities or play materials are available. Children are more likely to be disruptive on such occasions. A supermarket is perhaps the best-known parenting situation where children become bored, tired, irritable, and disruptive (Sanders & Hunter, 1984). Many parents fail to engage the child in the shopping activity and only respond when the child misbehaves.

The generalization of parenting skills to community settings enables parents to access social supports, complete necessary shopping or family business, and have a break from continuous home care of children. Some parents avoid taking their children anywhere because they are so disruptive that the parents feel embarrassed and stressed.

Planned activities training teaches parents to avoid these problems through a series of preventive measures used before entering social settings. Planned activities training as described here has been slightly modified from earlier research studies in which the procedure was employed (Dadds, Sanders, Behrens, & James, 1987; Sanders & Christensen, 1985; Sanders & Dadds, 1982; Sanders & Plant, 1989). Prior to receiving planned activities training, parents typically have been through 3 to 4 weeks of child management training in which they have received instruction in the use of reinforcement procedures, instructions, extinction, response cost, and time out as described in chapter 6. During this earlier phase, parents receive coaching, rehearsal, and in vivo feedback from the therapist (either in the home or in the clinic following direct observation of parent-child interaction) in the use of these skills for modifying different problem behaviors.

Planned activity training is designed as a generalization enhancement strategy that comprises the use of both stimulus control, situational inducement, and incidental teaching strategies (Hart & Risley, 1972). The process is accomplished in three discrete phases. Phase 1 focuses on instructing parents through the use of verbal instruction, modeling, behavioral rehearsal, and feedback. Phase 2 involves application of planned activity training skills in a variety of high-risk parenting situations. Phase 3 comprises fading of therapist cues and prompts and the development of self-management skills.

Overview of Session 1

Negotiate an Agenda. Greet parents and outline what will be covered in the session: review progress to date; identify situations in which difficulties are still being experienced; introduce some suggestions for coping with children's behavior in difficult home and community situations; and organize further feedback sessions. Review this proposed agenda with the parents.

Review Progress to Date. Invite the parents to comment on how they see their family's progress to date. Prompt the parents to describe any positive and negative changes in their child's behavior.

Identify Problem Settings. Invite the parents to mention any specific settings in the home and community where they currently experience management problems (e.g., shopping trips, visiting, getting the child to bed). Refer to prebaseline assessment data (e.g., behavioral checklists previously completed by the parents which identify problematic settings). Ask for the parents' opinions or views on why they experience difficulties, what they have tried to overcome the problem, and the effectiveness of these attempts. Rank order identified settings from most to least problematic.

Provide a Rationale for Planned Activities Training. Mention that you would like to discuss ways of dealing with children's behavior in situations mentioned by the parents. Outline briefly the basic ideas underlying the planned activities procedure. Examples include the following: (a) Prevention is better than cure. The task is how to prevent problems. (b) Encouraging children to become engaged in some activity that is interesting and absorbing reduces the opportunity for misbehavior. (c) Illustrate the preceding points by selecting examples that show how a lack of engagement can create problems (e.g., long shopping or car trips where child has nothing to do, becomes bored, tired, and irritable).

Discuss How to Prepare for Situations in Advance by Organizing and Managing Time More Effectively. Discuss issues relating to organizing time more effectively to avoid last-minute rushing. Invite parents to identify changes in their schedule or activities so time would be available to hold a discussion with the child prior to entering the situation. Reinforce parents for making suggestions that involve planning ahead to avoid problems (e.g., suggesting they set the alarm earlier the night before to avoid the rush of getting the kids off to school).

Discuss How to Talk About Rules Regarding Desired and Undesired Behavior in a Relaxed or Noncoercive Manner. Many parents have difficulty holding discussions with children. One parent in our program was asked to discuss the rules she would like her child to follow on a visit to her parents. The discussion consisted solely of listing in an angry, impatient voice all the things the child must not do, with occasional reminders to the child about how naughty he had been on their last visit. Model appropriate discussion skills, using prepared audiotapes of an ineffective discussion followed by a discussion that attempts to involve the child in the establishment of the rule. Invite the parents to comment on any differences between the two discussions and to identify their likely impact on the child. The discussion might begin by gaining the child's attention, describing the problem that arose previously in the situation, prompting the child to describe the appropriate or desirable behavior (i.e., the rules for the setting), praising the child for generating reasonable rules, suggesting specific rules if the child is unable to, and then ending with a summary of the agreed-upon ground rules.

Discuss How to Select Engaging Activities for Children in Specific Home and Community Settings. Introduce the concept of engagement (i.e., arranging practical, usable activities to keep a child busy in situations where activities are limited or unavailable). Alert the parents to the relationship between engagement and disruption (the more engaged the child is, the less opportunity for disruption). Provide some examples of activities that can be used in different situations (traveling in the car, shopping trips, visiting grandparents, when visitors arrive). Prompt the parents to identify other ways of engaging the child. Reinforce the parents for their efforts.

Discuss How to Encourage and Extend Children's Engagement in Activities Using Incidental Teaching. Having activities available is helpful, but it is no guarantee that children will use the activities appropriately. Many parents of difficult children have a room full of toys and then wonder why the child never plays with them. The goal of this phase is to make interaction with the materials more reinforcing for the child. This can be accomplished in a number of ways. Introduce the idea of incidental teaching as a way of increasing the child's interest in an activity. Discuss an example or show a videotape of a parent interacting with a child who is helping prepare dinner. In the first part of the tape, the parent primarily gives instructions on what to do and what not to do, and the child soon loses interest. In the second part of the tape, the parent responds to any initiation or comment by the child, answers the question, and then asks a further question about the food (color, taste, where it comes from) that extends the child's attention and involvement in the activity. The interaction ends with the parent praising the child for helping with dinner. Discuss with parents the differences between the two scenes.

Next, role-play a situation in which you play the parent and the parent plays the child. Attempt to extend the child's engagement. Then reverse roles, prompt, and provide feedback. Some parents, particularly those who rarely interact with their child, may require extensive subsequent coaching and feedback on how to respond to their child's play.

Another aspect of engagement relates to the use of novelty. Encourage parents to introduce a new activity before the child becomes bored with the old one. Finally, encourage parents to reinforce the child through praise and attention for participating in an activity.

Discuss How to Select and Apply Practical Procedures for Motivating Desired Behavior in Different Child-rearing Situations. Prior to this session, parents have been introduced to techniques for reinforcing desired behavior during child management training but may have had difficulty thinking of practical incentives in specific situations. Prompt the parents to identify possible reinforcers, stressing that the parents first try naturally available and nonintrusive consequences before tangible or material rewards are considered.

Discuss How to Select and Apply Practical Consequences for Undesired Behavior in the Same Settings. Review basic behavior correction routines such as terminating instructions, planned ignoring, and time out. Prompt the parents to adapt these skills to the particular setting where difficulties are still experienced.

Discuss How to Hold Discussions with Children Following an Activity to Give Feedback on Desired and Undesired Behavior. Model how to hold a discussion with the child after the event, activity, or outing to provide constructive feedback regarding desirable and undesirable behavior.

Written Summary. Answer the parents' queries. Provide a copy of the planned activities procedure in the handout "Guidelines for Using Behavior Correction Routines" (see Table 6.5 in chapter 6).

Overview of Session 2

During this session, review homework assignments from the previous session and then model how planned activities procedures can be used in different home and community settings. Introduce parents to several procedural checklists which detail how to use planned activities in different situations, and have parents select one home and two community settings to work on. End the session with the establishment of homework tasks and a summary of the main points covered in the session.

Negotiate an Agenda. Outline what will be covered in the session: review reading tasks; introduce some procedures for handling problems in a range of different settings. Review this agenda with the parents.

Review Homework. Discuss homework task from previous session. Answer any questions.

Model the Use of Procedural Checklists. With the parents, select one home setting from the list in Table 7.4. Give the parents a procedural checklist relevant to that setting (e.g., see Figure 7.1) and discuss each of the steps involved, highlighting the steps relating to incidental teaching and answering any queries. We have developed similar checklists for each setting. Therapists can generate their own as necessary to serve as a model for the parents.

Model the Use of Procedural Checklists for Community Settings. Repeat step 3, but focus on a community situation (see Figure 7.2).

Establish Goals. Ask the parents to implement the procedure in one home setting and to self-record their implementation of the steps on the checklist. Ask the parents to implement the procedure in two community settings using self-monitoring checklists. Remind the parents to read all of the training materials carefully before commencing the programs.

Table 7.4. Home and Community Settings for Generalization Programming

Home	Community
Getting ready to go out	Taking children shopping
Preparations for mealtimes	Traveling in the car
Handling mealtime disruptions	Visiting friends and relatives
Getting children to bed	Leaving children with friends, relatives, or babysitters
When visitors arrive	Taking children to religious groups
Encouraging independent play when you are necessarily busy	Children's birthday parties

Teaching Children to Pick up and Put Away									
Instructions: Each time you need your child to pick up and put away, mark yes, no, or NA (not applicable) for each of the steps below.									
Steps to be followed:	Date:								
	Time:								
1. Give your child an advance warning; calmly ask him or her to begin tidying up.									
2. If child does not know where to begin, suggest where to begin.									
3. Manually guide child's picking up, if necessary (physically guide the child through the motions).									
4. Handle whining or aggression through a terminating instruction and manual guidance, if necessary.									
5. When the child has finished, if misbehavior occurred, describe the behavior and withdraw games or toys for a brief period.									
6. Speak up and praise cooperative behavior.									
Number of steps completed correctly:									

FIGURE 7.1. Sample procedural checklist for one home setting.

Summary. Review main points covered. Answer questions and schedule the next appointment.

Overview of Session 3

During this session, parents practice using advance preparation, directed discussion, and incidental teaching skills with their child. This session can be held either in the child's home or in a clinic play room. Begin the session by establishing the agenda and then continue with two structured training exercises and a feedback session. Finish by establishing goals for between-session practice.

Negotiate an Agenda. Outline the proposed goals for the session: to practice setting up the child in a quiet activity while the parents and therapist

Traveling in the Car								
Instructions: Each time you travel in the car with your child, mark yes, no, or NA (not applicable) for each of the steps below.								
Steps to be followed:	Date:							
	Time:							
Before Leaving 1. Schedule the trip to avoid disrupting sleeping and eating routines.								
2. Explain the rules.								
3. Ask the child to repeat the rules. Prompt if necessary; then speak up and praise.								
4. Explain the consequences of both cooperative and disruptive behavior.								
During the Trip 5. Engage the child in activity shortly after leaving.								
6. Praise the child for desired behavior.								
7. Handle disruptions by gaining the child's attention and describing what he or she should do.								
8. If the problem continues, give a terminating instruction and a warning that the car will be stopped.								
9. If there are further disruptions, stop the car for 1 min. and state that the behavior must cease.								
After the Trip 10. Speak up and praise for appropriate behavior.								
11. Make available back-up rewards for good behavior.								
Number of steps completed correctly:								

FIGURE 7.2. Sample procedural checklist for a community setting.

review progress since the last session; to give the parents feedback on the use of the procedure for encouraging independent play when the parents are necessarily busy; to practice using incidental teaching skills during a structured play activity; and to give the parents feedback on their use of incidental teaching. Review this agenda with the parents.

Practice the Strategy for Encouraging Independent Play When the Parents are Necessarily Busy. Prompt the parents to explain the ground rules to the child and to set up the child in an activity (i.e., select a game, toy, or activity). Cue the parents to interrupt their conversation with the therapist to praise the child for not interrupting and for keeping the rules. Review how the child has been since the last session and how successful the parents' use of planned activities has been during the week. Prompt the parents to identify solutions to problems encountered and, if necessary, suggest alternatives the parents can try. During the discussions, prompt and reinforce the parents periodically for following the routine (i.e., reinforcing noninterruptive behavior). Give the parents feedback on their use of the procedures during your discussion time. ·

Discuss Practicing Incidental Teaching and Structured Play Activity. Ask the parents to set up the child in a new activity if the previous activity is no longer engaging the child. Briefly review with the parents incidental teaching strategies for extending play, language, and involvement in the activity. Instruct the parents to use these skills during the 15-minute observation. Begin the observation. During the observation, keep a record of specific examples of interaction that constitute correct and incorrect use of the procedure. At the end of the observation and before beginning feedback, prompt the parents to teach the child waiting behavior. Only use a prompt if the parents do not self-initiate.

Conduct Feedback. Prompt the parents to review their behavior during the observation. Reinforce the parents for identifying any strengths and weaknesses noted during the session. Prompt the parents to identify two things they feel they could have done differently. Identify specific steps in the incidental teaching routine that the parents wish to work on in subsequent sessions. Summarize main points.

Establish Goals for Between-Session Practice. Instruct the parents to apply the planned activities routine for two community settings and one home setting using the behavioral checklist for that setting. Summarize homework tasks.

Overview of Session 4

This session provides the parent with further in vivo coaching, practice, and feedback on the use of planned activities procedures. Begin the session with negotiating an agenda, and continue with practicing encouraging independent play when the parents are necessarily busy, incidental teaching in a structured play activity, and a routine for getting ready to go out.

Negotiate an Agenda. Outline the proposed goals for the session: to practice setting up the child in a quiet activity while you review progress since the last session; to review parents' use of procedures selected last week (two community and one home setting); to practice and get feedback on using incidental teaching in a structured play activity; to practice and get feedback on the procedure for getting ready to go out; and to establish goals for the next session.

Practice the Strategy for Encouraging Independent Play When the Parents Are Necessarily Busy. Use same format as described in session 3, step 2.

Practice the Routine for Getting Ready to Go Out. Arrange with the parents prior to the session to schedule a shopping trip or a visit to friends or relatives immediately after the session. Cue the parents to prepare the child in advance by holding a discussion of rules and to follow the procedure for getting ready to go out (see Figure 7.3).

Observe while the parents hold the discussion. During the observation, keep a record of examples of interaction illustrating correct and incorrect use of procedures. Complete the first part of the checklist.

Conduct Feedback. Keep feedback brief so the child does not have to wait too long. Give the parents feedback in the use of directed discussion skills.

Establish Goals for Between-Session Practice. Ask the parents to continue to work on the home and community settings selected last week. Remind parents of any additional goals relating to the planned activities procedure.

Overview of Session 5

The final phase of planned activity training involves teaching parents self-management skills and fading therapist prompts and cues. By the end of this phase, parents will be able to use planned activities skills independently with minimal reliance on the therapist.

Negotiate an Agenda. Outline the proposed goals for the session: to review progress from last week; to practice using planned activities skills with minimal help from the therapist; to develop problem-solving strategies for handling future problems; and to discuss parents' self-management skills. Review this agenda with the parents.

Review Progress to Date. Discuss homework tasks. Answer any questions.

Practice Planned Activities with Minimal Therapist Assistance. Introduce this exercise by telling the parents that it is important that they learn to use the

Taking Children on Shopping Trips								
Instructions: On each occasion you take your child shopping, mark yes, no, or NA (not applicable) for each of the steps below.								
Steps to be followed:	Date:							
	Time:							
Before Leaving 1. Schedule the trip to avoid disrupting child's nap or mealtime.								
2. Discuss rules with the child.								
3. Ask the child to repeat the rules. Prompt. Speak up and praise.								
4. Explain that good shoppers can earn special privileges for following the rules.								
5. Explain what will happen if the rules are broken.								
6. Before leaving, ensure that you have necessary materials ready (e.g., buttons, to be used later as rewards).								
During the Shopping Trip 7. Speak up and praise the child when he or she does something you like.								
8. If the child has kept the rules, after each 3-minute period, praise the child and then place a button in child's purse, explaining why.								
9. Involve the child in shopping.								
After the Trip 10. Count the number of buttons earned by the child.								
11. Allow the child to shop for some small item.								
12. Speak up and praise the child's accomplishments.								
13. Calmly describe any rules which the child forgot to follow.								
Number of steps completed correctly:								

FIGURE 7.3. Sample procedural checklist for a community setting.

procedures on their own with minimal help from the therapist. Give a general instruction that the parents are to interact with the child for about 15 minutes. Give no specific instructions. Observe this interaction, taking note of parents' unprompted use of discussion skills, incidental teaching, and behavior correction routines. Write down examples of correct and incorrect use of procedures.

Conduct Self-Evaluation. Following the observation, conduct a feedback session. Keep your feedback to a minimum. Prompt the parents to self-evaluate their performance during the observation. Use open-ended questions to structure the discussion only to the extent that the parents require it. "What were your goals? How did you feel the session went? What did you like about the way that you handled the situation today? What would you like to do differently if you did it again? What goals would you like to set for yourself at this point?" While such questioning serves as a prompt to the parents to self-monitor, self-evaluate, and self-select goals, they should be used sparingly and only if the parents are having difficulty self-generating answers. Finally, prompt the parents to summarize their self-identified solution and to write down goals for future practice.

Discuss Independent Future Problem Solving. Introduce this agenda item by saying that it is important that the parents become skilled at solving any future problems themselves. Review the basic steps in designing a planned activities intervention. Prompt the parents to self-select one remaining problem. Invite the parents to select one additional problem from a list of future problems they might encounter. Examples include how to prepare a child for school, how to manage homework problems, how to encourage independence in your child, how to prepare a child for a weekend away with friends, and how to help your child make friends at school. Then give parents a blank behavior checklist. Ask them to design a behavior change program for the two selected problems, to implement the program where applicable for one of them, and to self-monitor their implementation of their selected strategy.

Establish Goals for Future Practice. Prompt the parents to summarize and write down all homework tasks. Answer any questions.

OBSTACLES TO THE MAINTENANCE OF TREATMENT GAINS

Earlier in this chapter, we reviewed a number of interpersonal, affective, cognitive, and contextual obstacles to the maintenance of treatment gains that have been identified by recent research. Table 7.5 summarizes these obstacles. Many obstacles are associated with families dropping out of treatment, failing to change during treatment, or failing to maintain treatment gains. It is crucial that the presence of these risk factors is identified during initial assessment of the family, and that they are discussed with parents as part of the presentation of assessment findings and treatment planning (chapter 5).

When risk factors such as marital discord, lack of social support, or parental depression are identified, simply training the parents in basic child management skills may not be sufficient to produce maintenance of change. The parent-child training will need to be expanded to address these additional problems. A number of adjunctive interventions have been designed for this purpose. This does not imply that the parent-child focus should be abandoned or deferred pending successful remediation of the other problems. Parents are usually most concerned about the child problem, and shifting focus to other family problems without a mandate from the parents may increase the chances that they will drop out of therapy.

It is usually more acceptable to maintain the primary focus on the parent-child problem and to schedule focus on the other problems as parallel, contextual, or secondary areas for change. For example, when marital problems exist, the therapist can maintain the primary focus on parent-child problems while either dealing with the marital problems in parallel, as a contextual factor influencing parent-child problems, and/or scheduling the marital problems for later direct intervention. Chapter 9 discusses in depth the process of integrating marital and parent-child problems.

Anger control problems are commonly observed in parents of disturbed children, particularly in parents at risk for abuse (Wolfe, 1987; Wolfe, Edwards, Manion, & Koverola, 1988; Wolfe, et al., 1983). Similarly, depression in parents is a risk factor which has been repeatedly demonstrated

Table 7.5. Obstacles to Maintenance of Treatment Gains in Behavioral Family Therapy

Family and Interpersonal	Personal	Sociodemographic
Marital discord (Dadds, Schwartz & Sanders 1987)	Anger and self-control problems (Sanders & Glynn, 1981)	Low socioeconomic status single parenting, financial problems, and low education (Webster-Stratton, 1985)
Deficits in family communication and problem solving (Blechman & McEnroe, 1985)	Negative perceptions of the child (Wahler & Afton, 1980)	Lack of social support from family and friends (Webster-Stratton, 1985)
	Parental depression and other psychopathology (Griest, Wells, & Forehand, 1979)	Insularity (Wahler, 1980) Stressful life events (Webster-Stratton, 1985)
	Academic and peer problems in the child (Loeber, 1990)	

to have an adverse effect on parent-child interactions, child adjustment, and treatment outcome in behavioral family therapy (Downey & Coyne, 1990; Dumas, Gibson, & Albin, 1989; Griest & Wells, 1983). Strategies for helping parents cope with anger and depression are described below. We also present a brief intervention aimed directly at children who experience difficulties coping with problems. The intervention focuses on teaching children cognitive coping strategies that can be used to help manage emotional reactions to adverse experiences such as peer rejection, school failure, and family conflict. The process used to integrate child and marital treatments that is described in chapter 9 should be used similarly with the adjunctive treatments described here.

ANGER MANAGEMENT TRAINING FOR PARENTS

The following is a four-session, adjunctive module for parents who report persisting difficulties in controlling their anger when interacting with their children.

Overview of Session 1

This session is devoted to exploring the parents' existing methods of managing anger and to introducing a general model for anger control.

Negotiate an Agenda. Outline what will be covered in the session: to review parents' existing strategies in dealing with anger; to clarify the situational context within which negative affect occurs; to introduce parents to a rationale for anger management; to provide an overview of anger control strategies; and to introduce and practice the first phase of anger management.

Review Homework from Previous Week.

Review Existing Methods of Dealing with Anger. Ask the parents whether they have identified any difficulty in controlling their anger. Clarify dimensions of the expression of their anger (e.g., when, where, how much). Help parents identify the cues for anger, both internal and environmental. Summarize and draw together the main points.

Introduce Rationale for Anger Management. For example, "From what you have been saying, you seem to feel that you do have difficulties at times in keeping your cool and become more angry than you would like to. This part of the program looks at ways of helping you to identify those things that make you angry, to become aware of how you react, and to learn some different ways of expressing your annoyance or irritation.

Anger is a normal emotion. It's normal to become upset about some things. However, being angry and acting angrily toward others are two different things. In this part of the program we'll help you to handle angry feelings in ways that are not harmful to others." Give a brief overview and an example illustrating the steps involved in anger control: identifying cues to anger and high-risk situations; identifying how the body reacts in anger; identifying thoughts, beliefs, or assumptions that contribute to anger; planning each day to minimize hassles; preparing for provocations; handling criticism; learning to relax under pressure; and putting plans into action. Select one situation in which the parents report becoming angry (e.g., when children whine at bedtime; when criticized by spouse). Set up a baseline recording system to enable the parents to monitor their anger reactions during the next week in this situation.

Assign Homework. Remind parents to complete baseline record (see Figure 7.4).

Overview of Session 2

This session reviews the baseline recording task from the previous session. It teaches the parent self-coping skills (e.g., relaxation and cognitive self-statements) and plans a specific strategy for preventing anger outbursts in one situation.

Negotiate an Agenda. Outline what will be covered in the session.

Review Homework. Review parents' baseline record of anger-arousing situations.

Introduce Relaxation Training as an Anger Management Procedure. Give rationale for learning to relax (e.g., "If you are calmer you will be more able to deal effectively with your child's behavior."). Conduct a 20-minute relaxation session with parents and review their experience of the procedure. Give a relaxation audiotape, and establish a schedule for home practice (typically once each day for 20 minutes).

Introduce the Relationship Between Thoughts, Feelings, and Behavior. Explain how thoughts and feelings are related. Demonstrate this relationship by discussing a recent incident in which the parents became angry or irritated, and identify any maladaptive and irrational assumptions, beliefs, or self-talk. Introduce the notion of positive self-talk in preparing for and confronting provocative situations, and identify alternative self-statements the parents can use in the situation in the future. Write these on cue cards. Establish a schedule for future practice of the procedure.

Name: _____

Anger situation: _____

_____

_____

For each day this week, write down how angry you were every time the above situation occurred. Use the following scale.

5	4	3	2	1
Extremely angry	Very angry	Moderately angry	A little angry	Not at all angry

Occurrences					
	1	2	3	4	5	6
Day 1						
Day 2						
Day 3						
Day 4						
Day 5						
Day 6						
Day 7						

FIGURE 7.4. Anger self-monitoring form.

Assign Homework. Ask the parents to continue self-monitoring their anger reactions and to use their anger control strategy in one selected situation.

Overview of Session 3

This session introduces parents to the application of anger control techniques in two different situations. One situation is used for a behavioral rehearsal.

Negotiate an Agenda. Outline what will be covered in the session.

Review Homework. Check with parents regarding completion of the relaxation training task and their use of the anger control technique.

Identify Two Situations to Work On.

Demonstrate Anger Control Procedure for Self-Selected Situation 1. Using the general model, prepare a step-by-step behavioral checklist that the parents can follow in handling the situation (similar to the one in Figure 6.4). The checklist should include specific parenting techniques if the problem involves child management issues. Conduct a behavioral rehearsal with the parents until a reasonable level of mastery is obtained. Assign a specific homework task that involves using the procedure.

Select a Second Situation and Prompt Parents to Develop Their Own Strategy Using Situation 1 as an Example. Provide a blank behavioral checklist. Provide prompting and feedback only to the extent necessary.

Assign Homework. Ask the parents to continue self-monitoring of anger levels and to implement anger control strategies in the two situations worked on.

Overview of Session 4

This final session introduces the parents to one final situation and further fades therapist help and assistance. Progress to date is reviewed, and a maintenance plan is introduced.

Negotiate an Agenda. Outline what will be covered in the session.

Review Homework. Check with parents on progress with tasks from last session.

Review Progress to Date. Ask parents which techniques they found most and least helpful. Clarify the extent to which parents feel they have made progress. Summarize and draw together main issues.

Devise Anger Control Strategy for Situation 3. Prompt the parents to work out and write down steps in dealing with situation 3. Provide minimal guidance and feedback, but provide the parents with rationale for developing their own problem-solving skills.

Introduce Maintenance Plan. Provide the parents with an overview of the steps involved in maintaining gains. These steps are (a) continuing to use skills taught, (b) phasing out self-monitoring over the next 3 weeks, (c) detecting early if things start to deteriorate, (d) planning a strategy to prevent any deterioration from worsening, (e) implementing a plan, (f) evaluating the plan, and (g) revising the plan as necessary.

Closure. Prompt the parents to summarize key tasks.

COGNITIVE COPING SKILLS FOR CHILDREN

Some children with behavioral and emotional problems can benefit from brief, focal skills training in self-management or self-coping strategies that they can use in managing daily stress. For example, children who are depressed or have mixed disorders of conduct and depression often experience worrying or upsetting thoughts which contribute to their distress ("I'm dumb, useless." "Everyone hates me. I may as well be dead."). This three-session module teaches children simple cognitive restructuring techniques.

Overview of Session 1

This session provides a rationale for using cognitive techniques and identifies a frequently occurring problem situation which produces or contributes to the child's anger, anxiety, or depression.

Negotiate an Agenda. Outline the goals of this session: to review homework from previous week; to provide rationale to parents and child for use of cognitive techniques; to identify one situation that makes the child feel depressed; and to identify thoughts associated with the problem situation.

Review Any Homework from the Previous Week.

Provide Rationale to Parents for Use of Cognitive Techniques. For example, "An event can occur and different people can interpret the same event differently. For example, a shadow or cloud can be seen to represent a monster for one person and a tree for another. As another example, there are seven children in a swimming race; only one can win; the other six children will not get first place and can have different things they say to themselves after the race. These may range from a negative thought such as, 'I'm hopeless. I can't do anything right. I'm a loser. I'll never do it again.' to a positive thought such as, 'Oh well, I tried my hardest. I did as well as I could. There's always another time.' If people allow themselves to interpret life situations negatively, they will begin to feel bad about themselves. This could lead to feelings of sadness, lack of energy, an attitude of hopelessness, and poor eating and sleeping habits. This program is designed to help your child first identify his or her negative thoughts and then learn new and more positive ways of interpreting situations. The way we will do this is to have your child think of some recent situation and try to remember his or her thoughts about it. Then we'll introduce the idea of trying from now on to catch thoughts. We'll ask your child to write down his or her thoughts for the next week, and at the end you'll join us again and your child will show you what he or she has done."

Identify Problem Situation with the Child. Ask parents to leave the room. Prompt the child to identify problem situations. "Can you think of any situation that happens a lot where you might feel sad or upset? Tell me what happened." Introduce the child to the "Catch Your Thoughts" form (Table 7.6). Help the child record the situation on the form.

Discuss "Catch Your Thoughts." Probe for the child's thoughts in the situation described and explain, "Now we have caught your thoughts." Prompt the child to repeat the procedure for a different situation. Check for understanding, and praise the child.

Explain Procedure to Parents. Invite parents to rejoin the session. Encourage the child to demonstrate "Catch Your Thoughts" for parents. Explain further if necessary, and check for parent and child understanding.

Table 7.6. Catch Your Thoughts

Date	Time	What Happened?	How Did You Feel?	What Thoughts Did You Catch?

Assign Homework. Emphasize the need to practice this technique for it to be effective. Ask the child to record thoughts on the "Catch Your Thoughts" form. "It can be hard to remember all your thoughts because you have so many of them, so I want you to write them down, like I have, for all of next week whenever you feel sad or upset." Plan the next appointment.

Overview of Session 2

This session focuses on teaching the child basic cognitive restructuring techniques (changing to winning thoughts). It involves instructing the child, modeling the procedures for the child, and reviewing with the parents what the child has been asked to do.

Negotiate an Agenda. Outline what will be covered: to review homework; to teach the child a way of changing bad or upsetting thoughts; and to assign homework.

Table 7.7. Winning Thoughts Chart

Date	Time	Losing Thought	Winning Thoughts

Remember: To change losing thoughts into winning thoughts
1. Write down your losing thought.
2. Think of a way to say the opposite idea; that is, say a positive thought.
3. Write down your winning thoughts.

Review Homework. Review the child's homework (i.e., completion of thought-listing form). Answer any questions. Praise parents and child for completion of assigned task.

Teach the Child Cognitive Restructuring. Ask the parents to wait outside. Introduce the handout "Winning Thoughts Chart" (Table 7.7). Teach the child the three steps in the procedure:

1. *Notice:* Notice and observe what has been said or what has happened. Note how it makes me feel.
2. *Check:* What am I thinking that makes me sad? How can I think about this in a winning way? I'll use my "Winning Thoughts" chart.
3. *Reward:* Say to myself, "Well done."

Model Procedures. Model the procedures for the child and provide encouragement to rehearse the technique until mastery is achieved.

Instruct Parents. Introduce the ideas to parents and encourage the child to explain and demonstrate the procedure. Check for parent and child understanding.

Assign Homework. Ask the child to practice winning thoughts and record them on the "Winning Thoughts" chart. Plan the next appointment.

Overview of Session 3

This session reviews cognitive restructuring and teaches parents and child about how to maintain gains.

Negotiate an Agenda. Outline what will be covered: to review homework from last session; to prepare for other situations that may arise in the future; and to assign homework.

Review Homework. Review homework from previous session (i.e., completion of "Winning Thoughts" form. Check for understanding, and answer any questions.

Conduct Maintenance Training with the Child. Introduce the idea of preparing for other situations which may lead to feelings of sadness, anger, or upset. "Can you think of other things which might happen to make you feel sad?" Help the child identify potential problem situations. Help the child identify negative thoughts, and prompt the child to use winning thoughts to restructure negative thoughts. Model the procedure if necessary and rehearse with the child until the child can use the procedure in at least two situations.

Conduct Maintenance Training for Parents. Invite parents to rejoin the session. Explain the rationale for the child's continued use of procedures. Describe a scenario (for the parents) that the child has just worked on. Prompt the child to demonstrate what he or she will do in this situation. Check for understanding, and answer any questions.

Assign Homework. Ask the child to continue using the procedures.

COGNITIVE TREATMENT OF PARENTAL DEPRESSION

This module provides depressed parents of behaviorally disturbed children with a basic introduction to cognitive coping skills. It is not intended as a comprehensive cognitive therapy program to treat severe depression, and some parents may require more intensive individual therapy or pharmacotherapy to alleviate their depression.

Overview of Session 1

This session provides a rationale for the use of cognitive techniques and introduces the basic strategies of cognitive therapy.

Negotiate an Agenda. Outline what will be covered in the session: review homework from previous week; review evidence for depression in the parents; introduce the idea of cognitive distortions; teach the self-monitoring of thoughts.

Review Homework from Previous Week. Answer any questions the parents may have regarding their homework assignment.

Review Assessment Findings. Provide the parents with descriptive information from the relevant assessment techniques regarding the nature and extent of the parents' mood disturbance (e.g., BDI score, direct observation, or parental self-reports). Provide a concise summary of the problem and review this summary with the parents for accuracy and agreement.

Introduce the ABC Model of Emotions. Introduce parents to Ellis's (1962) ABC model of emotions. The event that upsets the parents is the Activating Event (A). The Beliefs held by the parents that are hypothesized to activate a negative emotional consequence are labeled B. The emotions resulting from the parents' beliefs about the activating event are the emotional consequences (C). Use an example to illustrate the model, and check for parents' understanding.

Introduce Cognitive Distortions. Introduce the parents to how ways of thinking (belief system) can affect emotions (e.g., negative automatic thoughts, core beliefs, logical errors). Discuss how cognitive distortions will negatively affect emotional state (e.g., all-or-nothing thinking, overgeneralization, mental filtering, magnification). Prompt the parents to discuss their experiences within this framework, and check for understanding.

Teach Self-monitoring of Thoughts. Teach the parents how to record their thoughts on the thought-listing form (Table 7.8). Check for understanding by asking the parents to fill in a sample response on the form, focusing on an upsetting event that occurred in the last week or two.

Assign Homework. Ask parents to record examples of any distressing thoughts on the thought-listing form until the next appointment.

Overview of Session 2

This session expands on the rationale presented in the previous session by training parents in how to change their thinking style.

Table 7.8. Thought-Listing Form

Name:		Week Beginning:	
Date	Event: What Happened	Feelings	Thoughts

Negotiate an Agenda. Outline what will be covered in the session: review homework; review and expand on techniques from the last session; teach a cognitive substitution technique; and assign homework.

Review Homework. Review the parents' completion of the thought-listing form. Answer any questions, and reinforce completion of the task.

Review Last Session's Work. Briefly review ideas covered in the last session. Check for understanding, and use data from the thought-listing form to illustrate the ideas presented.

Teach a Cognitive Substitution Technique. Explain the rationale for cognitive substitution. "This is a technique to help increase your awareness of the way in which you think which leads to unwanted, negative emotions." Help the parents to generate a list of substitute cognitions (e.g., "I am a loving and worthwhile parent; just because my child is occasionally noisy in public does not imply that I am a failure as a parent."). Teach the technique using an ABC event on the parents' thought-listing form. Model the procedure, and encourage the parents to attempt the method and continue it until they achieve mastery. Answer any questions.

Assign Homework. Ask the parents to continue completing the thought-listing form and incorporate cognitive substitutions when appropriate. Plan the next appointment.

Overview of Session 3

This session focuses on fine-tuning the parents' ability to challenge irrational or negative beliefs.

Negotiate an Agenda. Outline what will be covered in the session: review homework; review how to challenge negative thoughts; and demonstrate and rehearse the procedures.

Review Homework. Review completion of the thought-listing form. Answer any questions, and reinforce correct completion of the task.

Challenge Negative Thoughts. Check for understanding of information from the previous session. Review the notion of deciding whether beliefs are true or false according to facts, not feelings. When appropriate, discuss utility, consistency, and logical analysis of beliefs.

Review Procedures. Review the use of substitution techniques using an example provided by the parents from the previous week's homework sheet. Encourage parents to use the substitution procedure with another example, and check for understanding.

Assign Homework. Teach parents to use the thought-changing form (Table 7.9). Ask parents to record their thoughts, changing negative to positive thoughts. Plan the next appointment.

Overview of Session 4

This session reviews the progress to date and teaches the parents about the importance of maintenance.

Negotiate an Agenda. Outline what will be covered in the session: review homework; review understanding of work thus far; and discuss the issue of maintaining gains.

Review Homework. Review homework from the previous session. Answer any questions.

Review Understanding of Work Thus Far. Check that the parents understand the concepts and techniques taught in this module. Give further practice in challenging negative thoughts that arise in situations involving children. Answer any questions.

Table 7.9. Thought-Changing Form

Date	Time	Negative Thought	Positive Alternative Thoughts

Discuss Maintenance Training. Explain the importance of continuing to confront and challenge irrational or negative cognitions that arise in the future. Help the parents to identify potential future problem situations
which may lead to recurrence of negative thinking or depressed affect.
Select two situations to work on, and encourage parents to develop a
problem-solving plan for dealing with the situation. Model and rehearse
the proposed solution as necessary. Prompt parents to summarize the main
strategies they will use in the future to combat depressed feelings.

Assign Homework. Ask the parents to continue using the procedures.

SUMMARY

This chapter reviews a number of variables that may obstruct the generalization or maintenance of parent behavior to different parenting contexts. Affective, cognitive, social, parenting task, and physical environment variables may create social contingencies which are incompatible
with generalized implementation of parenting skills. Preliminary data
show that training approaches that seek to modify the impact of these
variables can be associated with improved generalization and maintenance.
However, effective generalization programming requires careful assessment of the interrelationships between variables that affect parenting, to
determine the optimal combination of strategies for a family. Hence, if
particular generalization strategies are to be effective, they must be derived
from a fine-grained functional analysis of each parent's ecological environment, and they must be individually tailored to that setting.

While generalized changes in parent behavior are often sought to facilitate robust changes in child behavior, a variety of other procedures may
be used to facilitate generalization of child behavior. Future research
should investigate the relationship between different categories of generalization. For example, does generalization across settings reliably predict
generalization over time? At present, these questions remain unanswered.

Chapter 8

Management of Home- and School-Related Problems

BEHAVIORAL PROBLEMS AT HOME AND SCHOOL

Children with behavioral and emotional problems often perform poorly at school. Many oppositional and conduct-disordered children experience problems with basic academic skills (Becker & Carnine, 1980; Maugham, Gray, & Rutter, 1985; Wheldall & Glynn, 1989). Academic failure is a significant risk factor for delinquent behavior in adolescence (Loeber, 1990). Burke and Simons (1965) found that 90% of institutionalized delinquents had a history of truancy and poor school adjustment. Other studies have shown that delinquents are more likely to be delayed in reading and writing skills than nondelinquent controls (Meltzer, Levine, Karniski, Palfrey, & Clarke, 1984). Furthermore, their disruptive and antisocial behavior can lead to major difficulties interacting with same-age peers in the school setting (Kazdin, 1987a; Matson & Ollendick, 1988). Children with severe behavior problems often have few friends, and many are eventually rejected by their peer group (Patterson, 1986). The disruptive behavior of children at school has other consequences in the school system. It is a major source of stress for schoolteachers at both primary and secondary levels (Wheldall & Merrett, 1988) and a common reason for teachers seeking to leave the teaching profession. School-aged children with adjustment difficulties and behavior problems may require concurrent interventions at the family and school level.

Parents of children with behavior problems are often concerned about their child's progress at school, and many family conflicts can revolve

172

around the child's attitude about school, attendance, behavior in class, and the completion of homework. Parents may also express a variety of complaints to a therapist about the child's teachers or school. This chapter does not provide a detailed description of procedures for school-based behavioral consultation, although the topic is clearly important. Instead, it details some strategies we have found useful in working with schools regarding the management of students who present with behavioral problems at home and school. A case example illustrates a relatively simple intervention strategy involving a contract for behavior at school and home.

Importance of School-Based Liaison

A child's experience at school can have a profound impact on the child's adjustment and view of his or her academic and social competence (Rutter, 1989). When a behaviorally disturbed school-aged child is referred to a clinic, liaison with the child's school is indicated when (a) there is a prior history of significant school-related difficulties (e.g., low achievement, disruptive behavior in class or on the playground, or peer interaction problems); (b) when the school has initiated the referral of the child; (c) when the child is obviously currently distressed about attending school or is refusing to attend; or (d) when the child has an attention deficit disorder, specific learning difficulty, or developmental disability. In each of these situations an initial meeting with the school should be considered to determine the extent of the difficulties and to gauge the likelihood of the school's cooperation in resolving the child's problem.

School-based consultation may be important for several other reasons. First, if the child is a major management problem both at home and at school, the effects of a home-based intervention may not generalize to the school setting if an entirely different management approach is used there. For example, one 9-year-old boy in our program was being handled by his parents with positive attention for good behavior and time out for aggression. At school, when similar outbursts occurred the teacher had no consistent plan for dealing with the problems. Sometimes the child would be reprimanded, but on other occasions he was sent out of the room, given a detention after school, or sent to the principal's office. While improvements occurred at home, there was little change in the child's disruptiveness at school until the teacher agreed to try a home-school behavioral contract which involved the child receiving back-up rewards for appropriate behavior at school.

Second, disruptions at school can serve as a setting event for subsequent problems at home. For example, the child arrives home from school in an obviously agitated state after being teased or bullied at school. The child in this situation may be much more difficult to control than usual. Third, a school-based intervention program that deals with both academic learning problems and behavior management issues may be needed to produce improvement in a child's overall adjustment.

The treatment outcome literature suggests that family interventions may not necessarily overcome school-related difficulties in children with conduct problems. For example, Forehand and Long (1988), in a long-term follow-up of children treated with a behavioral parent training intervention, found that while treated children were not significantly different from a nonproblem comparison group on several measures of adjustment, treated children performed more poorly academically. When children are failing educationally and have concurrent family problems, exclusive focus on the family may mean that the child remains at risk in the long term for problems such as low self-esteem, dropping out of school, and antisocial behavior.

Several lines of evidence show that children's classroom behavior, learning, and academic performance can be changed by the systematic application of stimulus control and contingency management (Sulzer-Azaroff, & Mayer, 1977; Wheldall & Glynn, 1989). The behavior modification literature contains many examples of how children's academic performance and classroom behavior can be improved by providing better feedback and reinforcement for academic work completed (Scriven & Glynn, 1983), by using peers and parents as tutors (Limbrick, McNaughton, & Glynn, 1985; Topping, 1987), by rearranging classroom seating arrangements (Krantz & Risley, 1977; Moore & Glynn, 1984), and by using contingency contracts (Glynn, Thomas, & Wotherspoon, 1978). While a technology has developed which could potentially be used in assisting children with behavioral and learning problems, the challenge remains one of ensuring that it is available when it is needed.

Obstacles to Effective School-Based Behavioral Consultation

Numerous writers have discussed the complex issues involved in consulting with teachers or a school system about the psychological or educational needs of individual children (Bergin & Kratochwill, 1985; Johnson, 1988). Many clinicians who have attempted to set up management programs for difficult youngsters in a school have been surprised at the complexity of the consultative tasks involved. Liaison with school personnel about the behavior of a particular student can be a frustrating experience if the clinician blindly ignores the school as a social system. Like any organization, schools have a hierarchical power structure which influences how decisions are made and by whom. Increasingly, schools are responsible for monitoring and organizing their own resources, including the use of external consultants. School staff can initially seem uncooperative and defensive, particularly when they perceive the parent to have obtained help for their child from outsiders without the teacher's knowledge or to have complained about the teacher's or school's handling of a child. In liaising with schools, we typically contact the principal as a courtesy to let him or her know we would like to speak to a child's teacher about a particular student.

There are several interpersonal and organizational obstacles to the development of better coordination of mental health services for children and families. First, the teacher and the parents may have different views on the nature and magnitude of the child's problem. For example, it is inappropriate to assume that the teacher will see the child as a special case needing extra attention or assistance within the school. The child may not be seen as a problem at all. Second, teaching is a demanding and stressful profession. Arranging a mutually convenient time to discuss a particular student can be a problem. While face-to-face contact with teachers is best, in many situations the time required to set up such a contact is precluded, which forces clinicians to rely on telephone contact unless other personnel are available to visit the school. Third, many teachers in their training may have been exposed to behavior modification approaches in a fairly negative light, and there may be some suspicion of the clinician and the use of behavioral approaches to resolve the problem. Fourth, a history of negative encounters with the child's parents makes the task more difficult. Not infrequently, a parent's concern for the child's welfare can lead to the parent appearing demanding or critical of the school's handling of the child. This criticism, in turn, produces defensive behavior in the teacher, and there is no satisfactory resolution of the problem. (Table 8.1 lists topics parents should avoid when discussing their child with school staff.) Fifth, the school may have an unsympathetic principal who tends to side with parents and be critical and unsupportive of school staff.

Finally, clinicians working in mental health clinics, hospitals, or in private practice usually do not have any institutionally or professionally sanctioned mandate or authority to consult with or advise teachers about educational matters. Furthermore, they are rarely trained in the school-based consultation skills required to carry out this task properly. While schools are generally able to liaise with whomever they consider can be of assistance to an individual student, professional boundaries between clinical child psychologists, educational psychologists, and school guidance services are frequently blurred. This sometimes means that individual children are not adequately serviced by any group. Close interdisciplinary collaboration is often required in individual cases. This ideal is sometimes achievable, but often a coordinated, across-service approach is difficult to attain, particularly when professionals have competing theoretical orientations.

Despite these limitations, we have found that if teachers are approached appropriately it is possible to develop an intervention program involving collaboration between the child's home and school.

Disruptive Behavior at School

One of the most worrisome problems for parents is a child's conduct at school. Children can be considered disruptive in school for a variety of reasons. Common problems include inattentiveness, not following teacher's directions, distracting other children through silly behaviors such as swinging on chairs, making faces, making loud noises, getting into fights on the playground, failing to complete work, speaking out of turn, and wandering around the classroom. Most teachers expect a certain standard of conduct from pupils. A large-scale survey of primary schoolteachers in 32 schools in the United Kingdom found that 46% of teachers nominated talking out of turn as a major problem. This category included behaviors such as yelling, talking about non-work-related matters, and making inappropriate comments and remarks (Wheldall & Merrett, 1988). Fewer than 1% of teachers cited aggression as the most troublesome behavior. Over half the teachers surveyed (51%) felt that they spent more time on problems of order and control than they should. If the disruptive behavior is persistent and severe, the child may be suspended or expelled from school.

Children can be disruptive for a variety of reasons. The disruptive behavior of conduct-disordered children at school can be an extension of their disruptive behavior at home. These children are generally uncooperative and defy adult authority. Other children can be disruptive because the work is too hard or not challenging enough (in the case of gifted children).

Table 8.1. Guidelines for Discussing Your Child's Problems with Teachers

---

1. Avoid making negative comments about your child to the teacher. Most teachers react negatively to parents abusing their children even if the child has been difficult to deal with at school.
2. Avoid criticizing the school or the teacher's handling of your child, even if you feel your criticisms are justified.
3. Avoid trying to make excuses for your child's conduct.
4. Avoid becoming irate or angry. This strategy often backfires and can make others irritated and defensive.
5. Avoid claiming that your child has special gifts or abilities unless you know this for certain. Some teachers become annoyed by parents who claim their child is bright but has never done well at school. Parents can easily overestimate their child's ability. Teachers see your child's performance in relation to hundreds of other children of the same age.
6. Avoid giving teachers advice on how they should teach. Teachers, as professionals, often react negatively to well-meaning advice from parents about how they should run their classroom.

Sometimes disruptiveness is due to teachers trying to enforce excessively rigid rules. The same factors that can contribute to behavior problems at home can occur in the classroom (e.g., the teacher only attends to children when they are disruptive and ignores desirable behavior). A child may also have lower intellectual ability or a specific learning difficulty in one or more subject areas, such as reading or math, which influences the child's behavior in the classroom.

Several strategies can be used in resolving a school-related behavior problem. These include referring the child to school or educational psychologists, remedial teachers, or other programs or agencies which run programs for children with special needs. These referral options require active liaison and good communication between the parties involved and the consent of the parents. The active cooperation of a child's teacher is important to effect long-term improvement.

A home-school behavior contract is another strategy which involves working concurrently with the family and school. It involves establishing a regular system of two-way feedback from home to school, and vice versa, regarding the child's attainment of agreed-on goals in each setting.

HOME-SCHOOL CONTRACT:
CASE EXAMPLE

The following example illustrates some of the consultation process steps involved in liaising with schools regarding an individual student's difficulties.

Problem

Roger was a 10-year-old boy of normal intelligence who was repeating grade 5, in part because of the insistence of his single-parent mother that the boy could not cope with the work in grade 6. Roger was initially referred because of behavior problems at home involving refusal to help with chores, complaining about school, and refusing to do homework and to wear corrective lenses in the classroom. In class (according to his mother), Roger had been insolent and disruptive. Mrs. Smith, Roger's teacher, reported that Roger frequently disrupts the class by getting out of his seat, talking to his neighbors, failing to begin work on time, and making rude gestures to her behind her back.

Home Intervention

This involved holding several sessions with Roger's mother following the basic child management strategy discussed in chapter 6. A simple

points system with daily and weekly back-up rewards had been established which involved Roger receiving positive attention and points for
half-hour periods when he kept to three basic house rules: no tempers or
swearing, completing chores for the day without protesting or complaining, and completing homework. Each half-hour time block was worth 100
points, which could be exchanged for TV time the next day.

School Intervention

Initial Preparations. Telephone contact with Roger's teacher was made to
explain our involvement with Roger and to arrange a convenient time to
meet to discuss Roger's behavior at school. The teacher preferred to meet
after school, as she felt it would be impossible to have a prolonged discussion during the school day. Prior to contacting the child's classroom
teacher, we had requested the parent's consent to do so.

Initial Phase of the Consultation. The therapist arrived at school at the scheduled
time and followed the teacher's directions to her classroom. After greetings
and initial pleasantries, which included showing the therapist some of
Roger's artwork displayed on the wall, an agenda for the session was
negotiated. The agenda proposed by the therapist included (a) discussing
the nature of his involvement with the child, (b) discussing the teacher's
view on the nature of Roger's difficulties at school, and (c) discussing a
strategy for the further assessment of Roger's difficulty at school.

The therapist explained that the parent had been referred to our service
from her family doctor. The parent's main concerns were summarized and
an outline of the probable causes of some of the difficulties was discussed
as well as previous attempts to overcome the problem. The teacher was
then asked to comment on Roger's behavior at school, and the therapist
attempted to obtain a clear description of the teacher's concerns and the
salient antecedents and consequences of the problem behavior. The
teacher mentioned the problem behaviors of failing to begin work
promptly, silly disruptive behavior in small-group work (making faces,
talking), and not bringing homework to school.

The therapist asked the teacher to describe what strategies she had tried
to deal with each of these and how successful these had been. The teacher
commented that she had tried to talk to Roger outside class to find out if
anything was troubling him and had yelled at him frequently. Her opinion
was that neither of these strategies had worked. She expressed an interest
in finding out what had been tried at home. The therapist then described
the basic approach that was being used and asked the teacher whether she
would be interested in a program which would involve a two-way communication system between home and school regarding Roger's daily homework requirements and his behavior at school and home.

It was agreed that a baseline record would be useful for a period of a week to establish how frequently Roger engaged in major disruptive behaviors. The recording form shown in Figure 8.1 was provided. The results appear in Figure 8.2. The teacher was also asked to complete the Teachers Report Form Checklist (Achenbach & Edelbrock, 1986). A schedule of further contact was negotiated which involved the therapist agreeing to prepare the details of a draft home-school program for discussion at the next meeting. The teacher was asked to write down a list of rules she wanted Roger to observe in class during the program.

Further Assessment. After 3 days, the therapist recontacted the teacher to check on how the baseline recording was proceeding, to troubleshoot any difficulties that may have arisen, and to confirm the next meeting. The teacher described three specific instances of problem behavior so far

Date	Behaviors	How often did they occur?	Total
8/17	LS		
	D		
	DG		
	HW		
8/18	LS		
	D		
	DG		
	HW		
8/19	LS		
	D		
	DG		
	HW		
8/20	LS		
	D		
	DG		
	HW		
8/21	LS		
	D		
	DG		
	HW		˚

Key LS: Late starting assigned work; D: Disobeys specific instructions;
DG: Disrupts small-group activity; HW: Does not complete homework.

FIGURE 8.1. A sample event record for monitoring classroom behavior.

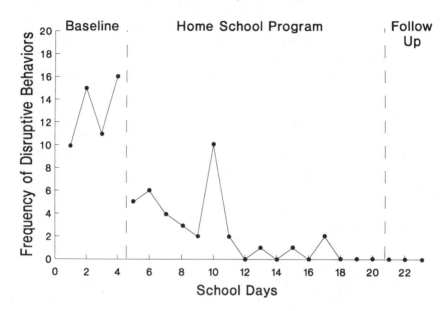

FIGURE 8.2. Frequency of Roger's disruptive behavior in
different treatment phases.

on the day in question and had written each example on the form provided.

Designing, Implementing, and Monitoring the Intervention. The next step involved
discussing the details of the proposed home-school behavior contract.
Prior to meeting with the teacher again, these details had been checked out
with Roger's parents over the telephone. Figure 8.3 shows a sample page
from Roger's program booklet.

The details were discussed with the teacher, as well as a mechanism for
monitoring the program in the early stages. The teacher agreed to contact
the therapist if any difficulties arose in the first few days, and the therapist
called the parent to check on daily progress for the first few days.

Troubleshooting and Monitoring Progress. Inspection of Figure 8.2 shows that the
program led to an immediate reduction in episodes of disruptiveness at
school. Roger liked the new system and earned almost maximum points.
A telephone call to the teacher on the third day revealed that Roger's
teacher was pleased with his progress. On the fifth day Roger arrived home
from school in tears. He had torn up his program booklet and announced
his arrival home by slamming the back door. That night he refused to do
his homework, and the mother provided the necessary consequences. The
mother called the therapist the next morning to explain what had hap-

HOME-SCHOOL PROGRAM

Day [＿＿＿] Date [ ][ ][ ][ ][ ]   Phase of program: Baseline [ ]
                                                              Treatment [ ]

Home Goals   Points   Parent's comments

1. Takes homework to school   [ ]   [＿＿＿＿＿＿]

2. Ready to leave for school by 8.20   [ ]   [＿＿＿＿＿＿]

3. Music practice   [ ]   [＿＿＿＿＿＿]

Home points earned [ ]   Parent's signature [＿＿＿＿＿＿]

Classroom Goals   9.00–10.45   11.00–12.30   1.20–3.00

1. Begins assigned work promptly. [ ]   [| |]

2. Obeys teacher's instructions . . . [ ]   [| |]

3. Attempts all assigned work . . . . [ ]   [| |]

4. Cooperates in group work . . . . . [ ]   [| |]

5. Keeps his or her area tidy. . . . . [ ]   [| |]

6. Completes set homework . . . . . [ ]   [   ]

Overall Rating of Behavior

[1] [2] [3] [4] [5] [6] [7]

Very poor   Satisfactory   Excellent

School points earned [ ]   Teacher's signature [＿＿＿＿＿＿]

Total Daily Points Earned: Home Points [ ] + School points [ ] = [ ]

FIGURE 8.3. Sample page from a home-school contract.

pened and expressed some doubt about the program's effectiveness. The
therapist agreed to call the teacher at lunchtime to find out what had
happened at school the previous day. The teacher reported that Roger had
been disruptive in class by swearing loudly at another boy after an incident
at lunchtime when he had been teased by a sixth-grade boy. It was agreed

that the consequences the teacher provided were appropriate and that the program should continue unaltered for the next 10 days, at which point the program would be reviewed.

Termination of Intervention. A review following 3 weeks of the program showed that Roger's behavior at school had improved markedly. Both his mother and teacher considered his behavior to be satisfactory, and a proposal to phase him off the program while maintaining the behavior change was discussed. This phasing off the program was tackled in a stepwise fashion, as follows. First, the home back-up rewards were phased out so Roger received a reward every third day instead of daily. Daily praise and positive attention for good performance were maintained. Next, Roger's teacher encouraged Roger to make his own self-assessment at the end of the day regarding following classroom rules. For the first 2 days, the teacher reinforced accurate self-reports by giving Roger feedback on whether he was being too lenient or harsh. Finally, the back-up rewards were ceased, the program booklet was withdrawn, but Roger's teacher continued to praise him occasionally for complying with rules. Roger's teacher and parent agreed to maintain contact on an informal basis, and his teacher agreed to notify Roger's mother if a further problem arose. Follow-up of Roger 6 months later showed that Roger's behavior had continued to improve, and neither his teacher nor his parent considered him to be a management problem.

TRAINING PARENTS AS REMEDIAL TUTORS

Some parents present to mental health professionals with concerns regarding their child's academic progress. Poor academic performance is a major contributor to children dropping out of school, which in turn increases the risk of a variety of antisocial behavior problems (Loeber, 1990). Reading is perhaps the most important academic skill children are expected to learn at school, as children who are poor readers find it increasingly difficult as they progress through the school system to keep up with work required in virtually all subject areas. Despite its generally recognized value, a significant number of children experience difficulties in learning to read. The reasons for children's failure to become proficient readers are complex. However, research shows that parents can play an important role at home in helping children with reading problems. A useful method known as Pause, Prompt, Praise was developed by McNaughton et al. (1987) for training parents of 8- to 12-year-old children to become remedial tutors for their own children at home. The procedures were devised to help children who had failed in the regular school system and had fallen several years behind in their reading.

The basic principle behind Pause, Prompt, Praise is that parents should regularly listen to children read material that is at an appropriate level of difficulty, in a positive social context. Parents learn how to attend positively to correct reading performance and how to correct their child's mistakes. Children's ability to read is strongly influenced by motivation. Children feel discouraged and do not enjoy reading when their efforts are unsuccessful or meet with disapproval. Children with reading difficulties are often afraid of making mistakes, and it takes patience and persistence to help them to regain their confidence, to sit down and tackle the task again. Figure 8.4 summarizes the key steps involved for a parent in using the Pause, Prompt, Praise strategy. Table 8.2 includes some guidelines on how to set up a remedial reading program using Pause, Prompt, Praise.

Managing Homework Problems

As children progress through school, they are expected to spend at least some time after school doing homework and independent study. Schools and teachers vary in the amount of such work expected. Children in grades 4 through 7 can expect anywhere from 10 to 60 minutes of homework each night. However, it is important for all children to develop good study habits and complete homework if they are to make satisfactory progress in their studies. Most homework is revision work, and children will normally have done similar examples or exercises at school.

Many parents experience occasional difficulty concerning their child's homework. Children sometimes tell parents at the last minute that they need help with a project which requires a trip to the library. Some children refuse to do homework, or do it carelessly. Parents often blame the child's attitude for such problems and accuse the child of being lazy and irresponsible. This often makes the problem worse. One father in our program required his 10-year-old to do at least 1 hour of math study each day. He sat next to the child with a ruler and quizzed the boy on his times tables. Every time the boy answered incorrectly, the father would yell at him and whack him with the ruler. The child did not learn his tables correctly and became so anxious about school work that his grade became worse and worse. While this example is extreme, it reflects a common problem. Parents often feel their job is to correct mistakes in homework, and they rarely balance criticism with praise and encouragement. As a result, the child often refuses to do homework and the nightly routine becomes fraught with conflict.

Parents, nevertheless, play an important role in helping their children develop proper study habits and routines. This includes arranging a well-lit space where children can work free of distractions, taking an interest in their work, assisting children to find resources and other materials

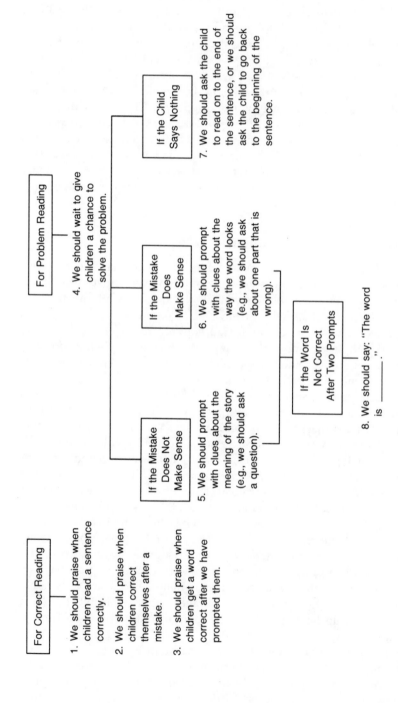

For Correct Reading

1. We should praise when children read a sentence correctly.

2. We should praise when children correct themselves after a mistake.

3. We should praise when children get a word correct after we have prompted them.

For Problem Reading

4. We should wait to give children a chance to solve the problem.

If the Mistake Does Not Make Sense

5. We should prompt with clues about the meaning of the story (e.g., we should ask a question).

If the Mistake Does Make Sense

6. We should prompt with clues about the way the word looks (e.g., we should ask about one part that is wrong).

If the Child Says Nothing

7. We should ask the child to read on to the end of the sentence, or we should ask the child to go back to the beginning of the sentence.

If the Word Is Not Correct After Two Prompts

8. We should say: "The word is ———."

FIGURE 8.4. Pause, prompt, and praise procedure. From McNaughton, S., Glynn, T., and Robinson, V. (1987). *Pause, prompt, praise: Effective tutoring for remedial reading.* Birmingham, England: Positive Products. Reproduced with permission.

184

Table 8.2. Guidelines for Using Pause, Prompt, Praise

1. Arrange a suitable time and place to hear your child's reading for 10 minutes 3 to 4 times weekly. Make sure the TV is turned off to minimize distractions.
2. Select suitable books for your child to read. Most schools use a series of learning-to-read books that are graded from simple to difficult. Contact your child's teacher and ask him or her to send home a book that is at an appropriate level of difficulty.
3. Check on the difficulty level of the book. Count off 50 words. In a notebook, write the date and the name of the book. When your child begins to read, put a check mark in the notebook for each mistake made. Mistakes can include leaving words out, adding words, or reading words incorrectly. Count one mistake for each word read incorrectly. If your child corrects a mistake, don't count this as a mistake. Count the number of mistakes and subtract this number from 50. This will show you the number of words read correctly. If there are more than 10 mistakes, the book is too hard; if there are fewer than four, it is too easy. For books that are too hard or easy, speak to the teacher to get a book at the right level of difficulty.
4. Use Pause, Prompt, Praise to help your child become an independent reader. When your child reads correctly, praise him or her. When your child makes a mistake, wait a few seconds (pause) to give your child a chance to correct the mistake. If your child does not self-correct, then prompt (give a clue). When your child gets the correct word(s), offer praise and encouragement.
5. Check on your child's progress. Repeat step 2. Remember not to give any praise or assistance during this check.
6. If you are feeling irritable or impatient, do not listen to your child's reading.

needed, and establishing consistent rules relating to completion of homework.

It is important to remind parents that they are not the child's teacher. Even though parents may be convinced that the way they were taught as children to solve math problems is the right way, children will generally be expected to tackle problems in the way they have been shown at school. Children differ widely in their abilities and how quickly they grasp concepts and new ideas. Homework should not be a time of stress or pressure. It should be a pleasant interaction in which parents act as a resource person who encourages and offers help if the child needs it. Table 8.3 provides some guidelines for parents in dealing with homework problems.

SUMMARY

Children with concurrent behavior and learning problems may require active liaison between clinical staff and school-based psychological, guidance, and special education services. It is not uncommon for children to have been referred previously or concurrently to school-based guidance or psychological services. In such instances, appropriate interdisciplinary or interagency liaison is essential, particularly when other professionals are concurrently involved in the case.

Therapists can often help parents prepare for parent-teacher meetings,

Table 8.3. Guidelines for Overcoming Homework Problems

1. Let your child relax on arriving home from school. Do not make children start their homework as soon as they walk in the door.
2. Arrange a proper place to study. Primary school children often want to do their homework in family living areas rather than their bedroom. Clear a space at the kitchen table and eliminate distractions. Buy or build your child a desk with a desk lamp for working on projects. However, it is not until high school that children can be expected to work independently in their bedroom.
3. Select a specific time for doing homework (after relaxing but before going out to play or watching TV).
4. Ask your child whether he or she has any homework today. Find out when the work must be completed.
5. Help your child get started. Be prepared to sit down at the table with your child. Helping doesn't mean doing the work for them. Ask your child what needs to be done. Remind your child of the ground rules (TV comes after homework is done).
6. Offer praise and encouragement while your child is working—for example, "You're working well on your homework tonight, Brian."
7. Wait until your child asks for help before giving it.
8. Deal with requests for help by using incidental teaching (see chapter 6).
9. Avoid criticizing messy or incorrect work. Criticism often backfires with a child who is reluctant to do homework. Suggest that children do rough copies, and then a final, neater copy for handing in.
10. Check your child's work before finishing. Try to find something positive to say. When checking work, correct only a few mistakes if you must.
11. Offer a reward following the completion of homework. This might include being allowed to go out and play, or watching TV. For some children, an extra incentive such as a behavior chart can be used initially to establish a new homework routine.

---

clarifying the nature of the parents' concern and the purpose of the meeting. It is not uncommon for parents to adopt a confrontational approach to such meetings that will probably alienate the teacher and produce guarded or defensive behavior. A discussion and behavioral rehearsal of what the parents want to say at the meeting can reduce parental anxiety and aggressiveness. Some parents have minimal involvement with their child's education, and almost all contact is initiated by the school staff, who are concerned about the child's conduct. In many instances, this lack of involvement is a result of a skills deficit (parents are unaware of what they can do to help) rather than a motivational deficit (a lack of interest in their child's education).

There is little controlled research on the effects of behavioral family intervention on children's academic progress when there are concurrent behavioral and learning difficulties. Consequently, the proposed conditions under which dually focused interventions may be desirable must be viewed as speculative. However, we believe that when children have severe learning and academic deficits, an exclusive focus on behavior management is inappropriate and unlikely to resolve the problem in the long term. Perhaps the best hope is for the child's parents and teachers to work together in creating a learning and instructional environment that is appropriate to the child's level and will engender academic success.

Chapter 9

Adjunctive Assessment and Treatment of Marital Problems

MARITAL DISTRESS AND TREATMENT OUTCOME

Despite the claims of a number of psychotherapists (e.g., Framo, 1975), child behavior disturbances are not always associated with marital dysfunction (Dadds, Schwartz, & Sanders, 1987; Emery, 1982; Johnston, 1988). Marital dysfunction is only one variable among many that may be associated with child behavior problems. Further, the relationship between marital distress and child disturbance appears to be mediated by the type of marital conflict, the sex of the child, family socioeconomic variables, and the type of child behavior disturbance (Dadds & Powell, in press; Dadds, Sheffield, & Holbeck, 1990; Emery, 1982; Grych & Fincham, 1990). For some families, however, marital conflict has a substantial influence on the child's behavior and may interfere with parents' capacity to implement treatment procedures. In this chapter we discuss the role of marital variables in the treatment of child behavior problems as a general model for integrating family contextual factors in treatment. This model can be applied with minor modification to the treatment of child problems in which a range of other family problems (e.g., depression, financial stress, insularity, and so on) must be considered.

Few studies have assessed the effects of marital distress on either adherence to treatment or therapeutic outcome. Further, these studies have yielded inconsistent results. Oltmanns, Broderick, and O'Leary (1977) found no correlation between marital satisfaction and self-reported treatment outcome for a mixed sample of disturbed children. However, a number of design shortcomings make the results inconclusive. Two further studies used quasi-experimental manipulations by assigning families to groups on the basis of level of marital distress. Brody and Forehand (1985) found only minimal differences in the outcome of a parent-training group for maritally distressed (MD) and nondistressed (ND) mothers of noncompliant children. Dadds, Schwartz, and Sanders (1987) also found no differences between MD and ND parents immediately following treatment. However, the MD group showed significant relapse to baseline levels compared to the ND group at 6-month follow-up.

Dadds, Sanders, Behrens, and James (1987) observed marital interactions in four MD families containing a conduct-disordered boy throughout their involvement in behavioral family therapy. During baseline observations, high rates of parent-parent conflict were observed to occur contemporaneously with parent-child conflict. During training in child management skills, the parent-child conflict decreased, but surprisingly the parent-parent conflict continued concurrently with the reduced incidents of parent-child conflict. Following a brief marital intervention, the marital hostility ceased and remained at low levels through 3-month follow-up.

This study, while based on a small sample, suggests an explanation for the poor durability of treatment effects for MD couples observed by Dadds, Schwartz, and Sanders (1987). Behavioral parent training may reduce parent-child conflicts but not generalize to other conflicts in the family which are functionally related to the former. As time progresses following treatment, the parent-child conflict increases to resume its pretreatment associations with the contextual family distress. In support of this contention, previous data have shown that providing child management training (CMT) does not necessarily produce reliable increases in marital satisfaction (Griest & Forehand, 1981; Griest & Wells, 1983). The combination of CMT and a marital intervention used by Dadds, Schwartz, and Sanders (1987) and Dadds, Sanders, Behrens, and James (1987) did result in increases in marital satisfaction, but not to levels reported by nonclinic well-adjusted couples. The combination did appear, however, to minimize the open display of marital conflict that was occurring simultaneously with parent-child interactions.

Attempts to expand behavioral interventions to maximize their impact on the family system have shown considerable promise. The most common strategy has been to add supplementary interventions to CMT, including marital conflict resolution (Kelley, Embrey, & Baer, 1979), self-control and self-management training (Sanders & Glynn, 1981; Wells, Griest, & Forehand, 1980), review training (Wahler & Graves, 1983), planned activities training (Sanders & Dadds, 1982), parent enhancement (Griest et al., 1982), and partner support training (PST; Dadds, Sanders, Behrens, & James, 1987; Dadds, Sanders, & James, 1987; Dadds, Schwartz, & Sanders, 1987). Given that all of the aforementioned have been shown to produce benefits over and above CMT alone, the unfortunate conclusion that more is better seems inescapable. An alternative and more productive approach might be to assume that either these treatments contain common beneficial elements or contain different elements which are useful to different subsets of families.

To clarify this dilemma, a number of methodological improvements must be incorporated into future research. The first concerns the selection of families for whom the adjunctive treatment is designed. Evidence should be provided that the target families have characteristics which require intervention over and above CMT. Research into families with maternal depression (Griest & Wells, 1983; Griest, Wells, & Forehand, 1979), marital distress (Brody & Forehand, 1985; Dadds, Sanders, Behrens, & James, 1987; Dadds, Schwartz, & Sanders, 1987), and insularity (Wahler, 1980; Wahler & Graves, 1983) are productive examples of this logic. Second, measures must be taken to ensure both the validity and impact of the adjunctive intervention (independent variable). Specifically, it must be shown that the intervention was delivered as described and produced the changes it was intended to produce (e.g., marital communication, problem solving, community contact), which subsequently led to change in parent-child interactions. Without these measures, no conclusion can be made about the specific role of the variable of interest (marital communication, self-control, insularity) on the outcome.

Third, the adjunctive treatment should be compared to state-of-the-art behavioral family intervention. It is pointless to add interventions to produce effects which could have been achieved by providing higher quality, more intensive, or more frequent CMT. Much research indicates that the effective training of behavior change agents, in this case parents, requires a multicomponent training format (instructions, modeling, rehearsal, and feedback) which is applied across multiple behavior change skills (Sanders & James, 1983). Parent-training programs should routinely incorporate these training procedures, especially if they are to be used as control conditions for evaluating the effectiveness of adjunctive techniques.

The final point concerns the conceptualization and technology of providing families with multiple interventions. Interventions have been described as adjunctive to CMT, and attempts have been made to formalize decision rules for moving families from one treatment to another (Blechman, 1981). Unfortunately, this creates notions of distinct treatments with clearly differentiated boundaries. This is the antithesis of the underlying rationale for providing broader family-focused interventions; that is, the contextual family variables are functionally related to parent-child problems. Clinical experiences with the adjunctive use of CMT and PST (Dadds, Sanders, Behrens, & James, 1987; Dadds, Sanders, & James, 1987; Dadds, Schwartz, & Sanders, 1987) have shown that the benefits of this approach are associated with a treatment process that integrates the two. Further, it is hypothesized that a number of critical points occur in the treatment process, at which time this integration can either facilitate or hamper the family's adherence to the broader focus of the treatment.

The goal here is to elaborate on the integration of treatments applied to families who present with a behaviorally disturbed child and also evidence marital distress, and to discuss the process by which these two areas of family conflict can be successfully integrated into a comprehensive family intervention.

CLINICAL INTEGRATION OF CHILD AND MARITAL FOCI

1. *Facilitate father's involvement in treatment.* Therapy process issues have been discussed in chapter 5, but some elaboration is necessary here to focus on specific problems of multiply distressed families. It is common practice for fathers to be encouraged to attend treatment. However, it is common for mothers to present with a child and the message that the father is not interested or is unwilling to be involved. Specific family therapy groups have been known not to accept families in which all members will not attend. This extreme contradicts the ethic ensuring an individual's right to treatment. A more practical approach is to maximize the likelihood that relevant family members attend treatment, but not refuse treatment to individuals in cases where one or more parties refuse to be involved. When fathers do not attend, we obtain permission from the mother to telephone the father regarding his involvement. In rare cases, mothers refuse permission, arguing that the husband's involvement in the family is minimal and participation in therapy would be destructive. If this view is maintained despite gentle pressure (information given about the importance of the father's role), the mother's position is accepted. In most cases, the mother is happy for the husband to be contacted.

When telephoning the father, the therapist can introduce himself or herself and then quickly get to the point that the therapist needs the father's help. That is, the father is an expert in that he has firsthand knowledge of family style and the child's problems. Further, the father will have a good idea about what sort of treatment can be implemented given the style and routine of this particular family. Clinical experience supports the effectiveness of this approach, and few fathers refuse to make at least one appointment to discuss the family's problem. The same role of family expert is equally assigned to the mother and the children; that is, the father is not implicitly given a unique and privileged role within the family. In summary, attempt to ensure the participation of both parents in treatment.

However, if this is impossible to arrange, the parent who is willing to attend should not be denied access to treatment.

2. *Develop a shared perception.* A wealth of data is available to indicate that adherence to treatment is facilitated by the establishment of a trusting, empathic therapist-client relationship (Lambert, DeJulio, & Stein, 1978). However, only recently has work begun on systematically analyzing therapeutic processes within family-based treatments (Chamberlain, Patterson, Reid, Kavanagh, & Forgatch, 1984). The establishment of a facilitative relationship is a critical factor in enabling parents to explore the relationship of the child's problems to their management of the problem and to contextual factors such as marital distress. The need to view family problems in an interactional or systemic way often inadvertently leads to therapists failing to form such a relationship with parents of problem children. If the parents begin treatment, as they often do, by complaining and blaming the child, the therapist may quickly focus on parents' management techniques, or worse, shift focus to other problems in the family to avoid blaming the child and to develop a focus on the system. Many parents will perceive these lines of questioning as an implicit communication that they are to blame for the child's problems. Clinics are full of parents who have dropped out of a previous treatment because they felt the therapist blamed them for the child's problems.

Ironically, most parents do tend to blame themselves, or at least wonder if they are to blame, for their children's problems. They will communicate this in the context of a supportive relationship but often deny it by dropping out of treatment if the confrontation is done without an initial acceptance of their perceptions of the problem.

The easiest way for a therapist to make the aforementioned mistakes is to have both parents and child in the first interview. Thus, if the parents openly complain about the child in his or her presence, the therapist may not feel able to explore the problem with the parents without further distressing the child and appearing to align with the parents. Many family therapists recommend always having all family members present, but it is gratifying to see that more and more are recognizing the benefits of splitting the system at various times and for various reasons. In summary, during the intake interview, split up the family and build relationships with the parents and children separately. Do not proceed into more formal assessments of parent-child interaction patterns until an open, trusting relationship with the parents has been established. Develop a shared perception of the problem by being client-centered during intake assessment. It is much easier to change people's perceptions when they feel that you understand them and have listened to their point of view.

3. *Integrate contexts with the child's problem.* Problems with contextual aspects of family functioning relating to the child's problem usually lie at two extremes. The first is when a therapist does not raise these issues for discussion, perhaps due to fear of discussing intimate family relations or due to conceptual biases about the role of these variables. The other extreme occurs when these issues are raised in such a way that causes the parents to deny their importance, existence, or the right of the therapist to focus on them. The approach we utilize is to raise questions about family functioning as follows: Inquire about other areas of family functioning after the parents' concerns about the child have been adequately addressed. Make the transition from the child focus to the marital and family focus as smooth as possible, preferably with a summary transition and brief explanation of why you are interested. Err on the side of asking about marital and family issues in the context of how they are affected by the child's problems, rather than to what extent they have caused the child's problems.

A useful way to raise the question of marital functioning and its relationship to the child's problems is to summarize information about the child's problem to show you have fully attended to the parents' concerns about the child. Then make a statement about how dealing with a problem child can place considerable stress on the rest of the family and, in particular, the marriage. Ask the parents to discuss this as it applies to them. Funnel questions; that is, proceed from the general (open questions) to the specific (clarification, elaboration), being client-centered and developing a shared perception of these aspects of family functioning.

It is easy to shift emphasis gradually from child problems causing marital distress to a more reciprocal conceptualization as the discussion continues. Many parents will raise the issue of the blame for the child's problems at this time and identify certain stressors that they have created for their child. For other families, it will be clear that the marriage is basically sound and the parents are jointly committed to the marriage or that the parent-child conflict is straining their relationship in the context of an otherwise harmonious family.

It is important to integrate parents' reports during this discussion with other forms of assessment regarding family functioning. It is not unknown for parents to report absolutely no problem during this discussion but to report marital distress on standardized marital adjustment inventories such as the Marital Adjustment Test (Locke & Wallace, 1959) or the Dyadic Adjustment Scale (Spanier, 1976). If this occurs, the discrepancy should be addressed with careful consideration of the individuals concerned. For example, care is needed with families in which the mother has been coerced by the husband into not talking about any problems except those concerning the child. The mother may complete the marital adjustment inventory honestly, however, providing evidence of marital or personal distress.

Confronting parents with this information within a session, however, may increase the risk of marital friction following the session, or subsequent dropout from therapy. In such cases, it may be advisable to schedule a visit with the spouse reporting marital distress (or depression, and so on) alone, perhaps in the context of assessing the child, to assess the extent of conflict, violence, and the possible implications of openly discussing these issues.

4. *Develop a plan for scheduling, sequencing, and integrating interventions.* At this point, it is assumed that the family has established an open, trusting relationship with the therapist; the child has been assessed as exhibiting behavior problems warranting a family intervention; and the parents also report marital conflict. If marital conflict exists, the parents can be asked to consider the following: Can they cooperate sufficiently, that is, put their marital problems aside for a couple of weeks, while they and the therapist work as a team together to help the child? The flavor of this is for the parents to "own" this decision, not for the therapist to be making directions about the role of their marital problems.

Clinical experience indicates that few families will say that they cannot cooperate for a few weeks. If they report they cannot, of course, the therapist must focus on the reasons for this and perhaps proceed to marital counseling prior to focusing on parent-child issues. However, no previous research was located which has assessed the efficacy of presenting marital interventions prior to parent training for maritally distressed people. In the majority of cases, however, the parents will agree to try to work as a team, by calling a moratorium on marital problems while they implement treatment for the child. It is argued that involvement in this decision is of great benefit in improving family relations.

5. *Stockpile examples.* Under conditions of a moratorium on marital conflict, the parents are then involved in a management program tailored to the parent-child problems and child disturbance. Marital issues are not ignored but, if and when they arise, they are carefully acknowledged and put aside for later consideration, as was agreed in the moratorium. In this way, the child management program is secondarily serving as an assessment phase yielding data on the relationship between parenting and marital issues.

When the child's behavior has improved (as it should quickly if management techniques have been appropriately selected, parents have been trained adequately, and they are consistently implementing techniques in their natural environment), the therapist can increasingly focus on the marital relationship via the stockpile of data generated during child management training. The likelihood of successfully intervening in the marital relationship has now been greatly enhanced by the following: (a) The child has improved; thus, a source of stress (noise level, coercion, demands) in the home is diminished; (b) the parents have worked as a team in producing this change; (c) the temporary cessation of marital conflict may have broken vicious cycles and allowed other positive forms of marital interaction to take place; (d) triadic forms of conflict have been altered by the successful reduction of child-initiated conflict; (e) the therapist's perceived credibility should be high following successful child intervention; and (f) the parents have been reinforced for compliance with therapeutic directives. In summary, do not "own" the scheduling of treatment interventions. Rather, ask parents to talk about the treatment foci of child and marital issues. Aim to achieve a moratorium on marital problems while working as a team with parents to help the child during CMT. During the child focus, acknowledge and stockpile any associated marital issues that arise for use later in the marital focus.

6. *Follow up with an integrated marital focus.* Research reviews of the interdependence of marital and child problems have emphasized the covariance of marital and parent-child interactions, parental personal adjustment, and the parents' pattern of social contacts. The marital relationship appears either to magnify or diminish the effects of various stressors acting on the child and/or the family. It can do this directly (e.g., through open displays of aggression) or indirectly (e.g., through its effect on parent-child interaction). The variables which appear to characterize families with marital discord and an oppositional child fall into three interdependent categories of parent-parent interactions.

First, there are the escalating sequences of coercion which appear to characterize distressed families (Patterson, 1982). Members are likely to initiate coercive attacks on each other, and these attacks are often followed by escalating aggression until a temporary resolution occurs which reinforces each participant's prior behaviors. One focus of intervention, then, must be to reduce the likelihood that family members will initiate or respond coercively to coercive behavior.

Second, marital discord and lack of social support appear to be associated with problem-solving deficits in families (Jacobson & Margolin, 1979). These preclude parents from constructively discussing, formulating, and implementing plans for dealing with family problems. In some families of oppositional children marked by discord and lack of social support, this role may have fallen entirely onto the mother, adding to her burden of managing the children (Patterson, 1980). Problem-solving training has been shown to be associated with increases in targeted problem-solving behaviors and general marital satisfaction in distressed couples (Jacobson & Margolin, 1979). For maritally distressed parents of oppositional children, such training may need to focus on increasing paternal involvement in problem solving and the communication skills required to accomplish this effectively.

Third, a marital relationship marked by positive father-mother engagement and effective communication appears to lessen negative mood states in individual parents (Emery, 1982; Schafer, 1985; Waring & Patton, 1984). As such, any procedure which increases parental communication or engagement may be beneficial to the parent-child relationship. The most widely used procedure aimed at achieving these goals is communication training that involves training parents in active listening and clear communication skills (Jacobson & Margolin, 1979).

Thus, marital interventions can incorporate these three factors and involve brief training in the following: (a) problem responses — the parents' ability to avoid initiating, or quickly resolve, an escalating conflict situation, and if necessary, schedule a discussion later when calm; (b) casual discussions — the parents' ability to communicate effectively on a day-to-day basis; and (3) problem-solving discussions — the parents' ability to schedule, formulate, and implement plans for dealing with family problems. The methods by which parents are trained in these skills are deliberately directive within the PST model (Dadds, Sanders, Behrens, & James, 1987; Dadds, Sanders, & James, 1987; Dadds, Schwartz, & Sanders, 1987); however, other researchers have chosen more client-centered procedures (e.g., Griest et al., 1982).

Griest et al. (1982) and Wahler and Graves (1983) used parent enhancement therapy and review training, respectively, to intervene with a focus on broader variables affecting the mothers of oppositional children. As with PST, these treatments are scheduled as adjunctive to the basic CMT procedure; however, they generally involve the therapist encouraging the mother to explore a range of variables which she identifies as adversely affecting her day-to-day coping and parenting. These variables can be marital, extended familial, social, personal, or whatever the parent sees as important. Given the plethora of variables that could be associated with the parent's difficulties and the child's problems, it may be advantageous to encourage parents to focus on those that are of concern to them rather than to set a uniform agenda for all parents. However, it is argued that the losses involved in using nondirective methods far outweigh this advantage. If a nondirective focus on broader family issues leads to improved treatment gains, we have gained no extra knowledge. However, if one schedules specific behaviors for change in families, the role of these behaviors in both the maintenance and treatment of child behavior problems can be more clearly delineated. The first approach may be clinically useful but is conceptually limited. While the directive approach might sacrifice somewhat a clinician's ability to respond to the subtleties of individual families, it allows the results of the intervention to be related back to the conceptual and empirical literature and be generalized to other clinical strategies.

SESSION OUTLINES

To allow therapists to make the most of the training time available, parents can be given booklets to read 2 or 3 days prior to each of the following three training sessions. The treatment procedures described, however, assume that these handouts to parents are not available to the therapist. The handout cards, which are presented in this chapter as tables and figures, can be used instead.

Overview of Session 1

Negotiate an Agenda. Introduce proposed agenda, giving an estimate of time involved: to review homework and baseline data (if relevant); to discuss ways of improving parents' responses to child behavior problems; to rehearse techniques; and to plan next session.

Review Homework. Check that parents have read the card titled, "When a Problem Occurs" (Table 9.1). If they have not read it, ascertain why and negotiate an alternative arrangement. Ask parents for comments, and check for understanding. Explain that this information will form the basis of the session.

Present Rationale for Partner Support. Explain that CMT produces child behavior change, not a cure, and that parents need to be able to (a) encourage each other to use positive parenting, (b) be consistent, and (c) problem solve together. Link this rationale with any available data on the parents' current patterns of marital interactions. Check for understanding, and prompt

Table 9.1. Parent Handout Card: When a Problem Occurs

---

1. Remain calm: Speak in a calm voice.
2. Try not to interfere if your partner is dealing with the child. That is, don't come to the rescue. The parent who gave the instructions to the child should follow them through.
3. Help your partner if you can see he or she needs it. For example, if your spouse is looking after the child and the other children start to misbehave, tend to the other children.
4. Back each other up by not giving contradictory instructions to the child.
5. Do not comment on each other's behavior until the problem is over and you are more relaxed. Do not blame or criticize each other.
6. After the problem is over, discuss it together, and if necessary arrange a problem-solving discussion.

---

parents to ask questions. If parents are agreeable, proceed to the next section.

Present Training Suggestions. Review the card entitled, "When a Problem Occurs" (Table 9.1). Work through the six suggestions one at a time. Explain the rationale, check for understanding, and prompt parents to ask questions and comment on each suggestion. Summarize the behaviors presented in the card and ask parents to identify some common situations in which these skills could be used.

Assign Homework. Explain the self-monitoring form to parents (Figure 9.1). Ask them to complete the checklist at the end of each day. Explain that it is vital that these skills are practiced every time a child behavior problem occurs. Give parents the next card, "Casual Discussions" (Figure 9.2). Explain that this should be read before next week's training session.

Plan the Next Session. Arrange a time for your next training session. This should be in 1 week. Explain that you will review parents' self-monitoring checklists at this meeting, so they should bring them. Explain that you will review progress on their behaviors in response to problems to see if any change has occurred.

Terminate. Prompt parents to ask any questions. Thank parents for attending.

Overview of Session 2

Negotiate an Agenda. Introduce proposed agenda and give an estimate of time involved (1½ hours): to review homework; to discuss ways of improving parents' casual discussions; to rehearse techniques; and to plan the next session.

Review Homework. Review homework (self-monitoring of implementation of problem responses). Ask open-ended questions about successes and problems. Review self-monitoring card. Inquire about parents' perceptions of the value of using these procedures. Discuss and integrate all data on parents' implementation of problem response techniques. Emphasize any positive change that was recorded. Identify any further improvements needed. Summarize last week's procedures and parents' implementation, and encourage parents to continue to use these problem response techniques so they become habits.

Introduce Casual Discussions. Check that parents have read the card "Casual Discussions." Ask parents for comments on its content, and check for understanding.

Name: _____   Date: _____

Think back to the worst instance of child misbehavior today. Did you:								
Steps to be completed Date:								
1. Remain calm								
2. Not interfere if your spouse was dealing with the child								
3. Help your spouse if they either requested it or obviously needed it								
4. Not give contradictory instructions to the child								
5. Not comment on your spouse's behavior until the problem was over								
6. If you did not know how to handle the problem, did you arrange a problem-solving discussion?								
Number of steps completed correctly:								

FIGURE 9.1. A partner support checklist.

Present Rationale for Casual Discussions. Explain that casual discussions are a way of increasing mutual understanding, communicating after parents have been separated during the day, encouraging each other's positive parenting behaviors, and promoting consistency of child management procedures. Link this with any available data on the parents' current interaction patterns, and with your own behavior as therapist (i.e., providing supportive encouragement by listening, asking questions, and so on). Check for understanding, and prompt parents to ask questions. If parents are agreeable, proceed to the next section.

Present Training Suggestions. Cue parents to the card "Casual Discussions." Work through the stages one at a time. Explain the rationale, check for

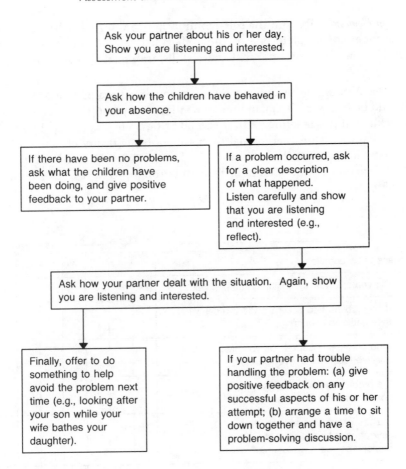

Ask your partner about his or her day. Show you are listening and interested.

Ask how the children have behaved in your absence.

If there have been no problems, ask what the children have been doing, and give positive feedback to your partner.

If a problem occurred, ask for a clear description of what happened. Listen carefully and show that you are listening and interested (e.g., reflect).

Ask how your partner dealt with the situation. Again, show you are listening and interested.

Finally, offer to do something to help avoid the problem next time (e.g., looking after your son while your wife bathes your daughter).

If your partner had trouble handling the problem: (a) give positive feedback on any successful aspects of his or her attempt; (b) arrange a time to sit down together and have a problem-solving discussion.

FIGURE 9.2. Parent handout card: Casual discussions.

understanding, and prompt parents to ask questions. Summarize the procedure and ask parents to identify typical home situations in which these discussions could be used (e.g., father or mother arriving home from work; on Sunday night to review the weekend; or on arriving home after a community outing).

Rehearse Procedure. Rehearse the procedure by (a) choosing a hypothetical situation for your rehearsal; (b) asking the mother or father to role-play the respondent while you role-play the initiating partner in the discussion; and (c) reversing roles until both parents have had a turn. Finally, rehearse the procedure with parents in their usual roles. Provide differential feedback on parents' use of skills. Continue rehearsal until reasonable mastery is obtained by both parents.

Assign Homework. Explain the self-monitoring form to parents (Figure 9.3). Ask them to complete one of these checklists at the end of each day. Explain that it is essential that these skills are practiced every day.

Plan the Next Session. Arrange a time for your next training session. This should be in 1 week. Explain that you will review parents' self-monitoring checklists at this meeting, so they should bring them. Explain that you will review progress on their casual discussions to see if any change has occurred. Give parents the next card, "Problem-Solving Discussions" (Table 9.2). Explain that this should be read and brought to next week's training session.

Name: _____   Date: _____

Steps to be completed	Date:							
1. Did you ask how the children had behaved?								
2. If no problem had occurred, did you ask what they had been doing?								
3. If no problem occurred, did you give positive feedback to your partner?								
4. If a problem occurred, did you give positive feedback to your partner?								
5. Did you give positive feedback to your partner for following the procedures you have learned?								
6. If your partner was not able to deal with the problem, did you arrange a problem-solving discussion for the near future?								
7. Did you offer to do something to help your partner deal with the problem the next time it occurs?								
8. Throughout your discussion, did you show your partner that you were listening and interested?								
Number of steps completed correctly:								

FIGURE 9.3. Casual discussion checklist.

Table 9.2. Parent Handout Card: Problem-Solving Discussions

1. Agree on a convenient time and place to talk to each other about any problems you are currently experiencing. It should be when you are both calm and will not be interrupted by the children.
2. Identify the problem behavior as specifically as possible. Try to deal with one problem at a time. Write down the problem as clearly as possible. Check that you both agree on what needs change.
3. Brainstorm together, thinking of as many solutions as you can. Write these down clearly.
4. Discuss each solution, weighing its pros and cons, its likelihood of success, whether it is practical to use, and any problems that might arise.
5. Choose the best solution(s) by mutual agreement.
6. Plan a strategy for using the solution. Be specific, working out exactly what you will both say and do when the problem occurs.
7. Review how the solution is working by arranging another meeting together.

Overview of Session 3

Negotiate an Agenda. Introduce proposed agenda and give an estimate of time involved (1½ hours): to review homework; to review baseline; to introduce problem-solving strategy; to rehearse techniques; and to plan a full review session.

Review Homework. Review implementation of "Casual Discussions." Review self-monitoring cards; inquire about parents' perceptions of the worth of using structured, casual discussions. Review all data on parents' implementation of casual discussions, emphasizing any positive change and identifying any further improvements needed. Summarize all review data and encourage parents to continue structuring their casual discussions until they become habits.

Introduce Problem-Solving Discussions. Check that parents have read the card "Problem-Solving Discussions." Ask them to comment on its content, and check for understanding. Explain that problem-solving discussions are a way of dealing with family problems without outside help. These discussions promote (a) parental agreement on household rules and discipline (as such they should help parents to be more consistent in their parenting); (b) parents' ability to formulate specific plans for overcoming family problems; and (c) a means of discussing family problems when both parents are relaxed and can concentrate. Link this rationale with any available data on the parents' current interaction patterns. Check for understanding. If parents are agreeable, proceed to the next section.

Present Training. Cue parents to the card "Problem-Solving Discussions." Work through the stages one at a time. Explain the rationale, check for understanding, and prompt parents to ask questions. Summarize the procedure and ask parents to identify typical family problems that could be used as an example. Identify a regular time that could be used for home-based, problem-solving sessions.

Rehearse the Procedure. Rehearse the procedure by (a) choosing a family problem; (b) role-playing with the mother and then the father; and (c) prompting the parents to hold a problem-solving discussion while you provide differential feedback on parents' use of skills. Continue this rehearsal until reasonable mastery is obtained by both parents.

Assign Homework. Explain the self-monitoring form to parents (Table 9.3). Ask parents to complete one form for each problem-solving discussion they hold. Ask parents to bring these forms with them to the next session for the final review of the program.

Overview of Session 4

Negotiate an Agenda. Introduce the agenda and give an estimate of the time involved (1 hour): to review homework; to review partner support; to review CMT; to conduct general counseling; to plan follow-up.

Review Homework. Review implementation of problem-solving discussions. Ask open-ended questions about successes and problems. Review self-

Table 9.3. Problem-Solving Checklist

Name: _____		Date: _____
Describe the problem.		
List possible solutions. 1.	Advantages	Disadvantages
2.		
3.		
Choose a solution.		
Describe your action plan.		
Review the outcome.		

monitoring cards. Inquire about parents' perception of usefulness of procedures. Review and discuss all data on parents' implementation of problem-solving discussions, emphasizing any positive change and identifying areas that require further improvement. Summarize, and encourage parents to continue using these discussions.

Review All Areas of PST. Assess (a) perceptions of change, (b) perceptions of worth, and (c) improvements still needed.

Review All Areas of Child Management. Assess as previously discussed, with the addition that all persisting problems can be scheduled for future problem-solving sessions.

Review Homework; General Counseling. Review the parents' implementation of all aspects of the parent support program and discuss parents' currently defined roles as disciplinarians, softies, decision makers, and so on in the family. Facilitate a positive discussion of perceived sources of stress in parental interactions. Problems identified should be scheduled for parental problem-solving discussions.

Plan Follow-up. Explain the structure and function of follow-up sessions. Encourage parents to continue to use all procedures. Explain that if problems are still occurring at follow-up, further help may be provided. Thank parents for attending.

SUMMARY

Marital difficulties remain a major obstacle to the effective resolution of children's behavioral problems. This chapter outlines several suggestions for dealing with such difficulties when they arise in the context of a referral of a child for behavior problems. Treatment outcome for the child is improved when these problems are addressed concurrently. However, some couples with long-standing discord will require a more intensive form of marital therapy than described here. For example, if there are problems of physical abuse, sexual difficulties, or extramarital affairs, more intensive relationship therapy may be required in addition to PST.

Chapter 10

Issues and Future Directions in Behavioral Family Intervention

LIMITATIONS OF A CLINICAL APPROACH

We have described an approach to family intervention that emphasizes the remediation of preexisting child and family problems by providing information and skills to the family. It has been argued that such an approach is the treatment of choice for children with conduct problems (Lochman, 1990) and can be readily applied with a range of other child and family problems. There is a substantial body of evidence to support the therapeutic value of the approach. However, our model of behavioral family intervention, like most other current models of clinical intervention, has its weaknesses and limitations. There is little room for complacency, as much more research and development are needed to improve clinical treatments and other mental health services for children and families. In this chapter, we explore current issues and possible future directions in the development of behavioral family intervention.

As with most psychological therapies, most time and energy are expended trying to overcome a problem that often has existed for years. While therapeutic work with children generally means the problem has a shorter history than is the case with many adult problems, clinical models of service delivery that involve working with individual families typically do not have a preventive focus (Orford, 1987). The clinician who spends a great deal of time and energy trying to help children with long-standing emotional and behavioral problems may understandably wonder whether many of these problems could have been prevented at some earlier time.

Such clinical approaches are resource intensive, involving large costs to the community in terms of the professional hours devoted to the family. Given the widespread nature of problems such as delinquency that result at least in part from family conflict, a clinical model of service delivery is likely to be an expensive solution to the problem.

This is well illustrated by Brunk, Henggeler, and Whelan (1987). They compared the effectiveness of multisystems therapy with a standard group parent-training program for parent-child problems in a sample of families at risk for child abuse and neglect. The multisystems therapy produced greater improvements in parent-child problems than the group parent training. However, this benefit did not come cheaply. The group program required one and a half hours of therapist time per family compared with 17 hours per family in the multisystemic therapy. It is important that economic considerations are included in the evaluation of alternative clinical treatments.

The majority of resources available to mental health services tend to be devoted to treating problems rather than preventing them. One reason for this is that it is difficult to evaluate whether preventive programs are effective. It takes great forethought and conviction on the part of administrators to divert resources away from pressing demands to programs that may or may not produce future positive benefits. However, a number of considerations can be derived from theoretical models and research into psychopathology in children and families that help guide the development of services for distressed children and families.

Accessing Children and Families at Risk

Research has indicated that it is often the families most in need of help with emotional and behavioral problems who do not have or seek access to mental health services (Sarason, 1974). Families who are socially and economically disadvantaged may be less likely to refer themselves for help and typically do not fare as well in treatment compared with middle-class populations (Dumas, 1986; Webster-Stratton, 1985). Simply establishing clinics that offer comprehensive services in disadvantaged neighborhoods may not be enough. Many families will not access the service, and for the ones that do, the service may be seen in a coercive, intrusive rather than a helpful light (Wahler, 1980).

Hence, an important area for research and clinical development is to improve our understanding of methods for encouraging high-risk families to access available clinical services. This process of improvement will involve evaluating methods for providing information about services, determining the optimal timing of such outreaches in terms of the family's life cycle and the child's stage of development (couple gets married, has first child, infant becomes mobile and explores environment, child begins school), and ways of identifying families at risk for problems who are not likely to seek help.

There are several possible means of accessing lower socioeconomic group families. These include making information about services more readily accessible at points of contact with families (e.g., in family doctors' waiting rooms; at daycare, preschool, and school facilities; at community health centers and neighborhood centers; or through community service announcements on television and radio). One useful but time-consuming method for accessing high-risk families is to have clinical staff, who are skilled public speakers and convincing, credible specialists in child problems, to speak regularly to parents of kindergarten and preschool children in lower socioeconomic areas. These parents can often be reached by holding a talk in their local childcare center on practical topics such as coping with children's behavior problems or fighting between siblings. Such talks often result in some parents seeking help for a problem that might have otherwise become unmanageable. Perhaps more importantly, these talks can facilitate discussion between parents about common problems and between parents and teachers about parenting, child development, how to deal with family problems, and where to seek help.

Adopting a Developmental Approach to Intervention

A strength of the behavioral approach is its focus on and applicability to the individual case (an idiographic approach), in contrast to models that emphasize normality and deviancy (a nomothetic approach). However, it would be foolish to ignore the wealth of theory and research available on the developmental aspects of health and psychopathology. Developmental aspects of childhood problems must be considered both in designing treatments for individual cases and in designing and evaluating preventive and treatment services at a community level.

At the level of the individual case, developmental considerations must be applied at various points in the consultation process. First, the child's current problems should be considered in terms of the problems that children of a similar developmental level commonly exhibit. For example, toileting and eating problems and some fears are common in preschool children and will usually decrease over time. However, it is not uncommon for parents to seek help with these problems, complaining that the child is disturbed and causing distress in the family. It is not appropriate to inform the parent that the child's problems are normal and offer no further help. However, it is useful to understand that such parents are not operating with accurate knowledge about their child's development and that the provision of information about normative patterns of development may facilitate a quick resolution to the problem.

In contrast, a family may be referred for help with a child who has exhibited aggression, stealing, firesetting, and learning problems since an early age. Knowledge of the developmental progression that is common in such conduct problem children (Kazdin, 1987a) will alert the clinician to the likelihood that this child is at risk for chronic problems. If in such a case the parents were labeling the problem as just a childhood phase or the innocuous results of a willful child, the clinician would be alerted to the need to consider the developmental aspects of the child's problems.

Thus, the second application of developmental considerations occurs in making predictions about the progression of the disorder. In this way, accurate information can be provided to caregivers and treatment can be planned over a longer course of time, in a preventive way. Follow-up visits can be scheduled for times in the child's development when problems may escalate. For example, conduct-problem boys often progress from oppositional behavior in the home to more severe delinquency when they fail to negotiate the developmental tasks of early adolescence, such as being part of a peer group and passing exams at school. Loeber (1990) clearly demonstrated that different risk factors impinge on the development of disturbed behavior at different times in the child's life cycle.

Finally, developmental data about child and family problems offer important guidance in the development of larger preventive and community treatment programs. Although more research is needed to make firm conclusions, it is likely that various critical phases occur in the development of child and family problems. The following are all likely to vary with the child's or family's stage of development: (a) the type, severity, and durability of childhood behavioral and emotional problems; (b) the salience of these problems to parents and the likelihood that parents will access services; (c) the ease with which the problems will diminish with the provision of clinical services; and (d) the likelihood that the results of intervention will be durable or will generalize to other problems, and thus function in a preventive mode.

From our experience, some critical phases can be identified at which time parents are likely to experience an escalation in problems and are more open to outside help. These include toddlerhood (from 12 to 36 months) when children first start to explore their environment. During this time parents are often making first contact with other parents and children at childcare groups and are eager to discuss child-rearing issues. The time when children make important transitions from preschool to primary and then to secondary school can also be associated with escalations in family conflict. Clearly, more research is needed to identify critical periods for intervention.

POSSIBLE FUTURE DIRECTIONS

Despite its limitations, behavioral family intervention can rightly claim to have developed a demonstrably successful approach to intervention with a variety of children's behavioral problems. However, there are several trends within the literature which point to some possible future directions that might benefit the field.

Applying Interventions Across a Range of Settings

Clinical treatments are often limited by the difficulty of intervening across a range of settings in the child's life. It is somewhat easier to work with childhood problems that are limited to one setting, such as noncompliance in the home. However, many children's problems occur in a range of home and community settings, and generally this is predictive of a poorer prognosis for the child (Kazdin, 1987a). Further, one of the most common frustrations for clinicians working with children with generalized problems is that several agencies may be involved in the case. For example, a depressed, aggressive boy may be receiving regular counseling from a school psychologist, be receiving medication from a psychiatrist in private practice, be attending a juvenile group program as part of a court recommendation, and then may be referred with the family for behavioral management of his problems.

In such scenarios, the need for effective communication and coordination of services between agencies is critical to our ability to provide the best possible intervention while using minimum resources and cost to the community. All clinical services operate within a larger mental health system, and resources must be devoted to establishing effective liaison with related services.

Applying High-Power Interventions

Kazdin (1987b) argued for the need to match the power of a clinical intervention to the severity and chronicity of the presenting problem. It is pointless to offer minimal interventions to children and their families whose problems are severe and persistent. Research into the effectiveness of various methods for training parents to implement child management skills has clearly indicated that a combination of information provision, modeling, rehearsal, and feedback is often required to teach basic skills such as praising a child (see chapter 2). Attending a series of lectures on child management skills may not be sufficient to help parents who are distressed and cannot manage their children. The group parent-training component described by Brunk et al. (1987) is an example of an intervention that lacked power in relation to the sample it sought to help.

It is our experience that some behavioral family therapists are moving to more complex treatment forms (e.g., Robin & Foster, 1989) after finding that parent training is not successful with their clientele. Often, however, the parent training is low power in that it does not include direct intervention (modeling, behavior rehearsal, feedback) in naturally occurring home and community settings. Many behavioral parent-training programs are solely reliant on the provision of written information, lectures, and video-taped presentations. While these may be of great benefit to parents who are coping fairly well and simply need to sharpen up their skills, they may be inappropriate for more distressed families. Consider a single mother who lives in a small apartment with three young children and has little economic or social support. The evening routine when she attempts to prepare dinner, bathe the children, and prepare them for bed may be an overwhelming experience for her that is high risk for escalating conflict and possible abuse. Providing this mother with modeled information on how to manage these routines will be unlikely to effect positive change. However, a training session followed by a series of home visits in which the therapist models skills, prompts the mother's implementation of skills, and provides supportive, constructive feedback is more likely to succeed.

Dealing with Educational and Learning Problems

Academic and peer relationship problems are clearly a risk factor for childhood emotional and behavioral problems, and nowhere is this relation more obvious than in delinquency (Loeber, 1990). Conduct problems and learning difficulties go hand in hand for many children, and a comprehensive approach to helping distressed children will necessarily involve a focus on the interaction of the two. This has clear clinical implications.

First, it is important that child and family therapists are either skilled in the assessment and treatment of childhood learning problems or can liaise effectively with an agency that possesses these skills. Second, it is important that treatment planning incorporates a comprehensive focus on the interrelationship of learning and behavioral problems. Third, treatment effectiveness will be enhanced by cooperation between intervention agents who are operating in different settings on different aspects of the child's problems. For example, a number of studies have provided evidence that reinforcement contingencies that span home and school settings are effective in decreasing generalized problems in the child (Shapiro, 1987). A teacher may be trained to provide contingencies for parental reports of improvements in child behavior in the home setting. Alternatively, a teacher can send home reports of the child's behavior and achievement in the classroom to parents who have been trained to apply effective contingencies. Interventions such as these that span learning and home settings show considerable promise, and further research and development should be encouraged in this area.

Research has also clearly established a link between poor peer relationships and behavioral and emotional problems in children (Rutter, 1989). A number of social skills programs are available for children who show problems of social withdrawal, depression, anxiety, and interpersonal aggression (Hersen & Van Hasselt, 1987). However, little work has been done examining how these programs can be integrated with family-based interventions for children whose problems span both domains.

Developing Programs for Alternative Family Models

The last few decades have witnessed an increase in the percentage of children who are raised in single-parent and reconstituted families and other alternatives to the traditional nuclear family (Emery, 1982). Further, there is evidence that these families have special needs and problems and that children in such families may be at risk for psychological problems (Coleman & Ganong, 1990; Emery, 1982; Fergusson, Horwood & Shannon, 1984). For example, one of the largest longitudinal studies of the relationship between childhood problems and family breakdown indicated that (a) children who experience marital breakdown are at higher risk for aggressive behavior, and (b) this risk increases further if the parents reconcile or remarry rather than remain as single parents (Fergusson et al., 1984).

It is crucial that child and family clinicians are knowledgeable of and sensitive to the changing demographics of families that the next few decades are likely to witness. More data are needed to help delineate the special problems of children from single-parent and reconstituted families. Further, program development that progresses hand in hand with the collection of data is sorely needed before we can offer comprehensive services to these children and their families.

Improving Diagnostic Systems

A controversial point concerns the use of diagnostic taxonomies with children and families. Early behavioral models were outspokenly opposed to diagnostic systems that assumed the diagnosable existence of various discrete categories of disorder. However, the last few decades have witnessed a return to the popularity of using such diagnostic systems, especially the DSM-IIIR categorization. While there is some evidence that the DSM system is improving with respect to childhood dysfunction, it is still fraught with problems relating to interrater reliabilities, coexisting psychopathology, labeling effects, and symptom-disorder specificity (Kazdin, 1988).

It is crucial that clinicians share a common language about psychopathology, and a diagnostic taxonomy greatly aids our communication. However, present systems are far from adequate, and more research and creativity are needed to develop a diagnostic system that truly reflects the nature of childhood emotional and behavioral problems.

Applications Combining Individual and Family-Focused Interventions

In general, the model of family intervention described in this book focuses on working with children through their parents. As mentioned in chapter 7, as children move toward adolescence some may benefit from concurrent individual sessions with the therapist. For example, children with somatic complaints such as abdominal pain of nonorganic origin, or depression or anxiety problems, can be taught self-coping, self-management, or problem-solving skills relevant to the problem. However, such individual therapy works most effectively if parents are trained to support and encourage children's application of skills they have acquired during individual therapy. Future research must determine what combinations of child- and family-focused treatments might be effective in the treatment of a variety of disorders.

SUMMARY AND CONCLUSION

Behavioral family intervention with individual children and families aimed at remediating preexisting problems is a promising treatment approach for a variety of childhood behavior disorders. This approach involves a consultative process which requires effective communication between the child's family, the therapist, and other significant people in the child's social network. While the techniques of behavior change described

earlier constitute the therapeutic centerpiece of the intervention, the consultation process (including the methods of training parents) strongly influences the treatment's acceptability to parents and therefore has an important role in the overall therapeutic strategy. Future research into
behavioral family intervention should attempt to define the specific strategies therapists employ in dealing with issues such as client nonadherence
to therapeutic tasks and other types of client behavior that create obstacles
for the smooth progression of therapy. Skill in dealing with such problems
should not be explained away as simply reflecting a therapist's experience,
intuition, or personal qualities. Some strategies may work more effectively
than others and are clearly worthy of empirical study in their own right.

There are several major challenges in delivering better treatment services to children and families. These concern the need to develop more
effective ways of accessing the many high-risk families who at present
receive no treatment. Unless disadvantaged families can be encouraged to
seek help, it will not be possible to investigate methods of improving
services to such families. Effective treatment is also limited to the extent
that we can liaise with other relevant treatment agencies and provide
treatment across a range of childhood problems that are sensitive to the
developmental aspects of the child's problems and that are appropriately
matched in power to the severity of the child's problems. While prevention
of children's psychological and behavioral problems sounds like an attrac-
tive alternative, it is by no means clear whether preventive interventions
will reduce the prevalence of children's behavioral problems in the community. More research and creative development of preventive programs
are needed to address the aforementioned limitations in light of the changing demographics of families in most Western countries.

References

Achenbach, T. M., & Edelbrock, C. S. (1983). *Manual for the Child Behavior Checklist and the Revised Child Behavior Profile.* Burlington, VT: University Associates in Psychiatry.

Achenbach, T. M., & Edelbrock, C. (1986). *Manual for the Teacher's Report Form.* Burlington, VT: Department of Psychiatry, University of Vermont.

Ambrose, S., Hazzard, A., & Hayworth, J. (1980). Cognitive behavioral parenting groups for abusive families. *Child Abuse and Neglect, 4,* 119–124.

American Psychiatric Association. (1987). *Diagnostic and statistical manual of mental disorders, Third Edition, Revised.* Washington, DC: Author.

Anderson, J., Williams, S., McGee, R., & Silva, P. A. (1987). The prevalence of D.S.M. III disorders in a large sample of preadolescent children from the general population. *Archives of General Psychiatry, 44,* 69–76.

Azrin, N. H., & Foxx, R. M. (1974). *Toilet training in less than a day.* New York: Simon & Schuster.

Baer, D. M., Wolf, M. M., & Risley, T. R. (1968). Some current dimensions of applied behavior analysis. *Journal of Applied Behavior Analysis, 1,* 91–97.

Bandura, A. (1973). *Aggression: A social learning analysis.* Englewood Cliffs, NJ: Prentice-Hall.

Bandura, A. (1977). *Social learning theory.* Englewood Cliffs, NJ: Prentice-Hall.

Bateson, G., Jackson, D. D., Haley, J., & Weakland, J. (1956). Towards a theory of schizophrenia. *Behavioral Science, 1,* 251–264.

Beautrais, A. L., Fergusson, D. M., & Shannon, F. T. (1982). Family life events and behavioral problems in preschool children. *Pediatrics, 70,* 774–779.

Beck, A. T., Ward, C. H., Mendelson, M., Mock, J., & Erbaugh, J. (1961). An inventory for measuring depression. *Archives of General Psychiatry, 4,* 561–571.

Becker, W. C., & Carnine, D. W. (1980). Direct instruction: An effective approach to educational intervention with the disadvantaged and low performers. *Advances in Clinical Child Psychology, 3,* 429–473.

Bergin, J. R., & Kratochwill, T. R. (1985). *Behavioral consultation in applied settings.* New York: Plenum Publishing.

Berkowitz, B. P., & Graziano, A. M. (1972). Training parents as behavior therapists: A review. *Behavior Research and Therapy, 10,* 297–317.

Bernal, M. E., Klinnert, M. D., & Schultz, L. A. (1980). Outcome evaluation of behavioral parent training and client centered parent counseling for children with conduct problems. *Journal of Applied Behavior Analysis, 13,* 677–691.

Bijou, S. W., & Baer, D. M. (1961). *Child development: A systematic and empirical theory: Vol. 1.* New York: Appleton-Century-Crofts.

Billings, A. G., & Moos, R. H. (1983). Comparisons of children of depressed and non-depressed parents: A social environmental perspective. *Journal of Abnormal Child Psychology, 11,* 463–486.

Blechman, E. A. (1981). Toward comprehensive behavioral family intervention: An algorithm for matching families and interventions. *Behavior Modification, 5,* 221–236.

Blechman, E. A. (1982). Are children with one parent at psychological risk: A methodological review. *Journal of Marriage and the Family, 44,* 179–195.

Blechman, E. A. (1984). Competent parents, competent children: Behavioral objectives of parent training. In R. F. Dangel & R. A. Polster (Eds.), *Parent training: Foundations of research and practice* (pp. 34–63). New York: Guilford Press.

Blechman, E. A., & McEnroe, M. J. (1985). Effective family problem solving. *Child Development, 56,* 429–437.

Blechman, E. A., Tinsley, B., Carella, E. T., & McEnroe, M. J. (1985). Childhood competence and behavior problems. *Journal of Abnormal Psychology, 94,* 70–77.

Bowlby, D. (1973). *Attachment and loss II: Separation.* New York: Basic Books.

Brody, G. H., & Forehand, R. (1985). The efficacy of parent training with maritally distressed and nondistressed mothers: A multimethod assessment. *Behavior Research and Therapy, 23,* 291–296.

Bronfenbrenner, U. (1977). Towards an experimental ecology of human development. *American Psychologist, 32,* 513–531.

Brunk, M., Henggeler, S. W., & Whelan, J. P. (1987). Comparison of multisystemic therapy and parent training in the brief treatment of child abuse and neglect. *Journal of Consulting and Clinical Psychology, 55,* 171–178.

Burke, N. S., & Simons, H. E. (1965). Factors which precipitate dropouts and delinquency. *Federal Probation, 29,* 28–32.

Chamberlain, P., & Baldwin, D. V. (1987). Client resistance to parent training: Its therapeutic management. In T. R. Kratochwill (Ed.), *Advances in school psychology* (Vol. 6). New York: Plenum Press.

Chamberlain, P., Patterson, G. R., Reid, J., Kavanagh, K., & Forgatch, M. (1984). Observation of client resistance. *Behavior Therapy, 15,* 144–145.

Christensen, A. P., & Sanders, M. R. (1985). Habit reversal and differential reinforcement of other behavior in the treatment of thumbsucking: An analysis of generalization and side effects. *Journal of Child Psychology and Psychiatry, 28,* 281–295.

Christoff, K. A., & Myatt, R. J. (1987). Social isolation. In M. Hersen & V. B. Van Hasselt (Eds.), *Behavior therapy with children and adolescents: A clinical approach* (pp. 512–536). New York: John Wiley & Sons.

Christophersen, E. R. (1982). Incorporating behavioral pediatrics into primary care. *Pediatric Clinics of North America, 29,* 261–295.

Christophersen, E. R., & Gyulay, J. E. (1981). Parental compliance with car seat usage: A positive approach with long term follow up. *Journal of Pediatric Psychology, 6,* 301–312.

Clark, H. B., Greene, B. F., Macrae, J. W., McNees, M. P., Davis, J. L., & Risley, T. R. (1977). A parent advice package for family shopping trips: Development and evaluation. *Journal of Applied Behavior Analysis, 10,* 605–624.

Cole, C., & Morrow, W. R. (1976). Refractory parent behaviors in behavior modification training groups. *Psychotherapy: Theory, Research and Practce, 13,* 162–169.

Cole, D. A., & Rehm, L. P. (1986). Family interaction patterns and childhood depression. *Journal of Abnormal Child Psychology, 14,* 297–314.

Coleman, M., & Ganong, L. H. (1990). Remarriage and step family research in the 1980's: Increased interest in an old family form. *Journal of Marriage and the Family, 52,* 925–940.

Conners, C. K. (1969). A teacher rating scale for use in drug studies with children. *American Journal of Psychiatry, 126,* 884–888.

Conners, C. K. (1970). Symptom patterns in hyperkinetic, neurotic, and normal children. *Child Development, 41,* 667–682.

Cummings, E. M., Ianotti, R. J., & Zahn-Waxler, C. (1985). Influence of conflict between adults on emotions and aggression in young children. *Developmental Psychology, 21,* 495–507.

Dadds, M. R. (1987). Families and the origins of child behavior problems. *Family Process, 26,* 341–357.

Dadds, M. R. (1989). Child behavior therapy and family context: Suggestions for research and practice with maritally discordant families. *Child and Family Behavior Therapy, 11,* 27–44.

Dadds, M. R., Adlington, F. M., & Christensen, A. P. (1987). Children's perceptions of time out. *Behavior Change, 4,* 3–13.

Dadds, M. R., & McHugh, T. (in press). Social support and treatment outcome in behavioral family therapy. *Journal of Consulting and Clinical Psychology.*

Dadds, M. R., & Powell, M. (in press). An examination of sampling and sex effects in the relationship of marital discord to childhood aggression, anxiety and immaturity. *Journal of Abnormal Child Psychology.*

Dadds, M. R., Sanders, M. R., Behrens, B. C., & James, J. E. (1987). Marital discord and child behaviour problems: A description of family interactions during treatment. *Journal of Clinical Child Psychology, 16,* 192–203.

Dadds, M. R., Sanders, M. R., & Bor, W. (1984). Training children to eat independently: Evaluation of mealtime management training for parents. *Behavioral Psychotherapy, 12,* 356–366.

Dadds, M. R., Sanders, M. R., & James, J. E. (1987). The generalization of treatment effects with multidistressed parents. *Behavioral Psychotherapy, 15,* 289–313.

Dadds, M. R., Schwartz, S., & Sanders, M. R. (1987). Marital discord and treatment outcome in the treatment of childhood conduct disorders. *Journal of Consulting and Clinical Psychology, 55,* 396–403.

Dadds, M. R., Sheffield, J., & Holbeck, J. (1990). An examination of the differential relationship of marital discord to parental discipline strategies for boys and girls. *Journal of Abnormal Child Psychology, 18,* 121–129.

Dangel, R. F., & Polster, R. A. (1984). *Parent training: Foundations of research and practice.* New York: Guilford Press.

Departments of Psychiatry and Child Psychiatry, Institute of Psychiatry and the Maudsley Hospital. (1987). *Psychiatric examination: Notes on eliciting and recording clinical information in psychiatric patients.* Oxford, England: Oxford University Press.

Derogatis, L. R., & Melisaratos, N. (1983). The Brief Symptom Inventory: A preliminary report. *Psychological Medicine, 13,* 595–605.

Dodge, K. A. (1985). Attributional bias in aggressive children. In P. C. Kendall (Ed.), *Advances in cognitive-behavioral research and therapy* (Vol. 4, pp. 73–110). Orlando, FL: Academic Press.

Donovan, W. L., Leavitt, L. A., & Balling, J. D. (1978). Maternal psychological response to infant signals. *Psychophysiology, 15,* 68–74.

Downey, A., & Coyne, J. C. (1990). Children of depressed parents: An integrative review. *Psychological Bulletin, 108,* 50–76.

Drabman, R. S., Hammer, D., & Rosenbaum, M. S. (1979). Assessing generalization in behavior modification with children: The generalization map. *Behavioral Assessment, 1,* 203–219.

Dumas, J. E. (1986). Indirect influence of maternal social contacts on mother-child interactions: A setting event analysis. *Journal of Abnormal Child Psychology, 14,* 205–216.

Dumas, J. E. (1989). Interact — A computer based coding and data management system to assess family interactions. In R. J. Prinz (Ed.), *Advances in behavioral assessment of children and families* (Vol. 3, pp. 177–202). Greenwich, CT: JAI Press.

Dumas J. E., Gibson, J. A., & Albin, J. B. (1989). Behavioral correlates of maternal depressive symptomatology in conduct disordered children. *Journal of Consulting and Clinical Psychology, 57,* 516–521.

Dumas, J. E., & Wahler, R. G. (1983). Predictors of treatment outcome in parent training: Mother insularity and socioeconomic disadvantage. *Behavioral Assessment, 5,* 301–313.

Edelstein, B. A. (1989). Generalization: Terminological, methodological and conceptual issues. *Behavior Therapy, 20,* 311–323.

Elder, G. H., Nguyen, T. V., & Caspi, A. (1985). Linking family hardship to children's lives. *Developmental Psychology, 56,* 361–375.

Ellis, A. (1962). *Reason and emotion in psychotherapy.* New York: Lyle Stuart.

Embry, L. H. (1984). What to do? Matching client characteristic and intervention techniques through a prescriptive taxonomic key. In R. F. Dangel & R. A. Polster (Eds.), *Parent training: Foundations of research and practice* (pp. 443–473). New York: Guilford Press.

Emery, R. E. (1982). Interparental conflict and the children of discord and divorce. *Psychological Bulletin, 9,* 310–330.

Emery, R. E., Weintraub, S., & Neale, J. M. (1982). Effects of marital discord on the school behavior of children of schizophrenic, affectively disordered and normal parents. *Journal of Abnormal Child Psychology, 10,* 215–218.

Eyberg, S. M., & Johnson, S. M. (1974). Multiple assessment of behavior modification with families: Effects of contingency contracting and order of treatment problems. *Journal of Consulting and Clinical Psychology, 42,* 594–606.

Feldman, M. A., Case, L., Rincover, A., Town, F., & Betel, J. (1989). Parent education project III: Increasing affection and responsivity in developmentally handicapped mothers: Component analysis, generalization, and effects on child language. *Journal of Applied Behavior Analysis, 22,* 211–222.

Fergusson, D. M., Horwood, L. J., & Shannon, F. T. (1984). A proportional hazards model of family breakdown. *Journal of Marriage and the Family, 46,* 539–549.

Finch, A., Jr., Montgomery, L., & Deardorff, P. (1974). Children's Manifest Anxiety Scale: Reliability with emotionally disturbed children. *Psychological Reports, 34,* 658.

Forehand, R. L., & Atkeson, B. M. (1977). Generality of treatment effects with parents as therapists. *Behavior Therapy, 8,* 575–593.

Forehand, R. L., Griest, D. L., & Wells, K. C. (1979). Parent behavioral training: An analysis of the relationship amongst multiple outcome measures. *Journal of Abnormal Child Psychology, 7,* 229–242.

Forehand, R. L., & Long, N. (1988). Outpatient treatment of the acting out child: Procedures, long term follow-up data, and clinical problems. *Advances in Behavior Research and Therapy, 10,* 129–177.

Forehand, R. L., & McMahon, R. J. (1981). *Helping the non-compliant child: A clinician's guide to parent training.* New York: Guilford Press.

Framo, D. L. (1975). Personal reflections of a therapist. *Journal of Marriage and Family Counseling, 1,* 15–28.

Furey, W. M., & Basili, L. A. (1988). Predicting consumer satisfaction in parent training for noncompliant children. *Behavior Therapy, 19,* 555–564.

Gardiner, F. E. M. (1987). Positive interaction between mothers and conduct-problem children: Is there training for harmony as well as fighting? *Journal of Abnormal Child Psychology, 15,* 283–293.

Garralda, M. E., & Bailey, D. (1986). Children with psychiatric disorders in primary care. *Journal of Child Psychology and Psychiatry, 27,* 611–624.

Glynn, T., Thomas, J. D., & Wotherspoon, A. T. (1978). Applied psychology in the Mangere Guidance Unit: Implementing behavioral programs in the school. *The Exceptional Child, 25,* 115–126.

Goldberg, D. (1972). *Manual of the General Health Questionnaire.* Manchester, England: University of Manchester.

Goldstein, A. P., Keller, H., & Erne, D. (1985). *Changing the abusive parent.* Champaign, IL: Research Press.

Goodyer, I. M. (1990). Family relationships, life events, and childhood psychopathology. *Journal of Child Psychology and Psychiatry, 31,* 161–192.

Goyette, C. H., Conners, C. K., & Ulrich, R. F. (1978). Normative data on the revised Conners parent and teacher rating scales. *Journal of Abnormal Child Psychology, 6,* 221–236.

Graves, T., Meyers, A. W., & Clark, L. (1988). An evaluation of parental problem solving training in the behavioral treatment of childhood obesity. *Journal of Consulting and Clinical Psychology, 56,* 246–250.

Graziano, A. M. (1977). Parents as behavior therapists. In M. Herson, R. M. Eisler, & P. M. Miller (Eds.), *Progress in behavior modification,* (Vol. IV, pp. 251–298). New York: Academic Press.

Griest, D. L., & Forehand, R. (1981). How can I get any parent training done with all these other problems going on? *Child Behavior Therapy, 4,* 73–80.

Griest, D. L., Forehand, R., Rogers, T., Breiner, J., Furey, W., & Williams, C. A. (1982). Effects of parent enhancement therapy on the treatment outcome and generalization of a parent training program. *Behavior Research and Therapy, 20,* 429–436.

Griest, D. L., & Wells, K. C. (1983). Behavioral family therapy with conduct disorders in children. *Behavior Therapy, 14,* 37–53.

Griest, D. L., Wells, K. C., & Forehand, R. (1979). Examination of predictors of maternal perceptions of maladjustment in clinic referred children. *Journal of Abnormal Psychology, 82,* 194–203.

Grych, J. H., & Fincham, F. D. (1990). Marital conflict and children's adjustment: A cognitive-contextual framework. *Psychological Bulletin, 108,* 267–290.

Hall, R. V., Axelrod, S., Tyler, L., Grief, E., Jones, F. C., & Robertson, R. (1972). Modification of behavior problems in the home with a parent as observer and experimenter. *Journal of Applied Behavior Analysis, 5,* 53–64.

Harris, S. L., & Ferrari, M. (1983). Developmental factors in child behavior therapy. *Behavior Therapy, 14,* 54–72.

Hart, B., & Risley, T. R. (1972). Incidental teaching of language in the preschool. *Journal of Applied Behavior Analysis, 8,* 411–420.

Hawkins, R. P., Peterson, R. F., Schweid, E. L., & Bijou, S. W. (1966). Behavior therapy in the home: Amelioration of problem parent-child relations with the parent in the therapeutic role. *Journal of Experimental Child Psychology, 4,* 99–107.

Haynes, R. B., Taylor, D. W., & Sackett, D. L. (1979). *Compliance in health care.* Baltimore, MD: John Hopkins University Press.

Hersen, M., & Van Hasselt, V. B. (1987). *Behavior therapy with children and adolescents: A clinical approach.* New York: John Wiley & Sons.

Hetherington, E. M., Cox, M., & Cox, A. (1982). Effects of divorce on parents and children. In M. E. Lamb (Ed.), *Nontraditional families* (pp. 223–288). Hillsdale, NJ: Lawrence Erlbaum Associates.

Hetherington, E. M., & Martin, B. (1979). Family interaction. In H. C. Quay & J. S. Werry (Eds.), *Psychopathological disorders of childhood* (pp. 30–82). New York: John Wiley & Sons.

Hoffman, L. (1981). *Foundations of family therapy.* New York: Basic Books.

Hudson, A. (1982). Training parents of developmentally handicapped children: A component analysis. *Behavior Therapy, 13,* 325–333.

Jacobson, N. S., & Margolin, G. (1979). *Marital therapy: Strategies based on social learning and behavior exchange principles.* New York: Brunner/Mazel.

Johnson, L. J. (1988). Barriers to effective special education consultation. *Remedial and Special Education, 9,* 41–47.

Johnson, S. M., & Christensen, A. (1975). Multiple criteria followup of behavior modification with families. *Journal of Abnormal Child Psychology, 3,* 135–154.

Johnston, C., & Mash, E. J. (1989). A measure of parenting satisfaction and efficacy. *Journal of Clinical Child Psychology, 18,* 167–175.

Kanfer, F. H., & Saslow, G. (1969). Behavioral diagnosis. In C. Franks (Ed.), *Behavior therapy: Appraisal and status* (pp. 417–444). New York: McGraw-Hill.

Kanfer, F. H., & Schefft, B. K. (1988). *Guiding the process of therapeutic change.* Champaign, IL: Research Press.

Kashani, J. H., Orvaschel, H., Rosenberg, T. K., & Reid, J. C. (1989). Psychopathology in a community sample of children and adolescents: A developmental perspective. *Journal of the American Academy of Child and Adolescent Psychiatry, 28,* 701–706.

Kazdin, A. E. (1980). The acceptability of time out from reinforcement procedures for disruptive child behaviors. *Behavior Therapy, 11,* 329–344.

Kazdin, A. E. (1983). Psychiatric diagnosis, dimensions of dysfunction, and child behavior therapy. *Behavior Therapy, 14,* 73–99.

Kazdin, A. E. (1987a). *Conduct disorder in childhood and adolescence.* Newbury Park, CA: Sage Publications.

Kazdin, A. E. (1987b). The treatment of anti-social behavior: Current status and future directions. *Psychological Bulletin, 102,* 187–203.

Kazdin, A. E. (1988). The diagnosis of childhood disorders: Assessment issues and strategies. *Behavioral Assessment, 10,* 67–94.

Kazdin, A. E. (1990a). Childhood depression. *Journal of Child Psychology and Psychiatry, 31,* 121–160.

Kazdin, A. E. (1990b). Premature termination from treatment among children referred for anti-social behavior. *Journal of Child Psychology and Psychiatry, 31,* 415–425.

Kelley, M. L., Embrey, H. L., & Baer, D. M. (1979). Skills for child management and family support: Training parents for maintenance. *Behavior Modification, 3,* 373–396.

King, N. J., Ollier, K., Lacuone, R., Schuster, S., Bays, K., Gullone, E., & Ollendick, T. H. (1989). Fears of children and adolescents: A cross sectional Australian study using the Revised Fear Survey Schedule for children. *Journal of Child Psychology and Psychiatry, 30,* 77–84.

Koegel, R. L., Glahn, T. J., & Nieminen, G. S. (1978). Generalization of parent training results. *Journal of Applied Behavior Analysis, 11,* 95–109.

Kolko, D. (1987). Depression. In M. Hersen. & V. B. Van Hasselt (Eds.), *Behavior therapy with children and adolescents* (pp. 137–183). New York: John Wiley & Sons.

Kovacs, M. (1980). Rating scales to assess depression in school aged children. *Acta Paedopsychiatrica, 46,* 305–315.

Krantz, P. J., & Risley, T. R. (1977). Behavioral ecology in the classroom. In K. D. O'Leary & S. J. O'Leary (Eds.), *Classroom management: The successful use of behavior modification* (2nd ed., pp. 349–366). Elmsford, NY: Pergamon Press.

Lahey, B. B., Hartdagen, S. E., Frick, P. J., McBurnett, K., Connor, R., & Hynd, G. W. (1988). Conduct disorder: Passing the confounded relationship to a parental divorce and antisocial personality. *Journal of Abnormal Psychology, 97,* 334–337.

Lamb, M., & Elster, A. B. (1985). Adolescent mother-infant-father relationships. *Developmental Psychology, 21,* 768–773.

Lambert, M. J., DeJulio, S. S., & Stein, D. M. (1978). Therapist interpersonal skills: Process outcome, methodological considerations and recommendations for future research. *Psychological Bulletin, 85,* 467–489.

Laski, K., Charlop, M. H., & Schreibman, L. (1988). Training parents to use the natural language paradigm to increase their autistic children's speech. *Journal of Applied Behavior Analysis, 21,* 391–400.

Limbrick, E., McNaughton, S. S., & Glynn, T. (1985). Reading gains for underachieving tutors and tutees in a cross-age tutoring program. *Journal of Child Psychology and Psychiatry, 26,* 939–953.

Lochman, J. E. (1990). Modification of childhood aggression. In M. Hersen, R. M. Eisler, & P. M. Miller (Eds.), *Progress in behavior modification* (Vol. 25, pp. 47–85). New York: Academic Press.

Locke, H. J., & Wallace, K. M. (1959). Short term marital adjustment and prediction tests: Their reliability and validity. *Journal of Marriage and the Family, 21,* 251–255.

Loeber, R. (1990). Development and risk factors of juvenile antisocial behavior and delinquency. *Clinical Psychology Review, 10,* 1–41.

Lutzker, J. (1984). Project 12 ways: Treating child abuse and neglect from an ecobehavioral perspective. In R. F. Dangel. & R. A. Polster (Eds.), *Parent training: Foundations of research and practice* (pp. 260–291). New York: Guilford Press.

Masur, F. T. (1981). Adherence to health care regimens. In C. K. Prokop & L. A. Bradley (Eds.), *Medical psychology: Contributions to behavioral medicine* (pp. 442–470). New York: Academic Press.

Matson, J. L., & Ollendick, T. H. (1988). *Enhancing children's social skills: Assessment and training.* Elmsford, NY: Pergamon Press.

Maugham, B., Gray, G., & Rutter, M. (1985). Reading retardation and anti-social behavior: A follow up into employment. *Journal of Child Psychology and Psychiatry, 26,* 741–758.

McFarland, M., & Sanders, M. R. (1990). *Child management training in groups: A therapist manual.* Unpublished manuscript, Department of Psychiatry, University of Queensland.

McGuire, J., & Richman, N. (1986). The prevalence of behavioral problems in three types of preschool group. *Journal of Child Psychology and Psychiatry, 26,* 455–472.

McMahon, R. J., & Forehand, R. L. (1978). Non-prescription behavior therapy: Effectiveness of a brochure in teaching mothers to correct their children's inappropriate mealtime behaviors. *Behavior Therapy, 9,* 814–820.

McMahon, R. J., & Forehand, R. L. (1983). Consumer satisfaction in behavioral treatment of children: Types, issues and recommendations. *Behavior Therapy, 14,* 209–225.

McMahon, R. J., Forehand, R. L., Griest, D. L., & Wells, K. C. (1981). Who drops out of therapy during parent behavioral training? *Behavior Counseling Quarterly, 1,* 79–85.

McManmon, L., Peterson, C. R., Metelinis, L., McWhirter, J., & Clark, H. B. (1982). The development of a parental advice protocol for enhancing family mealtime. *Behavioral Counseling Quaterly, 2,* 156–167.

McNaughton, S., Glynn, T., & Robinson, V. (1987). *Pause, prompt and praise: Effective tutoring for remedial reading.* Birmingham, England: Positive Products.

Meltzer, L. J., Levine, M. D., Karniski, W., Palfrey, J. S., & Clarke, S. (1984). An analysis of the learning style of adolescent delinquents. *Journal of Learning Disabilities, 17,* 600–608.

Miklowitz, D. J., Goldstein, M. J., Falloon, I. R. H., & Doane, J. A. (1984). Interactional correlates of expressed emotion in the families of schizophrenics. *British Journal of Psychiatry, 144,* 482–487.

Miller, G. E., & Prinz, R. J. (1990). Enhancement of social learning family interventions for child conduct disorder. *Psychological Bulletin, 108,* 291–307.

Miller, S. J., & Sloane, H. N. (1976). The generalization of parent training across stimulus settings. *Journal of Applied Behavior Analysis, 9,* 355–370.

Milner, J. S. (1980). *The Child Abuse Potential Inventory.* Webster, NC: Psychtec Corp.

Minuchin, S. (1974). *Families and family therapy.* Cambridge MA: Harvard University Press.

Molholm, L. H., & Dinitz, S. (1972). Female mental patients and their normal controls. *Archives of General Psychiatry, 27,* 606–610.

Moore, D. W., & Glynn, T. (1984). Variation in question rate as a function of position in the classroom. *Educational Psychology, 4,* 233–248.

Moos, R. H. (1974). *The Family, Work & Group Environment Scales Manual.* Palo Alto, CA: Consulting Psychologists Press.

O'Brien, M., Porterfield, J., Herbert–Jackson, E., & Risley, T.R. (1979). *The toddler centre: A practical guide to day care for one– and two–year-olds.* Baltimore, MD: University Park Press.

O'Connor, W. A., & Stachowiak, J. (1971). Patterns of interaction in families with high adjusted, low adjusted and mentally retarded members. *Family Process, 10,* 214–229.

O'Dell, S. (1974). Training parents in behavior modification: A review. *Psychological Bulletin, 81,* 418–433.

Ollendick, T. H., & Francis, G. (1988). Behavioral assessment and treatment of childhood phobias. *Behavior Modification, 12,* 165–204.

Oltmanns, R. F., Boderick, J. E., & O'Leary, K. D. (1977). Marital adjustment and the efficacy of behavior therapy with children. *Journal of Consulting and Clinical Psychology, 45,* 724–729.

Orford, J. (1987). *Coping with disorder in the family.* London: Croom Helm.

Panaccione, V. F., & Wahler, R. G. (1986). Child behavior, maternal depression and social coercion as factors in the quality of child care. *Journal of Abnormal Child Psychology, 14,* 263–278.

Parker, J. G., & Asher, S. R. (1987). Peer relations and later personal adjustment. Are low-accepted children at risk? *Psychological Bulletin, 102,* 357–389.

Patterson, G. R. (1969). Behavioral techniques based on social learning: An additional base for developing behavior modification technologies. In C. M. Franks (Ed.), *Behavior therapy: Appraisal and status* (pp. 341–374). New York: McGraw-Hill.

Patterson, G. R. (1980). Mothers: The unacknowledged victims. *Monographs of the Society for Research in Child Development, 45* (Serial No. 186).

Patterson, G. R. (1982). *Coercive family process.* Eugene, OR: Castalia Press.

Patterson, G. R. (1986). Performance models for anti-social boys. *American Psychologist, 41,* 432–444.

Patterson, G. R., & Brodsky, M. (1966). Behavior modification for a child with multiple behavior problems. *Journal of Child Psychology and Psychiatry, 7,* 277–295.

Patterson, G. R., Chamberlain, P., & Reid, J. B. (1982). A comparative evaluation of a parent training program. *Behavior Therapy, 13,* 638–650.

Patterson, G. R., McNeal, S., Hawkins, N., & Phelps, R. (1967). Reprogramming the social environment. *Journal of Child Psychology and Psychiatry, 8,* 181–195.

Patterson, G. R., & Reid, J. B. (1984). Social interactional processes in the family: The study of the moment by moment family transactions in which human social development is embedded. *Journal of Applied Developmental Psychology, 5,* 237–262.

Patterson, G. R., Reid, J. B., Jones, R. R., & Conger, R. E. (1975). *A social learning approach to family intervention: Vol 1. Families with aggressive children.* Eugene, OR: Castalia Press.

Petti, T. A. (1978). Depression in hospitalized child psychiatry patients: Approaches to measuring depression. *Journal of the American Academy of Child Psychiatry, 17,* 49–59.

Piacentini, J. C. (1987). Language dysfunction and childhood behavior disorders. In B. B. Lahey & A. E. Kazdin (Eds.), *Advances in clinical child psychology* (Vol. 10, pp. 259–284). New York: Plenum Publishing.

Pisterman, S., McGrath, P., Firestone, P., Goodman, J. T., Webster, I., & Mallory, R. (1989). Outcome of parent mediated treatment of preschoolers with attention deficit disorder with hyperactivity. *Journal of Consulting and Clinical Psychology, 57,* 628–635.

Porter, B., & O'Leary, K. D. (1980). Marital discord and childhood behaviour problems. *Journal of Abnormal Child Psychology, 80,* 287–295.

Procidiano, M. E., & Heller, K. (1983). Measures of perceived social support from friends and from family: Three validation studies. *American Journal of Community Psychology, 11,* 1–25.

Quay, H. C., & Peterson, D. R. (1983). *Manual for the Revised Behavior Problem Checklist.* Coral Gables, FL: Applied Social Sciences, University of Miami.

Reisinger, J. J., Frangia, G. W., & Hoffman, E. H. (1976). Toddler management training: Generalization and marital status. *Journal of Behavior Therapy and Experimental Psychiatry, 7,* 235–340.

Reynolds, C.R., & Richmond, B.O. (1978). What I think and feel: A revised measure of children's manifest anxiety. *Journal of Abnormal Child Psychology, 6,* 271–280.

Risley, T. R., Clark, H. B., & Cataldo, M. F. (1976). Behavioral technology for the normal middle-class family. In E. J. Mash, L. A. Hamerlynch, & L. C. Handy (Eds.), *Behavior modification and families* (pp. 34–60). New York: Brunner/Mazel.

Robin. A. L. (1981). A controlled evaluation of problem solving communication training with parent-adolescent conflict. *Behavior Therapy, 12,* 593–609.

Robin, A. L., & Foster, S. (1989). *Negotiating parent-adolescent conflict. A behavioral family systems approach.* New York: Guilford Press.

Rutter, M. (1989). Pathways from childhood to adult life. *Journal of Child Psychology and Psychiatry, 30,* 23–51.

Rutter, M., Cox, A., Tupling, C., Berger, M., & Yule, W. (1975). Attainment in two geographical areas — 1. The prevalence of psychiatric disorder. *British Journal of Psychiatry, 126,* 493–509.

Rutter, M., McDonald, H., Le Couteur, A., Harrington, R., Bolton, P., & Bailey, A. (1990). Genetic factors in child psychiatric disorders — II. Empirical findings. *Journal of Child Psychology and Psychiatry, 31,* 39–83.

Rutter, M., Tizzard, J., & Whitmore, R. (1970). *Education, health and behavior.* New York: John Wiley & Sons.

Sanders, M. R. (1982). The effects of instructions, cueing and feedback procedures in systematic parent training. *Australian Journal of Psychology, 34,* 53–69.

Sanders, M. R. (1984). Clinical strategies for enhancing generalization in behavioral parent training: An overview. *Behavior Change, 1,* 25–35.

Sanders, M. R., Bor, W., & Dadds, M. R. (1984). Modifying bedtime disruptions in children using stimulus control and contingency management procedures. *Behavioral Psychotherapy, 12,* 130–141.

Sanders, M. R., & Christensen, A. P. (1985). A comparison of the effects of child management and planned activities training in five parenting environments. *Journal of Abnormal Child Psychology, 13,* 101–117.

Sanders, M. R., & Dadds, M. R. (1982). The effects of planned activities and child management training: An analysis of setting generality. *Behavior Therapy, 13,* 1–11.

Sanders, M. R., Dadds, M. R., & Bor, W. (1989). A contextual analysis of oppositional child behavior and maternal aversive behavior in families of conduct disordered children. *Journal of Clinical Child Psychology, 18,* 72–83.

Sanders, M. R., Dadds, M. R., Johnston, B., Cash, R., Morrison, M., & Rebgetz, M. (1989). *Cognitive-behavioral treatment of childhood depression: A therapist's manual.* Unpublished manuscript, University of Queensland.

Sanders, M. R., & Glynn, T. (1981). Training parents in behavioral self management: An analysis of generalization and maintenance. *Journal of Applied Behavior Analysis, 14,* 223–237.

Sanders, M. R., Gravestock, F., & Wanstall, K. (1990). *Cystic fibrosis: A parent's handbook for dealing with compliance problems.* Brisbane, Australia: Behaviour Research and Therapy Centre, University of Queensland.

Sanders, M. R., & Hunter, A. C. (1984). An ecological analysis of children's behavior in supermarkets. *Australian Journal of Psychology, 36,* 415–427.

Sanders, M. R., & James, J. E. (1983). The modification of parent behavior: A review of generalization and maintenance. *Behavior Modification, 7,* 3–27.

Sanders, M. R., Le Gris, B., Shepherd, R. W., & Turner K. (1990). *Children with feeding problems: A guide for parents.* Brisbane, Australia: Behavior Research and Therapy Centre, University of Queensland.

Sanders, M. R., Patel, R., Le Gris, B., & Shepherd, R. (1991). *Children with persistent feeding difficulties: An observational analysis of feeding interactions of problem and non-problem eaters.* Manuscript submitted for publication.

Sanders, M. R., & Plant, K. (1989). Programming for generalization to high and low risk parenting situations in families with oppositional developmentally disabled preschoolers. *Behavior Modification, 13,* 283–305.

Sanders, M. R., Rebgetz, M., Morrison, M., Bor, W., Gordon, A., Dadds, M. R., & Shepherd, R. (1989). Cognitive-behavioral treatment of recurrent nonspecific abdominal pain in children: An analysis of generalization and side effects. *Journal of Consulting and Clinical Psychology, 57,* 294–300.

Sarason, S. B. (1974). *The psychological sense of community: Prospects for a community psychology.* San Francisco: Jossey-Bass.

Schafer, R. B. (1985). Effects of marital role problems on wives' depressed mood. *Journal of Consulting and Clinical Psychology, 53,* 541–554.

Scherer, M. W., & Nakamura, C. Y. (1968). A fear survey schedule for children (FSS-FC): An analytic comparison with manifest anxiety. *Behavior Research and Therapy, 6,* 173–182.

Scholom, A., Zucker, R. A., & Stollack, G. E. (1979). Relating early child adjustment to infant and parent temperament. *Journal of Abnormal Child Psychology, 7,* 297–308.

Scott, J. M., & Ballard, K. D. (1986). Training parents and teachers in remedial reading procedures for children with learning difficulties. In K. Wheldall, F. Merrett, & T. Glynn (Eds.), *Behavior analysis in educational psychology* (pp. 239–254). London: Croom Helm.

Scriven, J., & Glynn, T. (1983). Performance feedback on written tasks for low achieving secondary school students. *New Zealand Journal of Educational Studies, 18,* 134–145.

Seymour, F. W., Brock, P., During, M., & Poole, G. (1989). Reducing sleep disruptions in young children: Evaluation of therapist-guided and written information approaches: A brief report. *Journal of Child Psychology and Psychiatry, 30,* 913–918.

Shapiro, E. S. (1987). Academic problems. In M. Hersen & V. B. Van Hasselt (Eds.), *Behavior therapy with children and adolescents: A clinical approach* (pp. 362–384). New York: John Wiley & Sons.

Sines, J. O. (1987). Influence of the home and family environment on child dysfunction. In B. B. Lahey & A. E. Kazdin (Eds.), *Advances in clinical child psychology* (Vol. 10, pp. 1–48). New York: Plenum Publishing.

Skinner, B. F. (1953). *Science and human behavior.* New York: MacMillan.

Spanier, G. B. (1976). Measuring dyadic adjustment: New scales for assessing marital quality. *Journal of Marriage and the Family, 38,* 15–28.

Spielberger, C. D. (1973). *State-Trait Anxiety Inventory for Children.* Palo Alto, CA: Consulting Psychologists Press.

Spielberger, C. D., Gorsuch, R. C., & Lushene, R. E. (1970). *Manual for the State-Trait Anxiety Inventory.* Palo Alto, CA: Consulting Psychologists Press.

Spielberger, C. D., Jacobs, G., Russell, S., & Crane, R. S. (1983). Assessment of anger: The State-Trait Anger Scale. In J. N. Butcher & C. D. Spielberger (Eds.), *Advances in personality assessment* (Vol. 2, pp. 161–189). Hillsdale, NJ: Lawrence Erlbaum Associates.

Stokes, T. R., & Baer, D. M. (1977). An implicit technology of generalization. *Journal of Applied Behavior Analysis, 10,* 349–367.

Stokes, T. R., & Osnes, P. G. (1989). An operant pursuit of generalization. *Behavior Therapy, 20,* 337–355.

Strauss, C. C. (1987). Anxiety. In M. Hersen & V. B. Van Hasselt (Eds.), *Behavior therapy with children and adolescents: A clinical approach* (pp. 109–136). New York: John Wiley & Sons.

Sulzer-Azaroff, B., & Mayer, G. R. (1977). *Applying behavior analysis procedures with children and youth.* New York: Holt, Rinehart & Winston.

Sweet, A. A. (1987). The therapeutic relationship in behavior therapy. *Clinical Psychology Review, 4,* 253–272.

Tharp, R. G., & Wetzel, R. J. (1969). *Behavior modification in the natural environment.* New York: Academic Press.

Topping, K. (1987). Peer tutored paired reading: Outcome data from ten projects. *Educational Psychology, 7,* 133–145.

Twardosz, S., & Nordquist, V. M. (1987). Parent training. In M. Hersen & V. B. Van Hasselt (Eds.), *Behavior therapy with children and adolescents: A clinical approach* (pp. 75–108). New York: John Wiley & Sons.

Vikan, A. (1985). Psychiatric epidemiology in a sample of 1510 ten-year-old children: 1. Prevalence. *Journal of Child Psychology and Psychiatry, 26,* 55–75.

Wahler, R. G. (1969). Oppositional children: A quest for parental reinforcement control. *Journal of Applied Behavior Analysis, 2,* 159–170.

Wahler, R. G. (1980). The insular mother: Her problems in parent-child treatment. *Journal of Applied Behavior Analysis, 13,* 207–219.

Wahler, R. G., & Afton, A. D. (1980). Attentional processes in insular and noninsular mothers. *Child Behavior Therapy, 2,* 25–41.

Wahler, R. G., & Dumas, J. E. (1984). Changing the observational coding style of insular and non-insular mothers: A step toward maintenance. In R. F. Dangel & R. A. Polster (Eds.), *Parent training: Foundations of research and practice* (pp. 379–416). New York: Guilford Press.

Wahler, R. G., & Graves, M. G. (1983). Setting events in social networks: Ally or enemy in child behavior therapy. *Behavior Therapy, 14,* 19–36.

Wahler, R. G., Hughey, J. B., & Gordon, J. S. (1981). Chronic patterns of mother-child coercion: Some differences between insular and non-insular families. *Analysis and Intervention in Developmental Disabilities, 1,* 145–156.

Wahler, R. G., Leske, G., & Rogers, E. S. (1979). The insular family: A deviance support system for oppositional children. In L. A. Hamerlynck (Ed.), *Behavioral systems for the developmentally disabled: School and family environment* (pp. 150–177). New York: Brunner/Mazel.

Wahler, R. G., Winkel, G. H., Peterson, R. F., & Morrison, D. C. (1965). Mothers as behavior therapists for their own children. *Behavior Research and Therapy, 3,* 113–114.

Waring, E. M., & Patton, D. (1984). Marital intimacy and depression. *British Journal of Psychiatry, 145,* 641–644.

Warren, S. A. (1974). The distressed parent of the disabled child. In W. G. Klopfer & M. R. Reed (Eds.), *Problems in psychotherapy* (pp. 30–48). Washington, DC: Hemisphere.

Webster-Stratton, C. (1981). Modification of mothers' behaviors and attitudes through videotape modeling group discussion. *Behavior Therapy, 12,* 634–642.

Webster-Stratton, C. (1982). Long term effects of videotape modeling parent education program: Comparison of immediate and 1-year followup results. *Behavior Therapy, 13,* 702–714.

Webster-Stratton, C. (1985). Predictors of outcome in parent training for conduct disordered children. *Behavior Therapy, 16,* 223–243.

Webster-Stratton, C. (1987). *Parents and children: A 10 program videotape parent training series with manuals.* Eugene, OR: Castalia Press.

Webster-Stratton, C. (1989). Systematic comparison of consumer satisfaction of three cost effective parent training programs for conduct problem children. *Behavior Therapy, 20,* 103–115.

Webster-Stratton, C., Kalpacoff, M., & Hollinsworth, T. (1988). Self-administered videotape therapy for families with conduct problem children: Comparison with two cost effective treatments and a control group. *Journal of Clinical and Consulting Psychology, 56,* 558–566.

Wells, K. C., & Egan, J. (1988). Social learning and systems family therapy for childhood oppositional disorder: Comparative treatment outcome. *Comprehensive Psychiatry, 29,* 138–146.

Wells, K. C., & Forehand, R. (1981). Child behavior problems in the home. In S. M. Turner,

K. S. Calhoun, & H. E. Adams (Eds.), *Handbook of clinical behavior therapy* (pp. 527–567). New York: John Wiley & Sons.

Wells, K. C., Griest, D. L., & Forehand, R. (1980). The use of self control package to enhance the temporal generality of a parent training program. *Behavior Research and Therapy, 18,* 347–354.

Wheldall, K., & Glynn, T. (1989). *Effective classroom learning.* Oxford: Basil Blackwell.

Wheldall, K., & Merrett, F. (1988). Which classroom behaviors do primary school teachers say they find most troublesome? *Educational Review, 40,* 13–27.

Williams, C. D. (1959). The elimination of tantrum behaviors by extinction procedures. *Journal of Abnormal and Social Psychology, 59,* 269–270.

Winefield, H. R. (1984). The nature and elicitation of social support: Some implications for the helping professions. *Behavioural Psychotherapy, 12,* 318–330.

Wolf, M. M. (1978). Social validity: The case for subjective measurement or how applied behavior analysis is finding its heart. *Journal of Applied Behavior Analysis, 11,* 203–214.

Wolfe, D. A. (1987). *Child abuse: Implications for child development and psychopathology.* Newbury Park, CA: Sage.

Wolfe, D. A., Edwards, B., Manion, I., & Koverola, C. (1988). Early intervention for parents at risk of child abuse and neglect: A preliminary investigation. *Journal of Consulting and Clinical Psychology, 56,* 40–47.

Wolfe, D. A., Fairbank, J. A., Kelly, J. A., & Bradlyn, A. S. (1983). Child abusive parents' physiological responses to stressful and nonstressful behavior in children. *Behavioral Assessment, 5,* 363–371.

Wolfe, D. A., & Manion, I. G. (1984). Impediments to child abuse prevention: Issues and directions. *Advances in Behavior Research and Therapy, 6,* 47–62.

Wolpe, J., & Lang, P. J. (1964). A fear survey schedule for use in behavior therapy. *Behavior Research and Therapy, 2,* 27–30.

Zeanah, C. H., Keener, M. A., Stewart, L., & Anders, T. F. (1985). Prenatal perception of infant personality: A preliminary investigation. *Journal of the American Academy of Child Psychiatry, 24,* 204–210.

Author Index

Subject Index

Psychology Practitioner Guidebooks

Editors

Arnold P. Goldstein, Syracuse University
Leonard Krasner, Stanford University & SUNY at Stony Brook
Sol L. Garfield, Washington University in St. Louis

William L. Golden, E. Thomas Dowd & Fred Friedberg—
HYPNOTHERAPY: A Modern Approach

Patricia Lacks—BEHAVIORAL TREATMENT FOR PERSISTENT INSOMNIA

Arnold P. Goldstein & Harold Keller—AGGRESSIVE BEHAVIOR:
Assessment and Intervention

C. Eugene Walker, Barbara L. Bonner & Keith L. Kaufman—
THE PHYSICALLY AND SEXUALLY ABUSED CHILD: Evaluation
and Treatment

Robert E. Becker, Richard G. Heimberg & Alan S. Bellack—SOCIAL
SKILLS TRAINING TREATMENT FOR DEPRESSION

Richard F. Dangel & Richard A. Polster—TEACHING CHILD
MANAGEMENT SKILLS

Albert Ellis, John F. McInerney, Raymond DiGiuseppe & Raymond J. Yeager—
RATIONAL-EMOTIVE THERAPY WITH ALCOHOLICS AND
SUBSTANCE ABUSERS

Johnny L. Matson & Thomas H. Ollendick—ENHANCING CHILDREN'S
SOCIAL SKILLS: Assessment and Training

Edward B. Blanchard, John E. Martin & Patricia M. Dubbert—NON-DRUG
TREATMENTS FOR ESSENTIAL HYPERTENSION

Samuel M. Turner & Deborah C. Beidel—TREATING OBSESSIVE-
COMPULSIVE DISORDER

Alice W. Pope, Susan M. McHale & W. Edward Craighead—SELF-
ESTEEM ENHANCEMENT WITH CHILDREN AND ADOLESCENTS

Jean E. Rhodes & Leonard A. Jason—PREVENTING SUBSTANCE
ABUSE AMONG CHILDREN AND ADOLESCENTS

Gerald D. Oster, Janice E. Caro, Daniel R. Eagen & Margaret A. Lillo—
ASSESSING ADOLESCENTS

Robin C. Winkler, Dirck W. Brown, Margaret van Keppel & Amy
Blanchard—CLINICAL PRACTICE IN ADOPTION

Roger Poppen—BEHAVIORAL RELAXATION TRAINING AND
ASSESSMENT

Michael D. LeBow—ADULT OBESITY THERAPY

Robert Paul Liberman, William J. DeRisi & Kim T. Mueser—SOCIAL
SKILLS TRAINING FOR PSYCHIATRIC PATIENTS

Johnny L. Matson—TREATING DEPRESSION IN CHILDREN AND
ADOLESCENTS

Sol L. Garfield—THE PRACTICE OF BRIEF PSYCHOTHERAPY

Arnold P. Goldstein, Barry Glick, Mary Jane Irwin, Claudia Pask-McCartney
& Ibrahim Rubama—REDUCING DELINQUENCY: Intervention in
the Community

Albert Ellis, Joyce L. Sichel, Raymond J. Yeager, Dominic J. DiMattia,
& Raymond DiGiuseppe—RATIONAL-EMOTIVE COUPLES THERAPY

Clive R. Hollin—COGNITIVE-BEHAVIORAL INTERVENTIONS WITH
YOUNG OFFENDERS

Margaret P. Korb, Jeffrey Gorrell & Vernon Van De Riet—GESTALT
THERAPY: Practice and Theory, Second Edition

Donald A. Williamson—ASSESSMENT OF EATING DISORDERS:
Obesity, Anorexia and Bulimia Nervosa

J. Kevin Thompson—BODY IMAGE DISTURBANCE: Assessment
and Treatment

William J. Fremouw, Maria de Perczel & Thomas E. Ellis—SUICIDE RISK:
Assessment and Response Guidelines

Arthur M. Horne & Thomas V. Sayger—TREATING CONDUCT AND
OPPOSITIONAL DEFIANT DISORDERS IN CHILDREN

Richard A. Dershimer—COUNSELING THE BEREAVED

Eldon Tunks & Anthony Bellissimo—BEHAVIORAL MEDICINE: Concepts
and Procedures

Alan Poling, Kenneth D. Gadow & James Cleary—DRUG THERAPY FOR
BEHAVIOR DISORDERS: An Introduction

Ira Daniel Turkat— THE PERSONALITY DISORDERS: A Psychological
Approach to Clinical Management

Karen S. Calhoun & Beverly M. Atkeson— TREATMENT OF
RAPE VICTIMS: Facilitating Psychosocial Adjustment

Manuel Ramirez III—PSYCHOTHERAPY AND COUNSELING
WITH MINORITIES: A Cognitive Approach to Individual
and Cultural Differences

Martin Lakin—COPING WITH ETHICAL DILEMMAS IN
PSYCHOTHERAPY

Ricks Warren & George D. Zgourides—ANXIETY DISORDERS: A
Rational-Emotive Perspective

Emil J. Chiauzzi—PREVENTING RELAPSE IN THE ADDICTIONS:
A Biopsychosocial Approach

Matthew R. Sanders & Mark R. Dadds—BEHAVIORAL FAMILY
INTERVENTION

Philip C. Kendall—ANXIETY DISORDERS IN YOUTH: Cognitive-
Behavioral Interventions